T0271976

Crisis and Renewal
in Twentieth Century Banking

Crisis and Renewal
in Twentieth Century Banking

Exploring the history and archives of banking at times
of political and social stress

Edited by

EDWIN GREEN, JOHN LAMPE and
FRANJO ŠTIBLAR

Routledge
Taylor & Francis Group

LONDON AND NEW YORK

First published 2004 by Ashgate Publishing

Published 2016 by Routledge
2 Park Square, Milton Park, Abingdon, Oxon OX14 4RN
711 Third Avenue, New York, NY 10017, USA

Routledge is an imprint of the Taylor & Francis Group, an informa business

British Library Cataloguing in Publication Data
European Association for Banking History. 12th Conference (Lubljana, Slovenia: 2001)
 Crisis and Renewal in Twentieth Century Banking: Exploring the History and Archives of
 Banking at Times of Political and Social Stress. – (Studies in Banking History)
 1. Banks and banking—Europe—History—20th century—Congresses. 2. Financial crisis—
 Europe—History—20th century—Congresses. I. Title. II. Green, Edwin, 1948-. III. Lampe,
 John R. IV. Štiblar, Franjo. V. European Association for Banking History.
 332.1'094'0904

Library of Congress Cataloging in Publication Data
 Crisis and Renewal in Twentieth Century Banking: Exploring the History and Archives of
 Banking at Times of Political and Social Stress/edited by Edwin Green, John Lampe and
 Franjo Štiblar.
  p. cm. – (Studies in Banking History).
 Includes bibliographical references.
 1. Banks and banking—Europe—History—Congresses. 2. Financial institutions—
 Europe—History—Congresses. I. Title: Crisis and Renewal in Twentieth Century Banking.
 II. Green, Edwin. III. Lampe, John R. IV. Štiblar, Franjo. V. European Association for
 Banking History. VI. Series.

 HG2974.C75 2004
 332.1'094'0904–dc22

                                                                                    2003054481

ISBN 13: 978-0-7546-3358-7 (hbk)

Contents

List of Tables

List of Figures

List of Illustrations

Introduction

This book presents the proceedings of the annual conference of the European Association for Banking History – the twelfth in the series – in Ljubljana, Slovenia, in May 2001. The conference, generously hosted by the Bank of Slovenia and the Nova Ljubljanska Banka, met at a momentous time in the modern history of Slovenia. The year 2001 marked the tenth anniversary of Slovenian independence, the tenth anniversary of the Bank of Slovenia and the tenth anniversary of the Slovenian currency. Delegates to the conference were very fortunate to meet and to hear from senior bankers, economists and others who had participated in the events of 1991 and in the subsequent redevelopment of the Slovenian economy.

Independence had brought an immense shift in the political and economic landscape of the country. Slovenia's subsequent entry onto an international stage, especially in its preparations for joining the European Community, were no less challenging. Delegates to the 2001 conference could not have asked for a more vivid example of the way in which banking history is being created as every day passes. As our hosts in Ljubljana could confirm clearly from their own experiences, banking history is not a remote and narrow subject. It is an area of study which has direct and continuing relevance for countries in rapid political, economic and financial transition.

The recent history of Slovenia and the former Yugoslavia has such a strong historical resonance that the Association was keen to produce a conference programme which would include, learn from and build upon the experience of this phase of swift change. This was the spark for a conference on the theme of banking at times of political and social crisis. It is a rich topic for bankers, for historians and for archivists.

If this theme has been overlooked in the past, it may be that banking historians have been preoccupied with 'crisis' in its monetary dimension. Generations of banking historians, including the Association's own membership, have often met and debated the topic of financial crisis. The performance of banks and banking systems at moments of financial crisis and at times of banking crashes or scandals has received exhaustive examination (for example, Kindleberger, 1978).

The study of banking in these times of stress has been immeasurably improved as access to banking archives has widened to throw light on such emergencies as the first Baring crisis and the fall of the Creditanstalt. The greater availablility of original sources has also strengthened studies of the related field of war, political power and finance (Burk, 1985; Ferguson,

2001). Yet there has been no concentrated attempt to take a broad view of banking during non-financial crises – that is, during political and social crisis. The conference in Ljubljana was an excellent opportunity to explore this relatively uncharted territory: it was a setting in which both hosts and delegates were keenly aware of the modern relevance of the topic.

Potentially this theme is vast in its scope. In the very long run it should include an examination of banking during the Dutch Revolt and the Thirty Years' War, banking during the American War of Independence and the French Revolution, and banking during the colonial wars of the nineteenth century. It might move forward into the twenty-first century to consider financial markets under pressure in national crises (as in Argentina) or in the international confrontation with terrorism. For the purposes of a single conference, however, the Association believed that the twentieth century, with the main focus on Europe, offered a remarkable width of experience. Revolution, world war, social unrest, civil war, persecution and partition were on stage throughout that devastated century; so too were their counterparts of reconstruction and recovery in national and international contexts. South-eastern Europe alone had witnessed the full range of these categories of crisis.

In assessing all these experiences, the historian has a relatively higher chance of tracing documentation and other evidence than in studying examples from previous centuries. This does not mean that such sources are easy to find or use – and inevitably the chances of tracing sources which provide neutral or objective treatment are remote. Political and social upheaval is intrinsically linked with the distortion and destruction of evidence. The conference in Ljubljana addressed this important issue by attempting to identify sources which throw new and clearer light on the crises of the twentieth century. The European Association for Banking History, in addition to providing a forum for research and debate by historians, has always emphasised the importance of identifying and opening up bank archives. It is in that tradition that the conference (and these proceedings) attempted to give an archival perspective as well as an historical view of banking at times of political and social stress.

The conference papers are presented here in six groups, bringing together discussion on major categories of crisis such as revolution, civil war, and reconstruction, and containing contributions on historical and archival issues. So far as possible, the groups of papers are presented in approximate chronological order, beginning with war and revolution in the early twentieth century and moving forward as far as reconstruction in the former Yugoslavia in the 1990s. Hence the sequence opens with Orbell's account of the vital but neglected role of merchant banking – in the shape of Barings – in both the political and financial predicament of Russia during the First World War. Lebedev follows with a study of the chronology of the Russian Revolution's impact on banking and finance. This narrative, which will be new to many banking historians, could not have produced a more vivid example of the collision of banking and politics than the Russian bankers' dealings with Lenin, Dzerzinsky and their circle. Potier then demonstrates the value of a great variety of banking archives in Western Europe as a mirror to the cataclysm in Russia.

Similarly, in the second group of papers, Green introduces examples of banking 'intelligence' records as a source of data and opinion on the financial turmoil in Central and Eastern Europe between the two world wars. The first-hand reports of visiting bankers can shed light on banks and companies which have otherwise left little trace. Bićanić and Ivankovič then examine the response of Croatia's banking sector to the multiple strains of worldwide depression, the Creditanstalt failure in nearby Vienna, and the changing balance between private and state banking in the 'first' Yugoslavia. In the same period, banking fell under the hammer of civil war in Spain. The third group of papers begins with Buchanan's appraisal of the role of foreign banks in the Spanish conflict, uncovering banking archives inside and outside Spain which until now have not featured in this long-running debate. Tortella and García-Ruiz then tackle the issue of the measurable effects of civil war on Spanish banking, not only in the period of conflict but also in the long years of isolation and slow reconstruction which followed. For a contrasting example of civil war's impact on the banking industry, Kostis depicts the Greek experience in the 1940s. Again, the impact of conflict can be understood and measured in terms of the reconstruction of the financial system, especially in assessing the role of British and then American intervention.

The Second World War had no real precedent or parallel in terms of the scale and range of its effect and consequences for the banking industry. In the fourth group of papers in this collection, Müller investigates the fate of the German banking industry both at the centre of a world war and in the complex processes of reconstruction in a ruined economy. It is an area of study where the opening of banking and official archives (inside and outside Germany) has made it possible for historians to take large strides in unravelling the tangle of political, social and financial factors in global war and reconstruction. For a contrasting viewpoint – in the only paper in the collection which offers a perspective beyond Europe – King retraces the return of bankers in the East at the end of the Pacific War. This chapter looks at the role of banking in the post-war recovery of the social and economic framework of Hong Kong and in the reconstruction of business throughout the East – even in the face of war and revolution in China and the rise of nationalism and confrontation elsewhere in the East.

A regional framework is adopted in the fifth group of papers, with special emphasis on the experience of Slovenia, the conference's host country. Štiblar compares the crises which confronted Slovene banks in the 1930s and the 1990s. The comparison evokes the very different bequests of the Austro-Hungarian Empire and Tito's Yugoslavia in the two periods of crisis. Štiblar also extracts measurements of the banking sector in these two periods. Ribnikar then examines the 1990s in terms of the 'transition' process which was required in all economies emerging from communist structures in Central and Eastern Europe. As the process is far from complete, he also reviews the options for those banks in small economies which are ready and willing to compete in regional and international markets.

Similarly, recovery from the rupture of banking relationships and financial markets during political and social crisis is at the centre of Lampe's overview chapter in the final group in this collection. He identifies five periods of crisis in the relationship between South-eastern Europe's banks and the Western world between the 1920s and the 1990s. He surveys the repair of these relationships, from Bulgaria to Greece, showing significant national differences and priorities. The national identity and character of banking systems has played a significant role in that process. It is therefore appropriate that the final chapter in the collection, by Unwin and Hewitt, considers the way in which this identity can be remodelled or created from afresh. The authors present the initial results of their study of the design and issue of banknotes for the transition economies of Central and Eastern Europe. It is a topic – like all the chapters in this collection – in which the realities of banking history are closely intertwined with political and social considerations. It is also a new and interesting example of banking, in the aftermath of crisis and change, turning to cultural and artistic inspiration for the development of their business identity.

Clearly the relationship between banking and external political and social factors offers a huge opportunity for new research. This potential is obvious in the themes of this collection but historians and archivists can look beyond these topics to issues such as banks and nationalisation, banking and diplomacy, and banking and the rise of international non-governmental organizations and pressure groups. Banking historians might also take up the theme of political and social crisis as factors in the durability and longevity of financial institutions, a topic which is often seen more narrowly in terms of management and strategy. There are additional large opportunities to extend the study of banks under political and social stress into other periods and other regions of the world. In this, the European Association for Banking History hopes that these chapters will stimulate that wider interest and perhaps convince historians and other users that banking history and banking archives are a valuable (and neglected) mirror for political and social change. The Association also hopes that its own conferences and publications will play a part in that effort.

References

Burk, K. (1985), *Britain, America and the Sinews of War, 1914–1918*, Winchester, Massachusetts: Allen & Unwin Inc.

Ferguson, N. (2001), *The Cash Nexus. Money and Power in the Modern World, 1700–2000*, London: Allen Lane.

Kindleberger, C. P. (1978), *Manias, Panics, and Crashes. A History of Financial Crises*, London: Macmillan.

PART I

War and Revolution: Russian and Foreign Banks, 1917–30

CHAPTER 1

A Private Banking House at War: Barings and Russia, 1914–17

John Orbell

Introduction

'I should be much obliged,' wrote the senior partner of Barings, Lord Revelstoke, to the Imperial Russian Ambassador in London, Count Benckendorff, 'if you would take an early opportunity ... of assuring the Ministry of Finance how entirely we are at the disposal of the Russian Government.'[1] The circumstances were the outbreak of war and the reason for writing was to stake Barings' claim to financing the needs of the Russian government in the forthcoming conflict. Neither Revelstoke nor the government could then have realized the extraordinary magnitude and complexity of the role that the private banking house of Barings was to play in the service of the Russian government. From 1914 to 1917 it formed the conduit between Britain and Russia along which money and munitions flowed on a stupendous scale. It is a story that has gone largely untold.

This role was despite Barings' relatively small size and modest resources. The firm was a private bank owned and managed by its founding family. Its balance sheet in 1914 totalled some £16 million at a time when the balance sheet of a major British retail bank commonly totalled ten times as much. Barings was not a deposit taker of significant size and most of its resources derived from its share and loan capital – largely provided by its directors and their families – and from its accumulated reserves. Despite these relatively modest resources, the firm arranged both long- and short-term finance well in excess of what its balance sheet suggested was possible.

On the one hand, it provided long-term finance largely through the issue of securities for sovereign, quasi-sovereign and corporate clients and, on the other, short-term finance for international trade and currency transactions through guaranteeing – or 'accepting' – the bills of exchange of international traders and financial institutions. In other words, for the most part Barings arranged and managed finance while others provided the necessary funds.

The dynamic of Barings' business – and, indeed, of the whole constituency of London's family-owned and managed merchant banks – rested on two principles. First, Barings' business was underpinned by first-class reputation. This meant that the debt and equity it issued and the bills of exchange it accepted were readily taken up by investors in the security and bill markets and, consequently, on highly competitive terms beneficial for the firm and for its clients. Second, the firm deployed its own private capital in a range of products (loans, bills, bonds, shares, gilts, property, and so on) in a way that was both cautious yet sometimes distinctly entrepreneurial.

In terms of both banking business and prestige, the Russian government had been a highly important client of Barings since the 1850s. The firm had then been appointed the government's Financial Agent in London operating its bank accounts, holding deposits, providing overdrafts, making advances and arranging payments and collections. The latter could be in respect of a vast range of transactions, at the most basic paying the ambassador's salary and, at the most complex, arranging instalment payments in connection with the construction of a battleship. There was nothing unusual in this. It was common practice for overseas governments to appoint agents in the major centres of economic and political activity – especially London, Paris and Berlin – to handle their financial affairs. At different times in the hundred years prior to 1914, Barings represented governments as diverse as those of the United States and Argentina, Canada and Chile, and Venezuela and Portugal.

This work was quite distinct from bond issuance. Acting as a government's financial agent did not imply a monopoly of bond issuance or of the associated work of paying agent which involved payment of coupon interest to bondholders. The Russian government neatly illustrates this point. Whereas Barings lead-managed numerous bond issues for the government, and also for entities in Russia which benefited from government guarantees, such as railway companies, it had no monopoly of the business. Amongst others between the 1850s and 1914, Rothschilds handled several issues.

Notwithstanding the importance of Barings in Russian government finance in the London market, before 1914 London had a relatively small role to play in Russian government affairs. For example, in the ten years before the outbreak of war in 1914, Russian government issues took the form of international offerings spread between Paris and London, Amsterdam and Berlin, most especially the former. Of these issues, only a modest proportion found a home in the portfolios of British investors. Out of the last issue of £55.5 million Imperial Government Bonds offered on the international markets in 1909, only £6 million, or around 10 per cent, was offered for sale in London and much of this probably found its way across the Atlantic to New York.

The outbreak of war in 1914 created an entirely new situation. This war would be won as much by technology and munitions as by men and valour yet Russia had neither the manufacturing capacity nor raw material resource to equip her forces sufficiently. Much would have to be provided by the industries of France, Britain and, later, the United States. The scale of Russia's requirements relative to her resources quickly alarmed her allies. Shortly after the outbreak of war, the British Embassy in St Petersburg estimated Russian war expenditure at £1.3 million a day, while in the autumn of 1914 the government had at its disposal in Britain just £11 million. So virtually from the outset of hostilities, Russia's dependency on her allies was substantial.

Sterling funds were needed not just for the purchase of munitions. On the outbreak of war, the sterling–rouble exchange in effect collapsed, necessitating a mechanism for finance of pre-war Russian commercial debts. In November 1914, the Russian Ministry of Finance concluded that, in the next twelve months, £58 million of such debt would have to be settled. In addition, the coupon interest due on Russian government bonds and government-guaranteed bonds held in Britain and in neutral countries had to be paid. Without this, Russian credit faced total destruction and the British government recognized until the latter part of 1917 that this was far too high a precipice over which to allow a valued ally to fall.

Underpinning the British government's response to Russia was its wish for an effective Eastern Front, equipped from the factories of Britain and France, to take pressure off the hard-pressed Western Front. Britain, therefore, was enormously sympathetic to the needs of Russia for money and munitions. When Russia had virtually exhausted its sterling balances in early 1915 and faced the prospect of defaulting on its overseas debts, the Chancellor of the Exchequer 'expressed [to Barings] every desire not to have Russian credit damaged in any way and authorized Lord Revelstoke to communicate with him in case of need'.[2] A few months earlier the British Foreign Office had explicitly stated to the Russian government that

> the British government recognizes fully the supreme importance of assisting Russia in financing war expenditure. They are most anxious to do everything in their power to help the Russian government for they realize that the placing of their resources at the disposal of their allies is as paramount in its importance as the task of financing its own operations.[3]

As the war progressed, Russia was not slow to play this card in order to extract from Britain and France maximum finance and on favourable terms.

The Means of Finance

An early question was how to provide this finance but it was quickly apparent that few alternatives existed. Bond issues to investors were clearly impossible; London investors had little appetite for Russian bonds pre-war and this would only diminish given the uncertainty brought by war. When the Russian-Ministry of Finance suggested a £100 million bond issue in late 1914, Lord Revelstoke of Barings responded that only £2–3 million could be raised in this way and even then on exorbitant terms. Even the Russian Ministry of Finance representative in London, Michael de Routkowsky, regarded this proposal from St Petersburg as a 'visionary dream'.[4] Payment by means of shipment of Russian gold was considered early on – and in October/November 1914 a relatively small shipment seems to have been sent – but Russia throughout the war showed a marked and, at times, baffling disinclination to export its gold as payment for supplies. This was despite the extreme exhortations of her allies and it became a source of brinkmanship and grievance between the governments.

In the event, the financial instrument chosen was the Imperial Russian Government Sterling Treasury Bill discounted at the Bank of England and, for the most part, payable at Barings although some bills were payable at the Bank of England. These were of twelve months' duration and were renewable, on the same terms, should the government not have funds to settle them when they fell due. The first bills, issued in 1914, carried the same rate of discount as British Government Treasury Bills or, put the British Foreign Office's way, the Russian government was granted 'the full advantage which the credit of His Majesty's Government commands in the London market'.[5] For later issues the rate was 6 per cent (or 5 per cent against any bills covered by gold).

It is not always clear what happened to the bills after their deposit with the Bank of England. There appears to have been the occasional public offering of bills, most notably in February 1915 when £10 million was offered for sale, payable after twelve months at the Bank of England. The lists opened on 12 February and closed three days later with an over-subscription of £2 million. Another public offering of £10 million was made in February 1917 of which £8.6 million was subscribed. Most bills, however, appear to have been held in the Bank of England presumably against funds placed with the Bank by the British Treasury; certainly the Bank benefited from a British government guarantee in connection with its handling of all Russian bills. Such bills, in effect, represented unsecured loans by the British government to the Russian government.

The Treasury Bill financings took the form of a series of agreements between the British Treasury and the Russian Ministry of Finance between 1914 and 1917, each one for a new tranche of debt. In October 1914 the first tranche of £20 million was made available, followed by another £20 million in early February 1915 and another for £10 million in late February 1915. Later that month the British and French governments sought to put the arrangements on a longer-term footing, in place of the previous hand-to-mouth basis, and agreed to provide £100 million through to the end of 1915. By September 1915, this sum had been exhausted when, under a new agreement, this time without French involvement, a further £300 million was made available in twelve monthly instalments. Around £50 million of this amount was never drawn, testament to the increased scrutiny by the British Treasury of Russian purchasing to ensure that funds were used in a proper way and gave value for money. On the conclusion of the 1915 arrangements, in September 1916 a further agreement was negotiated to cover the next twelve-month period. Now £150 million was to be made available, again in twelve monthly instalments, in addition to the unused £50 million. It was the last such financing. In total, then, between 1914 and 1917 some £600 million was made available to the Russian government through the mechanism of Treasury Bill issuance.

These somewhat bland statistics mask high drama and brinkmanship. From the very start, Russian war expenditure ran hopelessly out of control. Funds were exhausted far more rapidly than anticipated. When larger amounts were made available they were used up in an even shorter period. Russia was prepared to purchase munitions even when moneys were not in place to cover the expenditure. Of the £300 million financing made available in September 1915, for example, almost £200 million of it had to be set aside to meet munitions contracts already entered into. Negotiations between the British and Russian governments grew increasingly acrimonious and bitter, especially when Britain's own financial situation grew more critical in mid-1915. Measured diplomacy gave way to surliness. 'I do not understand how the maintenance of a large gold reserve against the paper currency of a country which has never had a free market in gold can compare in importance with the successful prosecution of the war,' the Governor of the Bank of England told the Russian Minister of Finance in response to a point-blank refusal of the latter to ship gold to Britain, 'though,' the Governor added for good measure, 'I sincerely hope that the allied cause will have triumphed before your stock of gold is exhausted'.[6]

In late 1915, a web of bureaucracy was put in place to ensure value for money and to end misappropriation. The British Treasury was at the heart of this and pursued the Russian Ministry of Finance with vigour and in exacting detail. In late 1915, Sir Malcolm Ramsay, Assistant Secretary of the Treasury, advised them that they were paying over the odds for their barbed wire; 'the price,' he wrote, 'appears to be possibly 10 per cent higher than the British government have been paying'.[7] A more illuminating issue touched on the Czar. Whereas in early 1915 his household had been able to make a down payment on a new Rolls Royce, in July he discovered that he would not be able to complete his purchase.

Barings' Role

The role of Barings and of its senior partner, Lord Revelstoke, was pivotal in Russian financial arrangements between 1914 and 1917. It took several forms but at its heart was Revelstoke's work in advising the Russian Ministry of Finance in its negotiations with the Treasury and the Bank of England. In all negotiations with the Treasury Revelstoke sat alongside Russia's representatives in London, Count Benckendorff, the ambassador, and Monsieur de Routkowsky, the Ministry of Finance's London representative. He articulated the case for Russia to successive Chancellors of the Exchequer, David Lloyd George and Reginald McKenna, and civil servants such as Sir John Bradbury and John Maynard Keynes, and interpreted the British attitude to the Russians. This was certainly not work for which the aristocratic Benckendorff was well suited, while Routkowsky appeared never to have a real grip on the issues and had little stamina in negotiation. 'Personally I consider that the bargaining about the rate of interest is not dignified,' he told Lord Revelstoke in 1914, adding that 'If the British government has stipulated a certain rate ... it must have good reason for it.'[8]

Sometimes Revelstoke went to these Whitehall meetings alone. A case in point was in mid-1915 when the £300 million financing was under negotiation. It was a critical moment but with Routkowsky exhausted and ill in bed, it seems that Revelstoke, alone, handled the preliminary negotiations that laid down the heads of agreement for the pending inter-government conference. 'He [Lord Revelstoke] is the only person au courant with our negotiations,' explained Routkowsky to the Treasury.[9]

There are numerous other examples of Revelstoke's apparent indispensability. When the British Treasury pressed the Russians in mid-1915 to remove Barings and Revelstoke from the operation of the new £300 million facility – presumably as a cost-control measure – the Russians would have nothing to do with it or with the proposal that in future all payments would be made direct to the Russian government by the Treasury itself. 'The Minister of Finance ... would prefer the continuation of the co-operation of Messrs Baring,' they insisted to the Treasury. They had their way.[10] It was just as well, as days later, due to a Treasury oversight, £4 million stood idle for several days, leading Sir John Bradbury to accept responsibility and explain to Revelstoke that 'the Treasury is inevitably unfamiliar with details of banking arrangements and I am anxious to reduce our intervention into the machinery to the minimum. The difficulty is, however, to secure the closer control over advances ... while at the same time leaving the actual banking machinery to work automatically.'[11] In February 1917, Lord Revelstoke – now without question the undisputed British expert on Russian finance – emerged from the shadows as a plenipotentiary and deputy head of the British diplomatic mission to the Allied Conference in Petrograd called to consider strategy for the continuation of the war. Again he emerged as the key financial intermediary, urging the Russians – as it turned out unsuccessfully – to moderate their demands for future financing and entreating the Minister of Finance to regard him as being 'non son Procureur-General mais son avocat'.[12]

Inevitably he was feted in Petrograd, given gifts by the Czar and Municipal Duma, dined out by dignitaries, entertained with champagne and dancing girls at Cuba's, the fashionable night spot, and several times given use of the Imperial box at the opera. 'A ballet called *Paquita*,' he noted in his diary one night, 'very poor but the dancing quite admirable'. '*Rigoletto*,' he noted on another occasion, 'well sung with good tenor'.[13] Mercifully for him, it was audible above the sound of Eastern Front gunfire.

No one is indispensable, but it seems that Revelstoke was as indispensable as it was possible to be in working as an intermediary between the Russia government, his client, and the British government, his client's paymaster. But Barings had several other roles to play. One involved the management of the Treasury Bill issuance which embraced organizing the printing and verification of bills, their issue when necessary to the Bank of England, their renewal when they fell due, and so on. Although time-consuming, this work was largely routine.

Of greater importance was Barings' provision of temporary advances and overdrafts for the Russian government at vital moments when, with its sterling balances exhausted, it needed to make immediate payments to prevent default. Such crises in funding were regular occurrences in the first year of the war and were invariably the result of brinkmanship and delay in negotiations as the two governments haggled and haggled again over the terms for new Treasury Bill issuance. At one point in September 1915, the

Russian government's accounts in Barings' book were overdrawn to the extent of £750 000, no small amount when the firm's balance sheet totalled £20 million, but generally Barings' risk was guaranteed by the Treasury. Indeed the Bank of England sometimes provided the money – and indeed had to do so in view of the amount of funding required. Thus in October 1914, when Barings made an emergency £2 million advance to the Russian government, the firm was put in funds by the Bank of England to enable it to do so.

Underlying all of this was the work of handling the government's accounts and making payments on its behalf. This included receiving demands for payment from suppliers of munitions and raw materials, obtaining permission to make such payments from authorities in both London and Petrograd (the latter being no easy matter under wartime conditions), making payment, and undertaking the necessary currency transactions when payments were made outside Britain. Hundreds of thousands of transactions were handled embracing everything from army boots to ice breakers, from barbed wire to troop ships. There can be little doubt that the lion's share of Russia's external munitions purchases during the First World War was made through Barings' books and it involved a vast volume of routine work for the firm.

Added to this was the firm's continuing work as paying agents, paying interest to the Russian government's bondholders both in London and in neutral countries. This now had the added complication of ensuring that no such interest was paid to citizens of enemy countries who had deposited their bonds with custodians in Amsterdam and New York – a thankless and seemingly impossible task.

All of this business was undertaken at little risk to Barings. The Bank of England and the Treasury accepted the risk attached to the Treasury Bill operations and to advances and overdrafts. Elsewhere at Barings there was minimum exposure on Russian accounts. Examination of the year-end valuation of the firm's security portfolio reveals scarcely a single Russian security held for house account during the war years while the trade finance business's exposure to Russian business was steadily wound down from 1914 onwards from an already low level. Of the £5.5 million acceptances drawn on Barings for its sole account in 1914 (a figure which excludes the firm's large dollar acceptance business on joint account with Kidder Peabody), only £100 000 was for account of Russian clients.

Barings made a great deal of profit from its Russian business during the war years derived from commissions from two main activities, namely the management of Treasury Bill issues and the handling of payments on behalf of the government; both were of about equal size. The commission arising from Treasury Bills is the easiest to identify. Barings charged no commission for handling the first tranche of bills in 1914; it is not clear why this should have been so. Revelstoke negotiated a quarter per cent commission on the next tranche of £20 million; it totalled the not inconsiderable sum of £50 000. Commission at this level remained the norm until arrangement of the £300 million financing in September 1915. Then the Treasury, probably cognizant of the amount of commission being paid, endeavoured to marginalize Barings' role although with little success. The upshot for Barings was a reduction in commission to a sixteenth per cent. Nevertheless, on a sum of £300 million, the revenue generated fell not far short of £200 000. There can be no doubt that this was a generous sum but at a time when merchant bankers commonly thought of commissions in terms of whole percentage points, a sixteenth per cent commission was not unreasonably large.

At this time Barings' revenue was derived from three major sources. One was 'interest and discount' which came from money market activity; another was 'investments' which embraced security trading and issuance, and the third was 'commissions' derived, *inter alia*, from accepting, paying agency work, security transactions for clients and provision of routine banking services largely to private clients. In the years immediately before the war all three were roughly the same size at about £130 000 each. Of the three, investment revenue could vary considerably from year to year and under wartime conditions, which put an end to new issues, it collapsed in 1916 and 1917. Costs – mostly salaries and premises costs – stood at around £90 000 a year and remained remarkably stable throughout the war period. This meant that in the years before the war, net annual profit was in the order of about £300 000.

In 1915 revenue generated from Russian government business amounted to £718 000, falling to £518 000 in 1916 and to £136 000 in 1917. Put another way, the firm's net profit more than trebled to over £1 million in 1915 and then fell off to about £700 000 in both 1916 and 1917 before slipping back to pre-war levels in 1918. Some of this profit was paid away in tax; in 1915 and 1917, for example, £450 000 was either paid to, or set aside for, the tax authorities. More was used in 1915 to write off pre-war bad debts amounting to £350 000. However, with the business well capitalized and with adequate reserves, most of the profits were paid away as dividends to the ordinary shareholders of Baring Brothers & Co. Ltd or entities associated with them. The partners of Baring Brothers & Co., with their large shareholding, received the lion's share.

Significance of the Role of Financial Agent

The financial agency work of Barings for the Imperial Government between 1914 and 1917 was extraordinary in terms of its magnitude, complexity and political sensitivity and it highlights aspects of the work of London's merchants banks that have largely escaped the notice of historians. Leading houses such as Barings and Rothschilds held several such appointments although the number fell as the nineteenth century progressed and as governments handed their agency work to the London branches or representative offices of banks from their own countries. At the high point in the late 1850s, however, one partner could list the clients for which Barings acted as agent as Russia, Norway, Austria, United States, Chile, Buenos Aires, New Granada, Canada, Nova Scotia, New Brunswick and Australia. So while the work undertaken for Russia between 1914 and 1917 was extraordinary in magnitude, many other relationships and transactions were undertaken.

Often agency work did not stray far from the routine of account keeping, payment making, exchange transactions and the provision of temporary advances. When it did, it could involve maintaining or establishing the standing of a government through careful management of its debt issuance. The experience of Russia between 1914 and 1917 is an excellent example of this but others include Barings' work for the Government of the Province of Upper Canada in the 1830s and 1840s. In the mid-1830s, Barings with another London bank, Glyns, was appointed the government's joint financial agents in London and created for the first time a market in the government's debentures. As no Canadian securities had been issued in London before, much confidence building was needed so the method of issue initially chosen was private placements. When the market was satiated and could absorb no further debentures – except on poor terms that would do reputational harm – Barings and Glyns met any pressing government requirements, such as for funds to pay coupon interest, through advances. These would be paid off in due course through the marketing of further securities when the market for them had recovered. In this way Barings with Glyns created for the Canadian government a credit rating almost unsurpassed in the international markets. This work should not be confused with the more straightforward business of security issuance as it had at its heart an intimate client-banker relationship which aimed to achieve long-term strategic objectives.

At another level, as with Russia between 1914 and 1917, ING Barings' archives reveal support of many governments at moments of crisis. A case in point, reaching far back into the nineteenth century, is Barings' work for the United States government. The firm had been appointed the government's London financial agents in 1803, throughout the nineteenth century operated its bank accounts for payment making throughout Europe and generally used its influence on the government's behalf. The civil war period was one of several highlights. Credits were made available in Barings' books for both the government and US armaments manufacturers–Colt and Remington being two notable examples–for the purchase and supply of rifles and other war munitions. 'These gentlemen,' wrote William Aspinwall, a special Union emissary to Europe, 'unhesitatingly authorized us to draw on them ... for a very large amount–on terms at once liberal and most considerate. For motives of delicacy, no public mention has been made of this honourable act which certainly no other house in Europe could have or would have done.'[14] Here are reflections, albeit on a much smaller scale, of Barings' connection with Russia in the First World War.

The role of financial agent highlights a multiplicity of potential conflicts of interests. Looked at from the twenty-first century, it is the most extraordinary and fascinating feature of Barings' work for Russia between 1914 and 1917. It seems bewildering that Lord Revelstoke, in Petrograd in 1917, could have acted as both an official British government representative yet also as banker to and agent for the Russian government. Of equal interest is the Russian government's apparent satisfaction in having as its banker in London an establishment figure so close to the British government and civil service elite and allied to British strategic interests. Yet on the surface at least, Barings and Lord Revelstoke appear to have played an effective role throughout the war period without criticism from either side.

Once again, there is plenty of historical precedent for this ambiguity. So far as Barings and Russia are concerned, the issue first emerged during the Crimean War in the 1850s and touched on conflict with Britain's strategic interests. Tom Baring, the senior partner of Barings, was then accused across the floor of the House of Commons by Prime Minister Lord Palmerston of being 'the known and avowed ... private agent of the government of Russia' for allowing the Russian government to ship its gold from Barings' basement only hours before the declaration of war.[15] Reaching back further to 1803, another British prime minister, Henry Addington, obliged the firm to withdraw from financing the United States government's purchase of Louisiana from France, a transaction which was to put US$11 million into the French Treasury for use in funding war with Britain.

Another conflict of interest arose during the Russo–Japanese War in 1904 and 1905 but this time it touched on the competing interests of the two governments involved as well as on the strategic interests of the British government. The latter intimated a need for Barings to maintain a more or less neutral attitude but it is quite clear that behind the scenes both governments were supported. The Japanese were, for example, assisted in marketing their bonds in New York for the first time while the Russian war effort was lubricated via their accounts in Barings' books. And on the conclusion of the war, when the Russian government was obliged to make payment to Japan, it effected this payment by means of a Barings' cheque!

Another feature brought to the surface by financial agency work and especially by Barings' work for Russia is the extraordinary influence which firms such as Barings and bankers such as Lord Revelstoke were able to exercise. There can be no doubt that in the war period Revelstoke – as throughout he was the only partner involved – was the real man of influence in Anglo-Russian finance. He moved in the highest Russian and British political and diplomatic circles with the greatest of ease; he was the only bridge between the two sides so far as financial matters were concerned. Such influence was achieved despite the relatively modest resources of his firm with its balance-sheet total of around £20 million. The interaction of London merchant bankers with government – especially the British government – is most often obscure and undocumented, based as it was on quiet conversations in out-of-the-way places. The relationship between the Russian and British governments and Barings in the First World War period brings it to the surface.

These issues highlight the relevance of the archives of investment banks such as Barings for the study of political and diplomatic history linked to financial history. An analysis of users of the Baring Archives shows that scholars have been slow to recognize this connection; their interests most frequently focus on economic and commercial issues. As the connection of Russia and Barings between 1914 and 1917 illustrates, political historians have much to gain from consulting these archives.

Notes

1   ING Bank NV, London Branch, Historical Collections. The Baring Archive [BA] 203889. Lord Revelstoke to Michael de Routkowsky, 29 July 1914.
2   BA 303891. Memorandum of a conversation of the Chancellor of the Exchequer, Mr Montagu, Sir John Bradbury and Lord Revelstoke, 7 September 1915.

```
```


3 BA 203889. Draft Foreign Office telegram to HM Ambassador, St Petersburg, 18 December 1914.
4 BA 203889. Michael de Routkowsky to Lord Revelstoke, 15 December 1914.
5 BA 203889. Foreign Office Memorandum, 26 September 1914.
6 BA 203893. Lord Cunliffe to Peter de Bark, Russian Minister of Finance, 5 December 1916.
7 BA 203890. Sir M. Ramsay to Michael de Routkowsky, 25 November 1915.
8 BA 203889. Michael de Routkowsky to Lord Revelstoke, 29 December 1914
9 BA 203891. Michael de Routkowsky to Lord Revelstoke, 5 September 1915.
10 BA 203891. Memoranda of conversations of Conrad de Sahmen with Lord Revelstoke, 30 September–1 October 1915.
11 BA 203891. Sir John Bradbury to Lord Revelstoke, 21 October 1915.
12 BA 203986.01.
13 BA 203986.03.
14 *New York Tribune*, 15 October 1875.
15 *Hansard*, 2 August 1854.

CHAPTER 2

Russian Banks During the First World War and the Revolution

Sergei Lebedev

In the last third of the nineteenth century, Russia had become part of the European banking community. In this period there were already close ties between Russian banks and the Western economy; merchant bankers and private bankers – many of them coming from Western Europe – were dominant in Russian finance. Then, from the end of the nineteenth century, the largest Russian commercial banks evolved from the status of speculative banks to that of universal banks. This was partly reflected in the growth of the number of branches. By January 1890, 34 banks had 47 branches, while by the same date 20 years later, 31 Russian banks had 492 branches (Epstein, 1925, Appendix 1). In the 1890s, overseas branches were also established; on the eve of the First World War these branches were most numerous in Paris, where France had been the main creditor of the Russian Empire. The First World War then dealt a heavy blow to banking – essentially a cosmopolitan business – all over the world.

This paper focuses on several problems of the period of war, revolution, nationalization and the early years of the Soviet regime in Russia. These issues include the relationships between Russian bankers and Russian authorities, the debts of Russian banks to foreign banks, Russian government deposits abroad, and the development of Russian banks after 1917.

The First World War

At the beginning of the First World War, the absence of any moratorium on the withdrawal of deposits in Russia had a profound positive effect, helping to instil public trust in banks. Banks had turned to small investors, even though railway companies remained the main bank customers before the war. Railway accounts took up the largest part of the Russian banks' liabilities at that time.

During the war Russian banks underwent a phase of speculation and concentration. In 1914–17, the largest bank in the country, Russo-Asiatic

Bank (RAB), having lost its French partners' support, gambled on domestic backing and strengthened its ties with the business interests of I. I. Stacheev and P. P. Batolin. The resulting expansion of the group led by RAB influenced a number of other bank establishments such as the United Bank and Volga-Kama Commercial Bank (Kitanina, 1969). A. I. Putilov, chairman of RAB, preferred to let K. I. Jaroshinski's financial group acquire other banks which had been under the influence of RAB, allowing Jaroshinski to acquire the Russian Industrial Trading Bank and later the Russian Bank for Foreign Trade. The Siberian Commercial Bank was taken over by N. C. Denisov, who had made his fortune in army supplies (Bovykin and Petrov, 1994, p. 306).

With the help of the banks, giant trading organizations and holding companies had been formed before and during the war. These groups were able to continue their activities even after 1917. The Petrograd International Commercial Bank (PICB) established the Southern-Russian Community for Foreign Trade ('Juroveta') with branches all over the country, while the Petrograd Discount Bank created 'Technogor', a company running the bank's interests in various sectors. The Russian 'Trading and Industrial Bank' brought together 18 transport, insurance and steamer companies into a holding company, including in particular the management of more than 300 steamer companies between the Caspian and Baltic Seas. The company had 400 agencies in the cities of Russia. The huge firm of Stacheev and Co. was working its way through Siberia, the Far East and Middle Asia. Its income in 1917 reached 17 million roubles. It was on the initiative of P. P. Batolin, a prominent partner in Stacheev and Co., that the Buchora Bank was formed. By 1917 this bank, with a total of 110 million roubles in shares of different banks on its hands, was able to make use of a credit of 220 million roubles (Gins, 1992, pp. 61–2).

Before the war, Russian banks had a wide circle of correspondents abroad, with many respected firms among them. The Paris house of Rothschilds, for example, used Russian banks for settling its accounts with its Russian interests.[1] Parisian branches of Russian commercial banks dealt in a wide range of currency operations, buying francs in France on account of Russian banks in Russia. Furthermore, they invested their French liabilities in Russian securities, thereby attracting French investment in Russian business and crediting their head offices in Russia. They also carried out exchange arbitrage, cashed the coupons of government and railway loans, and acted as French representatives of Russian companies (Anan'ich and Lebedev, n.d., 'Consortia', pp. 434–60).

During the war the foreign branches of Russian banks made loans to finance the country's military needs, carrying out exchange operations through the trading of Russian shares. Currency operations were made easier through opening rouble accounts to be settled in francs or through placing short-term bills of exchange. Such speculative operations incurred considerable losses for the banks' clients. However, these deals were not forbidden by the French government, in contrast to speculation in the English pound sterling at that time (Ehrensberger, 1925, p. 358).

The First World War reduced the importance of foreign participation in the share capital of Russia's leading banks. This involvement had reached 30 per cent in the early 1910s but it fell away when foreign shareholders could not participate in shareholders' meetings and when it proved impossible to sell new Russian share issues to foreign shareholders. In the Franco-Russian RAB, the participation of French shareholders in the bank's capital fell from one half to one third. Meanwhile all the Russian banks had carried out new share issues. The Russian Finance Ministry was bound to view with suspicion those banks with large German shareholdings, notably PICB and the Russian Bank for Foreign Trade.

In 1916, Russia saw a rise in banking activity and a growth in turnover in trade and in the overseas markets for Russian securities abroad – particularly in France, where the prices of securities turned out to be much lower than in Russia. This discount decreased as the amount of commercial bills in circulation went down. Russian military supplies were basically underwritten by state treasury loans. As in all the combatant countries, banks in Russia invested in short-term state liabilities and in state military loans. The Paris branches of the Russian banks also played a significant role in attracting French financial support for Russia's new internal securities.

Nevertheless, the inability of Russian banks to pay out dividends for 1914 (in the spring of 1915) had caused a dramatic fall in their share prices. The fall was heavier in Paris than in Russia. For example, the RAB share price fell to 395 francs or lower, having been rated at 575 francs at the beginning of the war. But by June 1917 the RAB's share price recovered to 670 francs (even in Paris) as a result of RAB's reassuring annual report for 1916. It was a happy year for all Russian banks. It seemed as if the Russian economy had lived through the shock of retreat and the defeats of 1914–15. During the war the balance-sheet totals of Russian banks grew higher than in the previous 30 years. Liabilities had grown from 5.4 billion roubles to 12.8 billion roubles. Discount loan operations increased from 5.6 billion roubles to 10.6 billion roubles, while the total balance sheet grew from 7.3 to 17.9

billion roubles. It should be noted, however, that prices had risen by 28.7 per cent in 1914, 20.0 per cent in 1915, 93.5 per cent in 1916, and no less than 683.3 per cent in 1917 (Atlas, 1930, p. 81).

The ties between Russian banks and French and English banks had loosened during the war, while the relationships with banks in neutral countries became stronger. In December 1916, the rules for the operation and activities of the National City Bank of New York in Russia were agreed (Tkachenko, 1998). It was only the second time (after the arrival of Crédit Lyonnais in 1879) that a foreign bank was allowed to open an office in St Petersburg. This privilege was connected with the expectations of a new world economic order which might follow a victory over Germany. In 1916, there were also two Russo-Dutch banks in St Petersburg, preparing for the post-war battle for the Russian market after the defeat of Germany and the abolition of the Russo-German trading treaty of 1904.

During the war the Nordic countries strengthened their investment position in Russia. In the spring of 1917 the Russian-Norwegian Bank was formed in Petrograd (St Petersburg). Its founders aimed at financing light industry and advanced sectors such as electro-chemistry and electro-metallurgy. Using their connections in financial and industrial circles in Norway, the founders hoped to attract specialists in technology in Russia to stimulate the development of hydroelectricity. The founders of the new bank also intended to introduce the large Norwegian shipping companies to the Russian market.

Meanwhile, the activities of Swedish bankers were closely connected with American economic expansion in Russia during the First World War. U. Ashberg, a prominent Swedish banker in Russia at the time, had begun his career in Russia as a representative of J. P. Morgan. In contrast to American bankers, however, Ashberg was in close contact with Russian politicians. He supported the pro-German circle and his 'New Bank' was classified by the Entente countries an undesirable partner for business in neutral countries. Ashberg's ambitions were fully realized when he emerged from being the owner of a humble bank to the status of a key partner of Bolshevik interests. At the time the Bolsheviks were trying to find an outlet to the financial markets of the world through neutral countries (Ostrovski, 1993, pp. 3–18).

Nationalization

A day after the Bolsheviks took power on 9 November 1917, the banks in Petrograd began opening irregularly for an hour-and-a-half or two hours a day and with intervals of one day or more. The committee of bank representatives decided to limit operations and restrict daily cash withdrawals to 10 000 roubles per capita, although customers' access to bank safes was permitted. By 13 November, cash payments were reduced to 3000 roubles a day per head. Initially the turnover on current accounts remained stable and it was only on 25–26 November, as the Petrograd public grew increasingly nervous, that withdrawals outnumbered the deposits. After 1 December the situation changed entirely. The State Bank's accountants protested against the forced confiscation of 5 million roubles from the banks' cash resources for the needs of the new government of the Council of Peoples' Commissioners. Those who went on strike in protest were dismissed. The paralysis of the central credit system made life difficult for customers, especially private banks, which could not regularly stock up on cash and were therefore unable to supply provincial branches and make interbank compensation payments. The Azov-Don Commercial Bank actually created a special compensation department to substitute for the functions of the State Bank. However the inability to supply cash to bank counters forced banks to restrict cash payments to 1000 roubles a day for individuals and 20 000 roubles a day for firms. On 3 December, this maximum was lowered to 10 000 roubles.

On 14–16 December, private banks negotiated with the Bolshevik commissioner of the State Bank as to the regulation of their activity. From 17 December, the private banks were able to resume work under the control of the State Bank, ending the 15-day period in which the State Bank had not functioned. In Moscow the State Bank, having retained its personnel, continued to operate but with frequent breaks resulting from the shortage of cash. The maximum daily payment per head was reduced to 150 roubles (Epstein, 1925, pp. 75–8). Thus, although nationalization was not yet formally in progress, the banks themselves set limits for payments from the customers' accounts.

The Bolsheviks gave the nationalization of banks a wide berth until the beginning of December 1917, when coordinated steps were taken to enforce and authorize the wishes of 'the masses'. On 27 December, the private banks were taken over, marking the start of nationalization of private property (Shepelev, 1998, pp. 86–9).

The decree of 21 January 1918 abolished all state loans and also state guarantees on bonds of various enterprises. Short-term liabilities of the State Treasury remained in use, along with credit notes with no interest to be drawn from them. The 'low-income' holders of the cancelled state securities or internal loans costing less than 10 000 roubles were promised personal certificates of the new Russian Soviet Federated Socialist Republic

(RSFSR) loan. Deposits in state savings-bank branches (and the interest due on them) were to be protected but the bonds of cancelled loans held by savings bank offices were exchanged for book debts of the RSFSR. The State Bank was put in charge of the abolition of loans. It was required to register all the paper securities in circulation (no matter whether they were to be cancelled or not). Special committees were given the right, with the approval of the local Soviets, to define those who could be enrolled as 'low-income' citizens who would be exempt from charges. The last section of the decree of 21 January gave the committees the power to annul entirely those savings which had been acquired 'in a non-working way', even if they were less than the free-of-charge minimum of 5000 roubles. Moreover in January 1918 the radical Bolshevik leader Y. Larin introduced his proposals for the abolition of money and the monetary system. The authorities were also aware that hyper-inflation created suitable conditions for expropriation of the funds of all layers of society which had any significant savings on their hands.

The attack on the Petrograd banks was a severe shock for the banking world. The French military censors intercepted telegrams from Petrograd on 27 December 1917 relating to the arrest of Vishnegradsky, a director of the PICB. Similarly they halted press telegrams dealing with the seizure, on Lenin's orders, of the Petrograd banks ('Les gardes rouges ferment le Crédit Lyonnais de Pétrograd, arrêtent directeurs') on the grounds that the news would undermine the morale of the French armed forces.[2] The denial of the legitimacy of nationalization later formed the legal basis for the operation of foreign branches of Russian banks.

All the same, during the first half of 1918, there were hopes among Russian bankers that the authorities would distance themselves from the policy of nationalization. In March a new wind of Bolshevik economic policy was blowing. Between March and August, Y. E. Gukovski, a champion of the rouble, served as the People's Commissioner of Finance. He assumed that the apparatus of nationalized banks need not be very different from that of pre-revolutionary banks (Ol'shevski, 1999, pp. 29–31, 34–5, 37, 44). In April, in a closed-doors meeting between Lenin, the representatives of the Public Commissariat of Finance, Gukovski, and the Head Commissioners of the State Bank (A. P. Spunde and Ja. S. Ganetski), a unanimous decision was taken to combine all the banks in a single and united People's Bank of the Russian Republic. But opinions varied as to the transformation of the nationalized banks. Spunde and Lenin voted in favour, Gukovski was against, and Ganetski leaned to a neutral position, as he did not think the idea could be implemented in practice. The suggestions for the protection of deposits, the freedom of cheque payments and the need for subsidies to consumers needs were accepted. The meeting also considered the preparation of a law encouraging citizens to keep money in bank accounts.

On 15 April 1918, Gukovski presented the first unified statement of RSFSR financial policy. He suggested taking emergency measures to recreate the system of monetary credit. Gukovski indicated that denationalization was being considered, as nationalization had been crippling trade and the systematic confiscations in industry had ruined the whole credit apparatus. He believed that there was no hope of finding subscribers for Soviet loans after the annulment of earlier Russian state loans.[3] Lenin's view was more pragmatic, against the background of communist criticism of Gukovski's programme and the clamour for abolition of the monetary system in favour of a socialist model of economic management. Lenin was more concerned with working out non-socialist methods of attacking bourgeois finance.

Hence it is clear that the Soviet authorities' financial policy, until June 1918, was vague in its concepts. Inside Russia and at overseas branches, the administration of the banks was preserved with the same membership which had been decreed according to pre-revolutionary laws. Inside Russia, managers chose to sign separate treaties with the Soviet authorities. Then in March and April 1918, the bankers joined forces with the authorities. Those with foresight now started negotiations for the sale of Russian bank shares. N. C. Denisov sold his controlling shares of the Siberian Commercial Bank to English interests and K. I. Jaroshinsky attempted to trade his bank's shares, first to the Entente allies and then to German interests.

After bank nationalization, a number of famous financiers still remained in Moscow, notably A. N. Naidenov of the Moscow Commercial Bank and G. A. Krestovnikov, head of the Moscow Merchants' Bank, who died in 1918. In May 1918, N. A. Vtorov, an eminent Moscow industrialist owner and financier, was murdered in his office on Varvarskaja (St Barbara) square. Many high-ranking officials of the old banks who had stayed in Moscow were now prepared to deal with the Soviet government rather than being counted in with the bourgeoisie. Posner, the former director of Crédit Lyonnais, thus became an administrator of the People's Bank of the RSFSR; his office was authorized to issue permits for the export of roubles. Vinberg, director of the Siberian Bank in Petrograd, and Malevinski, director of the Moscow Merchants' Bank, joined the committee for the liquidation of debts to German banks.

The 'red terror' which began in the autumn of 1918 forced most of the business elite to move to territories not occupied by the Bolsheviks. About 40 representatives of the financial elite left the country in February 1920, along with the evacuation of the whites in the south of Russia. Scores of Russian bankers found shelter, bed and board throughout Europe (Bovykin and Petrov, 1994, pp. 309–11).

Meanwhile, in December 1919, the People's Bank needed to liquidate the balances of joint stock banks. By this time the People's Commissioner of Finance, in his statements and directives, announced the closure of all the other private banks in the territory of Soviet Russia. At the end of 1919, the People's Bank itself became *de facto* a branch of the Finance Head Office, united with the former State Treasury. The bank was required to plan the finance of the entire economy and state system, budget activity and monetary circulation.

The economic decrees of the Bolsheviks marginalized the legal framework of finance. Trading in securities now became a matter of direct personal deals and this status quo continued until 1919–20. Professor I. C. Ozerov stated that people from Petrograd, Moscow and Odessa at that time were busy trading shares, somehow managing to extract securities from Petrograd banks. When Ozerov planned to sell his shares in the Parviainen factory and buy currency at the beginning of the 1919, the representatives of RAB – its Petrograd managers A. Z. Ivanov and M. N. Miller – asked for a 30 per cent commission for the bank. Such rates were actually imposed at that time for loan payments on bills.

Attempts at Compromise

On 12–16 April 1918, six directors of the nationalized banks were invited to the State Bank to take part in the work of the committee which was researching the effects of the nationalization of private banks. They accepted the invitation readily, being worried about the interests of their staff and shareholders. The vice-director of RAB pointed out that the bourgeoisie was ready for compromise with the 'socialist regime as long as it was inspired with democratic ideals' (Verstraete, 1918). This statement by one of the leading Russian bankers is important for a general understanding of the relatively passive role of the Russian bourgeoisie during the civil war. Quite apart from idealism, for many it was merely a matter of saving their property.

In their report, the bankers stressed that it was necessary for private nationalized banks to state their balances on the day of nationalization in order to take account of all operations that took place after that date. To fulfil this requirement, all the banks needed to reinstate their managers, personnel and offices. Banks needed to take in deposits, whose safety had to be assured. As to active operations, it was argued, the banks were drifting towards total liquidation as a result of the concentration of all banking activities in the new national bank.

This conference, held in April 1918 (four months after the nationalization directive was implemented), brought together more than 50 people, including representatives of the government, private banks, educated economists, representatives of trade and industry and the high-ranking functionaries of the pre-revolutionary Finance Ministry and State Bank. The bankers opposed the destruction of records, which needed to be analysed to produce an accurate idea of shareholders' rights and to make the Bolsheviks act more systematically and fairly in cases of expropriation. This approach would be a precedent for shareholders in industry (Verstraete, 1918, pp. 288–9).

Step-by-step nationalization of the banks was to begin after April 1918. The old bank managers thereby had the opportunity to alter the Bolshevik commissars' banking decisions and to change the new personnel that had been introduced (Epstein, 1925, pp. 106–7). The owners of current accounts were eager to withdraw their deposits and, although payments were limited to very small sums, the commissars in the nationalized banks actually proved to be quite easy to deal with. Bank officials were paying out up to maximum of 750 roubles a month from each current account. Yet it was always possible to circumvent such rules, especially as the Bolsheviks and the commissars in charge of banks were ready to give the go-ahead for withdrawal of large sums of money, generating a 12–15 per cent commission in their favour. It was also possible to retrieve valuables and securities which had been left in bank safes.[4]

On 31 May 1918, Maurice Verstraete, vice-chairman of RAB, wrote to F. E. Dzerzhinsky, the chairman of the Cheka, enclosing a message for Lenin. This was by way of an answer to Dzerzhinsky, who on 28 May had encouraged Verstraete to write to him. At this time, Verstraete was himself under the spell of Lenin's ideas to some extent. In his letter to Dzerzhinsky on 31 May, Verstraete assumed that political unity had been split: the socialist regime existed only in several regions of the country while in others a capitalist regime had survived; in some parts the banks were nationalized, and in others the shareholders held their rights tightly in their hands. The financial and trading interests of the RSFSR abroad had to be preserved by capitalist means. From Verstraete's point of view, it was of importance to have a Russian bank across RSFSR borders, which could be given a free rein by foreign governments, which could maintain credits and connections, and which at the same time would stay in touch with the government of People's Commissioners. Verstraete suggested RAB for this role as it had 116 branches and agencies, 19 of them in China, Japan, Manchuria, India, France, England and Italy, not to speak of a special representative in New York and 20 agencies in Russian regions which had been captured by Austrian and German troops. It seemed to be a matter of convenience to use this bank as the French government had always regarded it as much a French bank as a Russian one 'as most of its shares were in France'. In England and the United States, bankers were also accustomed to treating RAB as one of the main ties between Russia and the allies.

Verstraete offered to protect the bank from nationalization and thus preserve its assets abroad, primarily in China. He suggested the reclassification of shareholders as creditors (also using this as a universal principle when nationalizing industry) so as to allow the replacement of shares with bonds with flexible income. He drew a parallel with Banque de l'Indo-Chine in France, whose position had much in common with RAB's; the administration was in Paris, while its main activity was concentrated in the Far East. The members of the RAB board and management would work and retire only with the agreement with the RSFSR government. Verstraete's project aimed to concentrate the bank's business activity abroad and to develop trading companies on this platform. The pragmatic views of the Bolshevik government should not be underestimated, as shown in the negotiations it held with RAB (Watson, 1993, p. 40). The most eminent figures of Russian financial world (V. V. Kuzminsky, N. W. Kutler, V. V. Tarnovski, W. V. Nekrasov, M. J. Bogolepov, A. A. Bachmanov and others) collaborated – as with S. W. Tretjakov – in this strategy for overseas banking.

Banks Without Bolsheviks

In reality, the question of Russian banks' foreign branches and their branches in territories not under Bolshevik control was put off until at least 1924, the year of France's recognition of the USSR. By this year the foreign branches had adopted French sets of rules. However, RAB and the Eastern China Railroad – its best foreign asset – remained the subject of international dispute until the end of the 1920s and the early 1930s.

The Paris branches of Russian banks kept functioning till the end of October 1924, when their business was sequestrated by the Departement of the Seine.[5] After the 'francization' of Russian banks' branches and the diplomatic recognition of the USSR by the French government, representatives of Soviet Russia systematically attempted to take control of all Russian credit establishments abroad. For that purpose identities were falsified to claim on packets of shares which had got into Bolshevik hands during bank nationalization in December 1917. As early as 1918, the Emergency Committee (Cheka) was busy tracing the shareholders of large enterprises (Lebedev, 1999, pp. 160–1). On 1 November 1924, the Commissariat for Finance issued instructions to the Commissariats of External Trade and Foreign Affairs, requiring the collection of information about Russian banks' branches abroad. The instructions called for the immediate delivery of information on foreign legislation; certificates of French courts' decisions as to Russian banks; evidence of whether the banks had become independent in 1917; balance sheets since 1917; the nationality of customers and general characteristics of branches' activities; shares issued since 1917; certificates on how the old shares were quoted and whether new issues had been made, and information about foreign participation in the capital of Russian banks abroad.[6]

The fate of the PICB's Paris branch, the second most important after RAB in the 1910s, was characteristic. Before 1917, the controlling tranche of the PICB's shares was in the directors' hands. A further 44 000 shares were held by K. I. Jaroshinsky and 17 000 were held by the Stacheev-Batolin group. By the spring of 1918, Jaroshinsky bought all these shareholdings and resold 80 000 shares to F. Leech, an English agent in Russia, together with the shares of the Siberian Commercial Bank and the Russian Bank for Foreign Trade (Fursenko, 1991, pp. 281–3; Bovykin and Petrov, 1994, p. 312).[7]

The nationalization of banks, declared in December 1917 by the Soviet Government, had been carried out in the Russian territory which it then controlled, although branches of the Petrograd and Moscow nationalized banks were able to continue their work in the areas which had been under the control of the Bolsheviks' enemies during the civil war. At the end of 1918, in territories outside Bolshevik control, temporary directorates of the PICB, Volga-Kama, Azov-Don, Russian Bank for Foreign Trade, and the Russian Trade and Industry Bank were created. On 7–20 October 1919, the representatives of private banks gathered in a Bolshevik-free region for a banking assembly. At this meeting it was assumed that in the territories between the Pacific and Urals the banks were doing their normal business. The White government gave credits to banks for current account payments, for opening credits and for commodity loans. It was also assumed that the question of the establishment of Russian Export Bank had been solved, with private banks participating in the establishment of a new credit institute in which 55 per cent of its shares were to be reserved for commercial banks. The issue of South-Siberian Railroad bonds for 72 million roubles was achieved at the entrance rate of 93 for 100. The temporary directorates were keen to recruit members of their central boards to their numbers.[8] In this way a consolidation of a wrecked banking system was being attempted. Russian banks were also functioning with the same independence in parts of the old empire which were now in 'border' states.

By 1918, the managements of the main pre-revolutionary banks began to function in Paris by consolidating the remaining assets of former branches which had escaped Bolshevik control. Thus a number of PICB departments in White territories from Simpheropol to Vladivostok maintained relations with bank managements in Paris until the end of civil war in Russia. However, it was seriously weakened after it had given a subsidy to its Geneva branch, possibly when it opened in 1917.

Daniel V. Jéquier, director of Banque Internationale de Commerce, offered the French a majority stake in the PICB, using the shares which had belonged to German holders and were under the control of the Commission des Reparations. The text of 'Resumé du Traité avec l'Allemagne. Partie IX, clauses financières' appeared to offer this possibility.[9] The project was not carried through. The French Ministry of Finance, always suspicious of the PICB's close relations with Germany, was hoping that the Banque Internationale de Commerce would be more orientated to the Allies.[10] The PICB (which had actually transferred its management to Paris) had shares of 13 million francs out of a total capital of 15 million francs. But by 1920, when the capital of the Banque Internationale de Commerce had risen to 30 million francs, the PICB no longer had the majority of its shares. Among the heads of the bank were Count V. N. Kokovtsov, the former chairman of the Council of Ministers and a Finance Minister, and long-serving directors of the International Bank such as A. I. Vyshnegradski, E. G. Shaikevich and J. J. Savich (Vitte, 1960, p. 541, commentary no. 77). The new bank inherited the majority of the PICB's personnel. In the early 1920s, the Banque Internationale de Commerce emerged as one of the most liquid banks of Paris. In 1922, it ranked as 25th among the 43 member banks of the clearing house.[11] Later on it became focused on exchange, arbitrage and speculation.

The PICB existed alongside the Banque Internationale de Commerce as a 'société de fait'. The bank rented rooms from the Rothschilds at 26 rue Lafitte, the address of its old Paris branch. The board controlled most of the shares and did its work without convening shareholders' meetings. In reality, any shares left in Russia could not be presented on behalf of their owners. This situation was later used by Soviet representatives, who used false identities to present receipts for 'nationalized' shares with the aim of obtaining influence over the business of old Russian private banks abroad.

On 17 August 1934, the liquidation of the PICB was announced by the commercial tribunal of the Departement of the Seine. German shareholders in the PICB acted jointly through Deutsche Bank to contest the liquidation decision in the French courts until the beginning of the Second World War.[12] It should be noted that there was also a committee of Russian banks in Paris, which regarded itself as a descendant of the old association of banks in Petrograd. After the Bolshevik Revolution, the bankers gathered at first in the RAB office at 9 rue Boudreau, Paris. After 1919, they met at the Russian Chamber of Commerce, the headquarters of Arthur Raffalovich, who was himself a very active member of the committee. After the recognition of the Russian government by France in 1924, this group no longer met.[13]

By 1925 the following banks with Russian connections operated in Paris:

- Rodocanachi & Cie
- Gunzburg & Cie
- Banque Générale pour le Commerce Étranger (formerly the Russian Bank for Foreign Trade)
- Banque Internationale de Commerce (created by PICB in 1919)
- Banque du Nord
- Banque des Pays du Nord (managed by Kamenka (Azov-Don Bank), Knut Wallenberg (Stockholm), Olaf Hambro (London))
- Banque Russe du Commerce et de l'Industrie
- Banque de Commerce de l'Azov-Don
- Société Franco-Russe de Prêts et Avances
- Banque Commerciale pour la Russie et le Levant (subsidiary of Hoskier & Cie)
- Banque Russo-Asiatique (with branches in ten cities in China)
- Société Mutuelle d'Epargne 'Kazna' (established 1926, with funds and securities deposited in the Banque Internationale de Commerce)
- Banque du Crédit Mutuel (established 1930)
- Crédit Mutuel du Commerce et des Métiers (established 1930).

Russian Deposits Abroad

Since the end of the 1760s, Russian state credit had developed in the monetary markets of the world with the help of first-rate banking firms.

Table 2.1   Russian government deposits in French banks, 1927

Bank	Total francs
Banque de l'Union Parisienne	262 838
Banque des Pays du Nord	2 790 185
Banque Générale pour le Commerce Etranger[14]	724 307
Banque Hoskier	8 983 994
Banque Privée (Lyon-Marseille)	8 396 222
Comptoir National d'Escompte de Paris	8 048 790
Crédit Industriel et Commercial	83 899
Crédit Lyonnais	996 470
Hottinguer	3 086 039
Louis Dreyfus	184 459
Paribas	571 176
Petrograd International Commercial Bank	23 786 404
Rothschild frères	1 778 786
Russian Bank for Commerce and Industry	20 794
Russian Bank for Foreign Trade	540 844
Russo-Asiatic Bank	425 422
Société Générale	2 525 022
Vernes & Co	1 386 324
Total	**64 591 975**

Source: Archives économiques et financières (AEF), Paris, B 33842.

With the appearance of joint stock commercial banks, the biggest credit institutes of the West had become partners of the Russian government (Anan'ich, 1970, 1991; Anan'ich and Lebedev, 1991, pp. 125–47, pp. 434–60; Lebedev, 2000, pp. 242–55).

The problem of Russian state debt also had another dimension – the large state assets of Russia abroad, which were necessary for exchange interventions and loans. These were used on a profitable basis by Russian banks, which were members of the issuing syndicates. No less than 13 per cent of the pre-war Russian budget was spent on state debt payments. By 1 January 1914, about 48 per cent of liabilities were inside the country and during the war that proportion was more than 50 per cent. In France alone the rates of interests and payment were as high as 400 million francs a year (Raffalovich, 1922, pp. 9–10).

With the beginning of the First World War, payments to banks in France were subject to a moratorium. This enabled French banks to freeze all cash payments of the Russian government. Not all banks took this step; the Rothschilds in Paris did not use the moratorium and continued to pay the current accounts of the Russian State Treasury (Soviet ministrov, 1999, p. 212).

By 10 November 1914, the bank deposits of the Russian government in France totalled 298.7 million roubles. The largest account was with Crédit Lyonnais, in total 31.8 million roubles or 74.7 million francs. A further 63.45 million roubles were held in Parisian branches of the PICB and RAB (Lebedev, 2000, p. 249). The cash available to the Russian treasury in Paris amounted to 300 million francs by 2 January 1915, one quarter of the level before the war (Sidorov, 1960, p. 223).

In January 1915, the moratorium was lifted and the turnover on the accounts revived. By contrast, in January 1927, the Russian government's deposits in French banks amounted to 64 million francs.

Conclusion

Historians argue that the Allied powers over-exploited Russia's potential resources during the First World War and that this was one of the causes of the social explosion in Russia and a trigger for the nationalism of all Russian governments, whether Bolsheviks or White. Clearly the war against Germany – Russia's main trade partner – was a catastrophe for Russia. The country was in an economic blockade as soon as Turkey became involved in the war in the autumn of 1914. After the Brest-Litovsk peace treaty with Germany was concluded by Lenin's government in March 1918, the Allied powers began to look at Russia as an enemy nation and hence the blockade became more intensive (Hogenhuis-Seliverstoff, 1981).

Yet relations between the Soviet economy (the 'economy without enterprise') and German and other Western banks were emplanted and even grew (Pohl, 1988; Shishkin, 1989, 1991; Carlbäck-Isotalo, 1997). The state credit system of the USSR certainly flourished in response to the new economic policy adopted after the end of the civil war, when the State Bank was formed on 3 October 1921. In this new environment other banks began to appear, including specialized banks (Gindin, 1986, pp. 261–9; Petrov, 1999, pp. 133–4; Gregory and Tikhonov, 2000, pp. 1017–40).

References

Anan'ich, B. V. (1970), *Rossija i mezhdunarodnyi kapital 1897–1914*, Leningrad: Ocherki istorii finansovych otnoshenij.

Anan'ich, B. V. (1991), *Bankirskije doma v Rossii 1860–1914*, Leningrad: Ocherki istorii predprinimatel'stva.

Anan'ich, B. V., and Lebedev, S. K. (n.d.), 'International banking consortia for Russian railway bonds up to 1914', *Problemy sozial'no-ekonomicheskoj i politicheskoj istorii*.

Anan'ich, B. V., and Lebedev, S. K. (1991), 'Kontora pridvornych bankirov v Rossii i evropeiskije denezhnye rynki (1798–1811 gg.)', St Petersburg: *Problemy sozial'no-ekonomicheskoi istorii Rossii*.

Atlas, Z. V. (1930), *Den'gi i kredit (pri kapitalizme i v SSSR)*, Moscow: publisher not known.

Bovykin, V. I. and Petrov, Y. A. (1994), *Kommercheskie banki Rossiiskoi imperii*, Moscow: publisher not known.

Carlbäck-Isotalo, H. (1997), *Att byta erkännande mot handel. Svensk-ryska förhandlingar 1921–1924 (Exchanging Trade for Recognition: Swedish-Soviet negotiations 1921–1924)*, Uppsala: publisher not known.

Ehrensberger, F. (1925), *Die Pariser Börse und die französischen Bankinstitute seit dem Weltkrieges (1914–1925)*, Zürich: publisher not known.

Epstein, E. (1925), *Les banques de commerce russes*, Paris: publisher not known.

Fursenko, A. A. (1991), 'The Russian Vanderbilt', *Problemy sozial'no-ekonomicheskoj istorii Rossi*. St Petersburg: publisher not known.

Gindin, I. (1986), 'Die Rolle der Banken bei der Finanzierung der sowjetischen Industrie 1917 bis 1927', *Jahrbuch für Geschichte der sozialistischen Länder Europas*, Berlin: publisher not known.

Gins, G. K. (1992) *Predprinimatel'*, Moscow: publisher not known.

Gregory, P. P., and Tikhonov, A. (2000), 'Central planning and unintended consequences: creating the Soviet financial system, 1930–1939', *Journal of Economic History*, 60 (4).

Hogenhuis-Seliverstoff, A. (1981), *Les relations franco-soviétiques 1917–1924*, Paris: publisher not known.

Kitanina, T. M. (1969), *Voenno-inflazionnye konzerny v Rossii 1914–1917 gg. Konzern Putilova-Stacheeva-Batolina*, Leningrad: publisher not known.

Lebedev, S. K. (2000), 'E. Hoskier & Cie – bankir russkogo pravitel'stva vo Francii', *Problemy vsemirnoj istorii; Sbornik statei v chest' A. A. Fursenko*, St Petersburg: publisher not known.

Lebedev, S. K. (1998), 'Die deutschen Beziehungen der St Petersburger Internationalen Handelsbank', *Deutsche Unternehmen und Unternehmer im Russischen Reich im 19. und frühen 20. Jahrhundert (hrsg. von D. Dahlmann, C. Scheide)*, Essen: publisher not known.

Lebedev, S. K. (1999), 'Alexei Frolovich Filippov: journalist, banker and member of Cheka', *Iz glubiny vremen*, 10, St Petersburg: publisher not known.

Ol'shevski, V. G. (1999), 'Finansovo-economicheskaja polytika sovetskoj vlasti v 1917–1918 gg.: tendentsii i protivorechija', *Voprosy istorii*, 3.

Ostrovski, A. V. (1993), 'Ulof Ashberg mezhdu Zapadom i Rossiei. Iz vospominanij "krasnogo bankira" ', *Iz glubiny vremen*, St Petersburg: publisher not known.

Petrov, J. (1999), 'Kommerceskii bank v epochu NEPa: Istorija Elektrobanka (1922–1928)', *Rossija na rubezhe XIX–XX vekov. Materialy nauchnych chtenij pamjati prof. V. I. Bovykina*, Moscow: publisher not known.

Pohl, M. (1988), *Geschäft und Politik. Deutsch-russisch/sowjetische Wirtschaftsbeziehungen 1850–1988*, Mainz: publisher not known.

Raffalovich, A. (1922), 'La Dette publique Russe', *La Dette publique de la Russie*, Paris: publisher not known.

Shepelev, L. E. (1998), 'Sovetskaja vlast' i nazionalisazija bankov', *1917 god iparlamentarism*, St Petersburg: publisher not known.

Shishkin, V. A. (1989), *Antisovetskaja blokada i ee krushenije*, Leningrad: publisher not known.

Shishkin, V. A. (1991), *Tsena priznanija. SSSR i strany Zapada v poiskach kompromissa (1924–1929 gg.)*, St Petersburg: publisher not known.

Sidorov, A. L. (1960), *Finansovoje polozhenie Rossii v gody pervoi mirovoi voiny*, Moscow: publisher not known.

Soviet ministrov (1999), *Rossijskoj imperii v gody Pervoj mirovoj vojny. A. N. Yachontov's papers (Zapisi zasedanij i perepiska)*, St Petersburg: publisher not known.

Tkachenko, S. L. (1998), *Amerikanskij bankovskij kapital v Rossii v gody pervoj mirovoj vojny. Dejatel' nost' National City Bank of New York*, St Petersburg: publisher not known.

Verstraete, M. (1918), *Mes cahiers russes*, Paris: publisher not known.

Vitte, S. J. (1960), *Vospominanija*, 1, Moscow: publisher not known.

Watson, D. R. (1993), 'The rise and fall of the Russo-Asiatic Bank. Problems of a Russian enterprise with French shareholders, 1910–26', *European History Quarterly*, 23.

Notes

1 Société Commerciale et Industrielle de Naphta Caspienne et de la Mer Noir, 'Standard Russe', BNITO, Archives Nationales, Paris, 132 AQ 130.
2 Archives de la Préfecture de Police, Paris, B A/761, ff. 2649, 2664.

3 Archives économiques et financières, Paris (AEF), B 33842.
4 Information sur la situation en Russie, Stockholm, 8 September 1918, AEF, B 31977.
5 AEF, B 33842.
6 Controle des succursales des Banques russes en France, 1916–1925, AEF, B 33842. Sous-dossier 2.
7 Note sur les achats de titres russes. Stockholm, 17 fevrier 1919, AEF, B 32005.
8 Telegram from Omsk, 28 October 1919 for A. I. Putilov, AEF, B 32820.
9 10 June 1919, AEF, B 33842.
10 AEF, B 33842. Sous-dossier 2.
11 AEF, B 33842. Sous-dossier 2.
12 Bundesarchiv (Berlin). 80 Ba 2; Deutsche Bank, 7158.
13 Archives de la Préfecture de Police (Paris). B A/1708.
14 Established in 1924 as successor to the Russian Bank for Foreign Trade (Bovykin and Petrov, 1994, p. 312).

CHAPTER 3

Witnesses to Revolution: The Archives of Foreign Banks in Russia

Catherine Potier

Introduction

At the end of the nineteenth century, many banks were interested in Russia; the transformation brought by the railways, the discovery of coal deposits and other industrial developments all promised a high return on investment. In this 'Russian fever' the foreign banks, and particularly European banks, played an important role.

The relations between foreign banks and Russia differed according to the degree of commitment which the banks were prepared to give. This commitment could be in the form of:

- financial connections with Russian banks such as the Banque Russo-chinoise or with Russian companies and especially railway companies;
- financial participations in Russian companies or financial operations such as loans, issues of shares and government loans (as, for example, the £3 million $4\frac{1}{2}$ per cent bonds of the Armavir-Touapsé railway issued by Midland Bank in 1909), or
- direct representation through the opening of branches.

Whatever their relationships with Russia, European banks were all witnesses to revolution, each one in a different way. Although many of them ended any business relations with Russia during the First World War, there are some banking archives which provide evidence of the revolution itself. In order to identify these archives, the following approach has been adopted. First, with the help of Cameron and Bovykin's research, it was possible to identify banks which had a relationship with Russia before the First World War (Cameron and Bovykin, 1991). Secondly, it was possible to identify existing banks or those that merged with current banks. Thirdly, I contacted the archivist or the person in charge of the historical heritage of these banks. Finally these archivists were asked to answer a questionnaire in order to locate the existing documents.

These investigations into archive resources showed that only a few banks have kept their archives over this period. Only nine out of nineteen banks could be identified; moreover, among the documents kept by the banks, few of them concerned the period of the revolution.[1] Nevertheless, even if a bank did not open a subsidiary or branch in Russia, that bank may still have been a witness to revolution. While it may not have experienced it in the same way as a company with branches, it may have paid special attention to current events through representatives or correspondents. Moreover, as few companies preserved their archives over this period, this study took into account all the elements which could have had connections with the subject – namely projects which did not succeed, documentation showing that banks were still interested in Russia and were waiting to resume relations at the right time, or payments or disputes relating to Russian loans in France. For these reasons the scope of this study has been widened in order to present all the sources about the relationship between Russia and European banks during and after the revolution.

This analysis of bank archives is presented in three parts:

1. banks with direct representation in Russia,
2. banks which had financial participations and subsidiaries, and
3. banks which had only business or financial relations with Russia.

This division is not necessarily distinct and some banks which had branches in Russia could also have participated in financial operations. In each case, a brief historical reminder is followed by a description of the most interesting documents held by the bank.

Banks with Branches in Russia

Unlike France, the Czarist government followed the American example and forbade the foundation of foreign bank branches in Russia. At the same time the government agreed to the foundation of branches of foreign industrial enterprises. However, there were two exceptions: the foundation of Crédit Lyonnais' subsidiaries in Petrograd (St Petersburg), Moscow and Odessa, and the foundation of National City Bank of New York's branch in Petrograd, in 1916. The Russian subsidiaries of Crédit Lyonnais and National City Bank of New York operated in Russia following the approval of the Russian authorities. These banks were distinguished from the Russian banks in that their capital was provided by foreigners.

The *National City Bank of New York* opened a branch in Petrograd in January 1917. Its archives, comprising about 38 items covering the period

1915–18, are kept in the 624 collection of the Russian State Archives in St Petersburg. These records include correspondence between the manager of the branch and the head office, comments on the economic and financial situation in Russia, and comments on the possibilities for American companies to invest there. This collection gives another point of view as American bankers were in less evidence than the Europeans at this time, even if their economic influence and their interest grew in the course of the First World War.

As for *Crédit Lyonnais*, the bank set up in Russia when it opened the St Petersburg agency, followed by offices in Moscow and Odessa in 1891. Ten years later, district offices were created in Moscow (Ilinka Street) and in St Petersburg (Vassilevski-Ostrov). Very few archives of the St Petersburg office were kept in the State Archives: the 621 collection contains only information about companies.[2] However, the Crédit Lyonnais Historical Archives have many interesting documents. The collection of the Direction des Agences Etrangères (DAE) is very rich. Indeed, in setting up in Russia, the aim of Crédit Lyonnais was to help French customers who tried to develop their business with Russian industry. The bank played an important role in the market for Russian securities in France and took part in the financing of Russian farming exports. As witnesses to the revolution of 1905, the Crédit Lyonnais offices suffered from looting and were then forced to close during the October Revolution in 1917.

The Crédit Lyonnais archives which have survived are from the bank's headquarters rather than from the branches. They describe, month after month, the chronology of the revolution. The reports from Mr Rotulo and Mr Mathey on the Russian offices – and more particularly on Petrograd – describe the chronology of revolution from 1917 till 1919. They recount the beginning of the Bolshevik Revolution, the occupation of banks by the army on 27 December, the publication of the decree for the nationalization of the banks on 28 December, and the subsequent strike of bank employees. Month after month, every political event affected the branches' activities, the daily difficulties confronting non-Russian bankers, and the bank's relationships with employees and with Russian political representatives. The manager was arrested in June 1919. Until 1921, other reports were sent to the DAE, with details concerning the problems of winding up the agency, the requisition of the building and especially the preservation of the branch records.[3]

Correspondence between Ulysse Baud and Rosselli (director of the DAE) mentions Baud's state of mind: 'However, after all that I've endured during nine months, I must still bear up, what happens is not so terrible and if it is the last step of the agony, I will not fail as it is necessary to resist to the end.'[4] The interest of these documents is obvious: day by day, because Baud sent his letters every week, the historian can observe the development of the revolution in the Petrograd region. It is also interesting to observe staff morale under the pressure of events. When the Bolsheviks took power, it appeared that the new regime was fragile and thus temporary; little by little, however, the regime consolidated its position and the staff and management recognized that it was necessary to deal with the new government.

Most information about the revolution itself is given by general correspondence and by other letters estimating the impact of the revolution on the activity of the bank:

- correspondence on food sent to St Petersburg and Odessa (notes, letters sent to the Swiss and Swedish consulates and foreign offices);[5]
- correspondence concerning the agency's staff and lists of mobilized French staff. In the staff correspondence of the Moscow agency there are letters about the openings of rented safes in January 1918 (in the manager's letters about liquidation), telegrams and staff notes in 1917–18, and also letters about the situation in a more balanced and less detailed way than the above letters.

Staff appointment records are also of special interest. Annual detailed salaries for each employee are recorded, with comments such as 'is in Paris', 'reparation', 'left us since is in Paris', 'mobilized' or 'naturalized Russian' in some cases. These records also show the way the agencies managed their employees.

In the accounting archives of the branches, and more specifically in the balances, the 'cash' line is described as 'available on the State Bank'; for deposits, accounts and bills at sight, 'transfer by the People's Bank of our sale creditors' is quoted in consequence of the measures taken by the state. Under the heading 'Russian portfolio', the bank's ledgers state that 'Treasury bonds [are] due but locked in Moscow'. In the current accounts of the Wassily-Ostroff sub-branch, the balances mention that deposit account creditors on 31 December 1918 do not appear in the balance of 20 December 1912 but should be stamped by the People's Bank in 1919. The same applies to all the balances (definitive balances and monthly balances) of the Odessa branch from 1918 till 1929. These records allow a comparative study of the branches.

The historical interest of these accounting archives, besides balances, is in the regularity of the information relative to the activity and results of the agency. The weekly reports of the branch supply a set of information on the source and use of funds (cash, portfolio, advances, current accounts), the exchanges and the values of stock exchange investments, and the state of advances on securities on call (amounts and rates), current accounts (new customers, foreign correspondents, service offers). Moreover the account registers of the customers of the Odessa branch give an idea of the customers' portfolio of securities, both for private individuals and companies, in the period from 1916 to 1928.

Another part of the archive includes DAE files about the Russian branches. These archives include correspondence with customers from 1917 till 1932, in particular correspondence with the customers of the Russian agencies after 1920. Most of these customers were worried about the future of the contents of their safes, asking that they be put in security: 'However, we have been told, that Mr Roth of the Odessa branch has been able to escape from Odessa, taking his archives and maybe a part of his deposits.' It is interesting to look into the answers given by the directors: 'In spite of the protests of our director – which cost him long months of prison or internment – the Bolsheviks took all the securities by force, deposited in our Petrograd's branch cash and we don't know what occured to them.' In most of their answers, the managing directors referred to the difficulties of communication with agencies: 'We do not have any other news of our Petrograd branch other than that given by one of our employees released by the Bolsheviks, who took possession of all the bonds ; we are not able to tell to you any more.'[6]

Finally, DAE's archives also include about 20 boxes of customers' files relating to the liquidation of the branches, as well as all the accounts of foreign correspondents of Crédit Lyonnais' agencies and documents relative to the liquidation of branches (such as various receipts, securities and valuables deposited in safes, and everything else that could be recovered). In addition, there are files relating to the lawsuits instituted against Crédit Lyonnais. We have also traced financial files from the Direction des Études Economiques et Financières (DEEF), which have been classified and listed in a database. These files, for the greater part, are available for research.

Midland Bank's relations with Russia began in 1907, followed two years later by the issue of the $4\frac{1}{2}$ per cent Armavir-Touapsé Railway loan. The success of the operation was such that the bank's chairman, Sir Edward Holden, decided to strengthen Midland's position in Russia. Although at this time direct investments in Russia were dominated by France, Holden organized several missions and serious negotiations were opened with the Union Bank of Moscow. This initiative and other associations with banking institutions were not fulfilled. Recognizing the opportunities for expansion in Russia for British manufacturers, Midland chose a permanent presence in Russia based on a relationship with the Azov-Don Bank. An office opened in 1916 with Frederick Bunker as representative of the Midland. The office was set up in the Moïka, St Petersburg, in February 1917, 'for the purpose of facilitating the business of the bank between Russia and the United Kingdom' (Holmes and Green, 1986, p. 140). Although the initial outlook was encouraging, after the October Revolution Bunker was forced to escape from Russia in 1918. The tracks of his flight through Finland and Sweden can be found in the bank's archives, in particular through his correspondence. Bunker was a privileged witness to these events; his papers (classification mark 151/2) refer to the political and economic conditions of the country and more generally to business in Russia from March 1917 until April 1918. Bunker's reports and economic studies are an important part of this collection. Another part of Bunker's papers (classification mark 151/3–4) are concerned more particularly with the bank's customers (in particular, their account books) but they also reflect the difficulties of developing the activities of the bank and they contain the statutes of the representative office.

These records – Bunker's papers as Midland's agent and representative in St Petersburg from 1913 to 1918 – are the principal documents concerning Midland's relations with Russia over this period. Documents about the relations of Midland before its office was established in Russia are also preserved, in particular those relating to the Union Bank of Moscow, some balance sheets, correspondence with the City of Moscow, files relating to Russian loans, reports written by Holden's right-hand man Samuel Murray in September and October 1909, and documents about proposals for the purchase and the issue of stock of the Russian government by Barings and other banks. This material amounts to approximately 16 boxes. These files are available for consultation at HSBC Group Archives, London.

It should also be remembered that the *Hongkong and Shanghai Banking Corporation* had an office in Vladivostock from 1918 to 1925 and that some records of that branch have survived. This indicates that a certain amount of banking activity continued in Russia's Far East over a long period. The files of such agencies, when they could be saved, are truly the witnesses of revolution and they represent a privileged source of information for historians.

Subsidiaries and Participations

This category comprises banks with financial participations in Russian banking houses and/or Russian companies, with representation through the boards of directors of these establishments. In some cases these participants also had representatives on the spot or banking correspondents.

Société Générale (SG) began its relationship with Russia in 1872, when it sponsored the Société minière et industrielle, followed in 1897 with the foundation of the Société générale de l'industrie minière et métallurgique en Russie (also known as 'Omnium'). This provided participations in several companies in the coal and metal industries; the Omnium developed gradually, and SG gave loans to its companies. This dynamism in business might seem paradoxical, in that SG did not have any office on Russian territory, unlike Crédit Lyonnais.

In 1901, SG created a subsidiary in St Petersburg, the Banque du Nord, in which the Banque de l'Union Parisienne also participated. Wanting to strengthen its basis on the Russian territory, SG moved closer to the Banque de Paris et des Pays-Bas (Paribas) which had patronized the launch of the Banque Russo-chinoise. A merger agreement between the Banque du Nord and Paribas was signed in 1910 for the formation of the Banque Russo-asiatique, with its head office in St Petersburg. The Banque Russo-asiatique participated in the establishment of companies, the issue of bonds, negotiations for railway concessions, and the temporary purchase of shares for third parties. However, the bank was not a finance company. It was above all a deposit bank. Its branches were 'not imposed branches from abroad and without roots in Russia; by their branches, by their credit operations for trade and industry, they are deeply integrated into the Russian expansion. SG remains responsible to the French owners of the Banque Russo-asiatique's capital, who hold the majority' (Paribas and its partners held 20 per cent of the capital) (Bonin, 1994). Just before the Russian Revolution, the Banque Russo-asiatique had become a great Russian bank in which SG was simply a founding member: 'it symbolizes both the emergence of the Russian economic power and the cooperation between the "two Europes" to settle an attractive growth' (Bonin, 1994, pp. 32–59). However, because of the war, the nationalization and the disappearance of banks in Russia, the Banque Russo-asiatique was not trading at the end of 1917.

Surviving archives give little information about the fate of the Banque Russo-asiatique. The branches' documents and those concerning the bank's activity were not preserved. Only some documents about the Banque du Nord in the State Archives – 564 items details for the 1901–13 period – provide information about the management of the bank, the evolution of the network, credits, the financial and administrative situation, capital and the shareholding. Besides these, the remaining documents are kept in the archives of the French banks, essentially for the pre-revolution period. These documents relate to the payment and to the liquidation of the bank by the Paris committee. No information about the revolutionary period – not even fragmented news – was sent to the Paris committee. In the same way, few documents were preserved in Paribas.

Nevertheless, much more information has been tracked down from participations in companies led either directly by banking institutions or through the Banque Russo-asiatique. For SG and the Banque Russo-asiatique, there are some brief notes and newspaper extracts on the situation of the country and on banking legislation. In these same archives of the former Direction Financière, there are notes by Maurice Verstraete, SG's correspondent at the Banque Russo-asiatique, as well as two files of financial records relating to increases in capital in 1918 and 1919.[7] Records of SG's financial participations through the Banque Russo-asiatique can be found in the Direction Financières's collection, mainly concerning the transactions that SG made for other companies or states. These files are principally concerned with financial participations, containing appraisals of the bank's role or a summary of its assets. These documents include:

- the 'flyleaf', often containing a note on the context (such as general information on each company's creation, business, board of directors, staff, and so on);
- details of the transaction itself (such as its value, members of the syndicate, the term of reimbursement, eligibility for refunds, and so on);
- correspondence between the various members of the syndicate, the representatives of the bank, the customer;
- details such as statutes, extracts of reports of the committee and of the board of directors;
- notes by protagonists and news cuttings from legal publications. In these notes we find information concerning the activity of factories and companies at the time of the revolution. For example, in the file 'Mines de houille de Kouznetzk', the Petrograd committee reported to the Paris head office in August 1917 that the situation of the company was affected by the problems of communication and aggravated by the strike of the staff: 'The fate of our company is too intimately bound with that of the country where we are working that we can't write to you about our company without explaining to you what is taking place here and without mentioning the general political problems which we can see in the repercussions in Makeevka.' There then follows a report on the development of the uprising and its effect on the factory's staff: 'workers

mistreat and sack engineers and foremen they don't like, they evict directors and owners in many places'.[8]

This type of information can be found in the general meeting records, as for instance in a report of an extraordinary general meeting of the 'Union minière et métallurgique de Russie' in July 1921:

> The last months' events in Russia may be the sign of the Bolshevik regime's end. This regime is facing important opposition in the whole country, from farmers as well as from workers ... Therefore, we can hope that a different political order will be soon set up in Russia and that manufacturing will be able to start again.[9]

This information may have been less reliable and more fragmented but it gives an idea of the situation of the country. In another example, the Union minière et métallurgique at its general meeting in June 1920 reported that 'since October 1917, when the Soviets of Makeevka grabbed mines and factories, the company could not regain possession of its factories'. The company also described the state of the machines in its factory and, more generally, the impact of transport problems.

Even when these companies halted their activities as a result of revolution and nationalization, the staff still needed to manage the liquidation of their business. In terms of archives, this work produced transactional payments files (mainly correspondence) concerning the enforcement of laws in order to obtain delays for the execution of their commitments. Payments of debts, notes, correspondence and balances have also survived, having special interest when they supply figures of activity from before the Revolution until 1920.

It is also interesting to compare companies for a study of the impact of the revolution on the economy. About 20 files in SG's Historical Archives, mainly about mines and metallurgy, cover the following examples :

- Union minière et métallurgique de Russie
- Usines de Briansk
- Forges et aciéries du Donetz
- Métallurgique de l'Oural
- Banque de Commerce de l'Azov Don
- Extraits de chênes en Russie
- Gaz de Petrograd (1919).

The accounting archives of these companies, such as analysis ledgers or general ledgers, give some figures about production, outgoings and expenditure (in the cases of the Minière et industrielle de Routchenko or the Hauts fourneaux, forges et aciéries en Russie). At present there are no finding aids but these classified files are listed in a database and available to historians.

The archives of the Banque de Paris et des Pays-Bas contain few documents on the Banque Russo-chinoise. Although there are some documents about companies with which the bank had relations, there are no documents referring to the situation in Russia. The collection comprises for the main part collections of notes, board of directors' reports, statutes, general meetings minutes, balances and correspondence with the other participants (including the Banque de l'Union Parisienne), and some significant documents relating to the mutual interests of merchant banks. The value of these documents lies in bankers' views on Russian companies at this time. The areas of the bank's activities are similar to those of SG's: the Russian banks, the electricity or tramway companies, mines, petroleum, Russian loans and particularly the correspondence with the Russian government.

Paribas' records relating to Russian banks deal with debts and legal judgments, but there are also details of the Russian banks' commitments in the Société Franco-russe de prêts et avances from 1919 until 1945.[10] Records about the Russian banks emphasize Paribas' concern to protect such relations in spite of political events, the objective being on one hand to find capital for the Russians and, on the other hand, for the Europeans to keep contact with Russia and to save French interests.[11] However, these efforts came to an end with the liquidations of the Azov-Don Bank, the Banque russe du commerce et de l'industrie and others. These liquidations generated records such as agreements for payments, liquidation papers and commercial litigation papers. In addition there is a series of documentation and press reports gathered from 1901 to 1960, including news cuttings, reviews and analysis of the French and foreign press, notes and studies relating to the economic and financial situation of Soviet Russia.

The archives from Paribas and those from SG differ as they reflect the interests on the one hand of a retail bank and on the other hand of an investment bank. All the files mentioned above are available at BNP-Paribas' Historical Archives.

Banque de l'Union Parisienne

The Banque de l'Union Parisienne (BUP) participated in the development of Russian business from the beginning of the century (in partnership with Société générale de Belgique) through La Providence Russe. Then with the Banque de l'Union à Moscou, this bank joined the Banque du Nord and the combined bank, with 70 branches, tried to compete with the Banque Russo-asiatique. But in December 1913 disagreements between Russian and French bankers led to the closure of the BUP. However, these files of the BUP are now kept at SG and contain a whole series of records of financial operations and participations in Russia, including some from the period of the Revolution. Files on BUP's financial operations relate to issues of stock, debts and credits, and also more specific details of the financing of assets, personal loans, liquidations, and studies of the economic and financial position. The surviving documents are comparable with those of Paribas, but perhaps the most interesting are the lists of the syndicate's members and the details of their commitments. These files also reflect the views of investment bankers.

Baring Brothers and Co. Ltd

In addition to the French banks, it is important to underline the presence of Baring Brothers and Co. Ltd. Indeed, this bank was the financial agent of the Russian Imperial Government in London. Barings also had links with several Russian banks and railway companies.

Some correspondence of James Wishaw, Barings' agent in Petrograd at the time of the revolution, are preserved in the archives of ING Baring. James Wishaw wrote regularly to the bank and about 100 of his letters have survived. Most of his letters concern customers' business but in several cases Wishaw also gave details of the economic, social and political situation in Russia. One letter in particular is dedicated to the revolutionary activity in November 1917. Other papers describe the revolution which brought the temporary government to the power at the beginning of 1917. The most significant of these is the detailed diary written by the senior partner of Barings, Lord Revelstoke, as a member of the conference of the Allied governments during its mission to Petrograd in January and February 1917. The diary gives details of the life of the upper and middle classes in the city and the negotiations of the Allied governments (see also Chapter 1). Finally, these archives contain interesting correspondence relating to the financial position of the Whites from 1919 until 1920. For the moment these papers are not open for research.

Business Relationships

A number of other banks had links with Russia but did not maintain important participations. In most cases these links did not survive the revolution.

Deutsche Bank

The Deutsche Bank cannot be considered a witness of the Russian Revolution as it did not have a subsidiary or branch in Russia before 1973. Mendelssohn and Disconto Gesellschaft (which merged with Deutsche in 1929) were more prominent but their records have not survived. However, Deutsche Bank had been among the first banks to invest in Russia in the 1880s, especially in the loan issues for railways, banks and government loans. By participating in the Banque Russe pour le Commerce Étranger de Saint-Petersbourg, one of the most important joint-stock banks, Deutsche Bank created a bridgehead in Russia. This bank provided advice and assistance regarding German industrial investments, for example, Siemens.

Even if it did not manage to break the ascendancy of the two Berlin banks, Mendelssohn and Disconto Gesellschaft, Deutsche Bank laid the foundations for an intense development of Russian business in the 1920s. Moreover, there were also rumours that the bank would open in its own name. The *Frankfurter Zeitung* reported on 29 June 1922 that 'an article in a Russian newspaper [which stated that] the Deutsche Bank maintains its own representation in Moscow and tries to open an agency is described by the administration of the bank as without foundation'.

The Historical Institute of the Deutsche Bank keeps some files. For the period before 1914, about 60 files relating to the loan issues for Russian railways, banks and government loans have survived. A small number of files belonging to consortia between 1926 and 1935 are also available for consultation. All these files are in German and all the sources from the period 1850 to 1945 are accessible for consultation.

Dresdner Bank

Dresdner Bank played a role in Russia before the First World War, in particular in the financing of railways, mechanical and electrical engineering. Important business connections had continued since the end of the nineteenth century, including business with Hartmann, an engineering company in Lugansk, and the Russian Electricity Company Union in St Petersburg. In the 1920s and 1930s, the Dresdner Bank participated in the reactivation of financial relations between Germany and Russia. The Dresdner Bank Archives, where collection and arrangement began in 1999, are not accessible for the moment.

Société Générale de Belgique

The Société Générale de Belgique, a mixed bank, was very active in Russia before 1917. Although it had no Russian branches and it had hardly any involvement in government loans, its role was to 'patronize' industrial companies in the sectors of electricity, tramways and metallurgy. It participated in 1895 in the creation of Métallurgique Russo-Belge, which aimed to establish a steel and iron industrial complex in the Southern Donetz region. In 1909, the bank took part in the foundation of the Compagnie générale auxiliaire d'entreprises électriques, to take the control of a Russian company. Three years later, the Société Générale de Belgique acquired a share in newly-established Imatra.

The Société Générale de Belgique also held interests in the transport sector, particularly when in 1910 it acquired control of the Mutual Tramways Company, a holding company specialising in the construction and the exploitation of tramway networks and overseas electricity projects. The Société Générale de Belgique also maintained relations with French banks in many Russian businesses – with the Banque de l'Union Parisienne in the syndicate of Russian businesses, and with the Banque Russo-asiatique in various sectors in Russia.

Traces of the activities of the Société Générale de Belgique in Russia can be found in the bank's archives, essentially from the period before the Revolution. The archives of the director and governor Jean Jadot consist of correspondence and papers on the Belgian companies which were active in Russia and more particularly on the projects of the steel and iron industry trusts. These documents are supplemented by the papers of the engineering consultant Serge Witmeur. In the financial secretariat's archives, files can be found on all the bank's participations and on those of the Russian companies. Finally, from the revolutionary period, some information may be found in Russian archives in the proceedings of the Committee of Defence of the Belgian Interests and its various sections. This Committee was created in May 1918 and its general secretary, Eugène Witmeur, was a consulting engineer in the Société Générale de Belgique and the right-hand man of Jean Jadot. The objective of this committee was to draw up an inventory of Belgian assets in Russia as a basis for negotiations with the Soviet government.

The bank's business connections with Russia were not resumed until 1936 and the Committee was then suspended temporarily. Finally, the Committee participated in the organization of help for the Belgians repatriated from Russia. Information about the economic and political environment of

Russia relates only to the period before the Revolution, especially the 1905–06 period, when the general manager faced strike actions and revolutionary threats. Moreover in 1906, he was a victim of an attack. Over the period from 1905 until 1929, there are some records of different projects and participations with the Banque de l'Union Parisienne, particularly the correspondence relating to the Syndicat des affaires russes and other companies such as the Dnieper Railways and Poutiloff's Manufactory. Finally, there is not much information about the Russian Revolution in these archives. However, in the bank's records of its financial and commercial relations it is interesting to note that, in spite of frequent breaks, financial interests were maintained despite the political situation. The surviving records are partially listed and some of them are kept in the Belgian government archives.

Rothschilds

The Rothschilds had interests in Russia but they withdrew before the First World War. The French branch was very active in Russian petroleum. The Centre des Archives du Monde du Travail, which holds the archives of the French branch of Rothschilds (classification mark 132 AQ), mentions that a sub-class 12 P comprises correspondence with the bank's agents and some big Russian banks in the years between 1843 and 1914. On the other hand, documents concerning Russian loans cover the wider period from 1848 till 1924 (classification mark 132 AQ 64–68). These include official documents, contracts and correspondence relative to the Russian loans (under the classification mark 132 AQ 67) from the loans department during the war, the records of the bonds department (in 1921), and files of the Association of the Bearers of Russian Assets and a committee of defence (in 1924). Finally, in 132 AQ 68, there are records (forms and notes) concerning an advance from the French state to Russia in 1927–28. These documents are accessible to the public with appropriate authorisation.

Banque Nationale du Commerce et de l'Industrie

The archives of this bank are also kept in the Centre des Archives du Monde du Travail, in the archive group 120 AQ, under the following classification marks:

- 120 AQ 587: financial department of the Banque Nationale du Commerce et de l'Industrie, documents relating to the Société commerciale industrielle et financière pour la Russie (1922–43) and the syndicate for electricity companies in Russia;

- 120 AQ 978: agreement as to debts to the Russian state before 1917 and their use for the compensation of French losses as a result of the revolution (1920–64), 8 December 1948;
- 120 AQ 984, Banque russe pour le commerce et l'industrie (1913 and 1922).

These documents are accessible to the public with appropriate authorization.

Conclusion

The banking archives which are witnesses to the Russian Revolution are not numerous but they are rich and diversified. They are not numerous because most of the banks which then had their activity in Russia do not exist any more; some of them, on the other hand, ended their involvement during the First World War. The Revolution ended these relations and except for the Crédit Lyonnais, few European banks were as well implanted in Russia.

However, the correspondence sent by representatives and managers gives some information about the revolution. Accounting records of financial operations, even though they do not include direct information on the revolution, are very interesting as they allow us to understand how the war and the revolution affected economic life and European interests in Russia.

Today, many banks have reopened offices and/or branches in Russia, for example, Crédit Lyonnais, Société Générale, Deutsche Bank and HSBC. It is likely that bankers working in Russia today do not know that, many years ago, their banks were already there. Archivists and historians can help them to rectify this oversight.

References

Bonin, H. (1994), *La Société Générale en Russie*, Paris: Mission Histoire Société Générale.

Bonin, H. (2000), *La Banque de l'Union Parisienne* (1874/1904–1973/1974), *Histoire de la seconde banque d'affaires française*, Bordeaux: Institut d'études politiques de Bordeaux, Centre d'histoire de l'Université de Bordeaux 4-IFREDE.

Cameron, R. and Bovykin, V. I. (1991), *International Banking, 1870–1914*, New York and Oxford: Oxford University Press.

Gall, L., Feldman, G. D., James, H., Holtfrerich, C. L. and Buschgen, H. E. (1995), *The Deutsche Bank 1870–1995*, London: Weidenfeld & Nicolson.

Girault, R. (1973), *Emprunts russes et investissements français en Russie, 1887–1914*, Paris: Publications de la Sorbonne, Armand Colin.

Holmes, A. R. and Green, E. (1986), *Midland, 150 years of banking business*, London: B.T. Batsford Ltd.

Nougaret, R. (1992), *Le Crédit Lyonnais en Russie, 1878–1920*, Paris: Archives Historiques du Crédit Lyonnais.

Notes

1   I am grateful to the following for their valuable collaboration: Melanie Aspey (The Rothschild Archive), René Brion and Jean-Louis Moreau (Société Générale de Belgique), Reinhard Frost (Deutsche Bank), Edwin Green (HSBC Group Archives), Mr Jurk and Mrs Erke (Dresdner Bank), Elise Lemarchand (Centre des Archives du Monde du Travail), Anne-Thérèse N'Guyen (BNP-Paribas), Roger Nougaret (Crédit Lyonnais Historical Archives), Dr John Orbell (ING Baring) and Cyrille Vivarelli (Banque de l'Union Parisienne). I am also grateful to Professor Boris Anan'ich, Sergueï Beliaef, archivist, and Professor Hubert Bonin for valuable information.

2   Information from Professor Boris Anan'ich.

3   Crédit Lyonnais Historical Archives, Direction des Agences Etrangères (DAE), DAE 08811-1.

4   DAE 08025-2, Letter of 2/15 January 1918.

5   In his letters, the Odessa manager wrote about the *Potemkin* far before the revolution.

6   DAE 8786 bis/2.

7   Société Générale (SG), Direction financière, B02646, B03291.

8   SG, Direction financière, B01357.

9   SG, Direction financière, B01365.

10 This company was a consortium of French banks created with the aim of getting immediate funds to Russians. BNP-Paribas, 5\Cabet-1\20.

11 Ibid., 5\Cabet-1\20 à 29.

PART II

Depression and Political Turmoil in Central Europe

CHAPTER 4

Under Western Eyes: Foreign Banks' Archives Relating to Central and Eastern Europe Between the Wars

Edwin Green

And while my eyes scanned the imperfect disclosures (in which the world was not much interested) I thought that the old, settled Europe had been given in my person attending that Russian girl something like a glimpse behind the scenes. A short, strange glimpse on the top floor of a great hotel of all places in the world ...

Joseph Conrad, *Under Western Eyes* (London, 1911, 1957 edition), p. 273

In contrast to many other chapters in this book, this essay steps aside from the behaviour and performance of banks at times of acute political and social stress. Instead, this chapter suggests ways in which bank archives can act as a window on outside events, with bankers observing and commenting on the world around them.

Throughout banking history, information gathering has been a vital ingredient of the profession and it has become an important but neglected part of the legacy of banking archives. The examples which follow are from the old Overseas Branch of Midland Bank, now HSBC Bank plc.[1] The Overseas Branch generated a remarkable series of reports on conditions in Central and Eastern Europe in the 1920s and 1930s. The collection is emphatically a Western version, from the viewpoint of 'the old, settled Europe' in Conrad's phrase. Yet this is one of the richest and most unusual seams of comment and analysis in the bank's records, clearly demonstrating the banker's instinct for accumulating intelligence about the societies where banks operated. To date, and even though the Group's archivists have mentioned these records in their talks to historians, archivists and students since the late 1970s, Philip Cottrell is the only historian to have referred to the collection (Cottrell, with Stone, 1992, pp. 51, 74). Other multinational banks surely have similar examples of this information gathering and one of the objectives of this chapter is to encourage further interest in these relatively under-used sources.

The business context of these records is important to their historical value. On the surface, the compilation of information about Central and Eastern Europe may appear to be an eccentric, wayward activity for a bank such as Midland. For much of the twentieth century, Midland was famous for its *lack* of involvement in overseas banking and its promise to 'refrain from competing with our foreign friends in their own country' (Holmes and Green, 1986, p. 165). In reality, however, Midland was not so distant from overseas banking. Behind the public stance, Midland had long experience and interest in the wider international picture. It was this legacy which was to sustain the gathering of intelligence by the Overseas Branch in the 1920s and 1930s.

Under the leadership of Sir Edward Holden, the bank's managing director from 1898 to 1919 and chairman from 1908 to 1919, Midland had greatly expanded its role as a correspondent bank (particularly in partnerships with North American banks) and it had also been the first of the major British banks to intervene in foreign exchange business.[2] Holden had also toyed with the idea of opening branches in New York and Chicago. Then in 1909 Midland came close to taking a one-third share in the Union Bank of Moscow. At that time Moscow and St Petersburg were the scene of intense competition for banking and loan business, with British and German financiers challenging the traditional supremacy of French banks in the Russian market. Holden's play for the Union Bank eventually came to nought – partly as a result of the reluctance of the Russian chancellor and partly as a result of some alarming discoveries which Holden's team came across in the Union Bank's balance sheet – but the episode suggested close rather than distant interest in overseas opportunities.

Holden and his colleagues did not give up their watch on Russia. In 1913, they seconded Frederick Bunker, a member of the bank's 'foreign banks department' to the Azov-Don Bank, St Petersburg. Bunker was appointed Midland's representative in St Petersburg three years later and, in February 1917, a representative office was opened in the Moika. A less auspicious moment for a new venture in Russia could not be imagined. Nevertheless, throughout the two revolutions which followed, Bunker delivered a lively stream of business and information about the turmoil in the East. He remained in Petrograd after most Westerners (including the British Embassy staff) had left, until eventually in 1918 he was forced to escape through Red and White Russian lines to Finland and Sweden. 'Actual banking business had come practically to a standstill and could only be done in fear and trepidation,' Bunker wrote to Holden in May 1918. 'Holding on therefore meant only keeping up appearances for one never knew when one might be forcibly closed up.'[3]

After this torrid experience of overseas banking – and after Holden also abandoned plans to open offices in Paris and Madrid during the First World War – Midland's non-interventionist orthodoxy became more pronounced. The bank's strategy was explained by Reginald McKenna, Holden's successor as chairman, in the early 1920s. Its essential features were concentration on correspondent banking (that is, acting as the bankers' bank in London) and avoidance of any direct presence overseas which would compete with or offend the bank's correspondents. It was a strategy which was to prove both successful and durable, giving Midland no less than 1200 correspondent banking partnerships by 1929 and the largest share of this business in London. This commitment to correspondent banking and to avoiding direct representation became an intrinsic part of the bank's view of the world at least until the early 1970s.

Midland's public orthodoxy of non-intervention should not be mistaken for isolationism. The bank's Overseas Branch, even if it did not have any overseas offices, could only operate successfully as a correspondent bank if it had sound information about its international partners and about the markets where they were active. Like the managers of a domestic branch bank, the managers of the Overseas Branch needed to know their customers and to know their customer's business. In other words the bank had a new and larger appetite for high-quality information.

Events and personalities now came together to answer this need. From 1918, Midland's Overseas Branch could call upon experience and expertise in international banking. J. G. Buchanan, the general manager responsible for the Overseas Branch, was a former manager in Crédit Lyonnais, and L. D. Anderson, manager of the branch from 1920 to 1934, had been one of the trailblazers in foreign exchange in 1905. Frederick Bunker, manager of the branch from 1934 to 1945, was the veteran of the Russian campaign. Carl Wurth, the bank's 'overseas representative' from 1920 to 1930, had spent 30 years with 'important foreign banks'; Wurth's skills included fluency in at least seven languages.[4] Not least, this team was reporting to a chairman with keen political and international instincts. Reginald McKenna had served as Chancellor of the Exchequer in the wartime Asquith government and he continued to be an authoritative commentator on political and economic affairs. Like his friend and ally John Maynard Keynes, he had a voracious enthusiasm for data and analysis (Green, 1985, pp. 33–7).

The needs of the business and the chairman's own demand for quality information allowed Midland's Overseas Branch to carry out regular overseas missions throughout the 1920s and 1930s. In the course of these missions, Bunker, Wurth and their colleagues gathered information about the political and social condition of each country which they visited, the economic and financial position of those markets, and the position and prospects of the central and commercial banks. Their reports were compiled from press sources and from their own interviews, particularly conversations with the representatives of Midland's correspondent banks. A total of 41 of these reports have survived in the archives of HSBC Group, beginning with Wurth's visit to Czechoslovakia in 1920 and continuing until Bunker's visit to Scandinavia in 1936.[5] Regionally, eleven of the reports relate to South America, six to Spain and Portugal and four to Scandinavia. For present purposes, the key feature is that all the remaining 20 reports are concerned with Central and Eastern Europe. Table 4.1 lists these reports in alphabetical order.

The format of the reports remained the same throughout the period covered by the collection. Wurth's report on Czechoslovakia in 1924, running to 46 pages, is typical and this model might be helpful to historians and archivists interested in the series. After introductory comments, Wurth provided statistics of 'Area and Population', followed by an assessment of the 'Political Situation' (which in this case includes an interesting commentary on Czech–German antagonism at that time). The report's section on 'Agriculture' provides crop-by-crop statistics and a summary of progress in land reform ('a powerful weapon to fight down communism'). Wurth then reported at length on 'Industry and Mining', including lists of the principal businesses, their performance and prospects, and on 'Trade and Trade Policy', with extensive coverage of Anglo-Czech trade. The 'Transport' section describes the failure of railway nationalization, while 'Social Questions' reviews the cost of living, unemployment and strikes. Wurth includes a lengthy section on 'State Finances' (which he found 'precarious' in the extreme), followed by a profile of 'Currency', 'Public Debt' and the 'State Bank'. The final section of the report, as with the others described here, contains bank-by-bank summaries of interviews with Czechoslovak bankers, with a mix of recent history and comments on the prospects for Midland's banking relationships. This data is not systematic in the manner of a modern questionnaire or credit-rating form but it was sufficient information for Wurth to make recommendations on the level of credits allowed to each bank.

Table 4.1 Midland Bank Overseas Branch reports on Central and Eastern Europe, 1920–31

Country	Date	Author	Pages	Number of banks	Reference
Austria	1931	F. J. Bunker	12	10	284/14
Bulgaria	1924	C. A. Wurth	25	25	192/4
Bulgaria	1931	F. J. Bunker	10	9	284/15
Czechoslovakia	1920	C. A. Wurth	31	25	192/4
Czechoslovakia	1924	C. A. Wurth	46	33	192/4
Czechoslovakia	1931	F. J. Bunker	12	13	284/18
Estonia	1925	C. A. Wurth	27	26	192/4
Greece	1924	C. A. Wurth	20	23	192/4
Greece	1931	F. J. Bunker	20	19	284/12
Hungary	1924	C. A. Wurth	33	25	192/4
Hungary	1931	F. J. Bunker	8	15	284/16
Latvia	1925	C. A. Wurth	14	25	192/4
Lithuania	1925	C. A. Wurth	15	8	192/4
Poland	1925	C. A. Wurth	59	103	192/4
Roumania	1924	C. A. Wurth	54	37	192/4
Roumania	1931	F. J. Bunker	17	28	284/17
Turkey	1931	F. J. Bunker	16	16	284/13
USSR	1929	C. A. Wurth	64	1	192/4
Yugoslavia	1924	C. A. Wurth	63	4	192/4
Yugoslavia	1931	F. J. Bunker	14	17	284/19

Source: HSBC Group Archives, Acc. 192 and Acc. 284.

The business use of these reports was directly related to Midland's correspondent bank relationships, giving the Overseas Branch managers additional information on creditworthiness and risk. Although L. D. Anderson and his colleagues operated from Old Broad Street in London, Bunker and Wurth gave them a window on conditions in a wide variety of different markets. It is also clear that the reports were seen by the bank's chairman, providing valuable background for the political commentary in his speeches to shareholders and other audiences. The quality of this briefing on international affairs equipped him especially well for his continuing participation on issues such as reparations, Anglo-Russian trade, and in the 1930s, the vexed question of the German and Austrian standstill arrangements (Forbes, 2000, pp. 33–46). The readership of the Overseas Branch reports also included the bank's Intelligence Department. This was a productive link at a time when Wilfrid Crick and his colleagues in the

Intelligence Department were acting as a *de facto* private office for McKenna, providing text and statistics for his speeches and meetings. The department was also the author and publisher of the *Midland Bank Monthly Review*, an outstanding example of the bank reviews of the period (Roberts, 1995, pp. 41–60). In Midland's case, the *Review* maintained an international as well as a domestic perspective, in which the high quality of reports from Bunker, Wurth and their colleagues were surely an important influence.

How can these records help the historian to portray episodes of political and social stress? The historical setting of the Overseas Branch reports shows that both the authors and readers of the reports gave great weight to the political, social and economic intelligence which they offered. All of the surviving reports, including those on Central and Eastern Europe, also focus upon countries which were undergoing intense readjustment and even crisis. The collapse of the Austro-Hungarian Empire after the First World War meant that Wurth, in particular, was reporting on entirely new political structures in the early 1920s. He responded in a vivid style, as for example in his introduction to the report on Hungary in 1924:

> The finances, the administration, the whole governmental machinery, were already in an almost chaotic state when in March 1919, to crown all, the Communist Bela Kun, with his few thousands of well armed ruffians, succeeded in seizing the reins of power, and subduing the country, which had been thoroughly stripped of all weapons and means of defence. Fortunately, the Bolshevik regime was short lived, but it was followed by the still more grievous Romanian predatory expedition and occupation, to which only the stern and repeated French representations finally succeeded in putting an end, but not before damage and wanton destruction estimated by the Finance Minister, Baron Koranyi, in the interview he granted me, at 3000 million gold crowns, had been wrought by the Romanian Military.

Bunker, reporting on Romania itself in 1931, used similarly strong language:

> The nation was faced with an immense task after the War in taking over, and finding an administration for, large provinces of varying cultures and traditions, which strained the official machinery almost to breaking point, and favoured the development of an unwieldy crowd of State employees, underpaid, and therefore easily corrupted. One of the first essential tasks is to reduce the ridiculous number of officials, but, as is usual in such circumstances, the Government hesitates; so they remain to cause one of the worst of the budget difficulties, and the cynics are to an extent justified who say that the Romanian atmosphere consists of three elements – oxygen, nitrogen, and backsheesh. The purifying of it from the last is not likely to be a matter of a year or a generation either.

Although Midland's emissaries were especially pessimistic about conditions in Hungary and Romania, they were much more positive about Czechoslovakia and Yugoslavia. In 1924 Wurth believed that Yugoslavia had made more progress since the First World War than any of its neighbours:

> If we remember that no belligerent country has been devastated during the War to the same extent, we cannot help admiring the energy and industry of the people who with scanty means and practically no foreign help have achieved so much during the past four years, in the way of repairing the damages and restoring gradually their country to normality and prosperity Foreign financial and technical help would be most welcome, and would certainly result in mutual advantage.

Even in the midst of the depression in 1931, Bunker stated that Czechoslovakia was 'clearly the strongest' of the countries to emerge from the old Austro-Hungarian Empire: 'It took over from Austria in 1918 about 80 per cent of all the latter's industries, as well as some of the most valuable agricultural land. In short the country constitutes a well-balanced and compact whole, to a great extent self-contained and self-supporting.'

For the historian, these commentaries provide an eyewitness context for the more specialist intelligence provided in the sections on the economy and the banking industry in each country. The stresses or strains detected in each society find an echo in the portraits of banking conditions or individual banks. For instance, in Wurth's report on Romania in 1924, the entry on the Banca Romaneasca describes it as 'Mr Ventila Bratianu's bank [which] therefore enjoys a privileged position'. The allusion only takes on meaning after Wurth's lengthy description of Bratianu's role as Minister of Finance in the liberal administration: 'I don't think there is in any country a more abused statesman ... he is obstinate in the highest degree; he never deviates from the course he has once adopted ... Most of all, he is blinded by his chauvinism and the morbid fear of intervention in Romania's economic affairs.' It is no surprise that Wurth was cautious about recommending credits to the Banca Romaneasca. Likewise, his recommendations on dealing with the other Romanian banks must be seen in the light of his lengthy exposition of the settlement of commercial debts owed abroad and the debts and obligations under the post-war peace treaties. Wurth describes these onerous and complex arrangements in impressive detail.

A parallel example is found in Wurth's report on Polish banks in 1925. This survey was strengthened by his willingness to look at the wider issues of Russo–Polish enmity, the long period of inflation which followed the First

World War, the customs war with Germany, and the cost of maintaining 'the second largest army in the world' (Wurth estimated that cost to be 40 per cent of the Polish total budget). On the banking scene the result was that the 'joint stock banks are all locked up' in their lending. Wurth came to the conclusion that 'generally speaking the pre-war banks may be considered well founded and well managed, whilst the post-war banks, with few exceptions, are weak and have little prospects'. Hence the Bank Malopowski, established in Cracow in 1869 and linked with the Credit Anstalt, had been 'well managed' whereas the Union Bank, founded in Warsaw in 1921, had proved to be 'very speculative' during the crisis.

In their surveys of local banks, Wurth and Bunker were able to comment on a surprisingly large number of financial institutions. The report on Poland quoted above, for instance, contains entries for 103 banks, ranging in size from the Bank of Poland and the Bank Handlowy to examples of 'very small' cooperative mutual and farmers' banks in the provinces. The coverage in the other reports was not so lavish (as can be seen in Table 4.1) but both Wurth and Bunker invariably considered a wide span of types and sizes of banks. As to the information which they offered, the reports provided details of capitalization and balance sheet totals, location and date of formation, and (where applicable) the level of activity on the correspondent banking account. In some cases, Wurth and Bunker ranged much further afield, noting connections with other local or international banks, referring to major shareholders, customers and officials, and assessing the business prospects of the banks. The following extract from Bunker's report on Romania in 1931 is typical of these more comprehensive descriptions:

Banca Marmorosch, Blank & Co

This is one of the great banks of the country, but through injudicious operations on a large scale in recent years, they have become very greatly immobilized, and it is only by the help of the Banque Nationale de Roumanie, always rendered in full measure because of Mr Blank's powerful Court influence and because the fall of such a great institution, with its repercussions on Romanian credit abroad, would be unthinkable if it could by any means be avoided, that it is maintained alive. It is quite certain that on a forced liquidation in present conditions they would be far from solvent; indeed, so far as can be foreseen, they are never likely to be able to get square again by any normal or natural economic process. But it is whispered that, because of their great services to Romania in the past and the very great pull they are still supposed to have on the people who govern the country, an opportunity will be sought at a convenient time to give them a kind of present of such value that by its aid they may be able to rehabilitate their position – something such as the Management of a future State Wine and Spirits monopoly, for instance. There will, of course, be opposition. In the meantime, I understand that the Government and the National Bank together have relieved Marmorosch, Blank & Co to the extent of over £500 000 by taking over from them for cash an immobilization in the shape of a big printing works and some quite frozen bills from their portfolio.

These sources have their drawbacks. They are no substitute for the political, social and business records of the home countries. They are also 'Western' in their point of view, carrying some of the prejudices of the Allied powers of the First World War and the post-war settlement. Certainly the reports were intended for a Western readership, concentrated in and around Midland's London offices.

This bias should not be exaggerated, as the authors had strong Central and Eastern European credentials. The multi lingual Wurth was Swiss in origin and had worked for European banks while Bunker had married a Russian and had spent five hectic years in St Petersburg. The Overseas Branch managers back in London to whom the reports were addressed were international both in origin and in outlook. It is perhaps more important that the reports contain information about banks and businesses which have otherwise left little trace. Some of the institutions visited or described by Wurth and Bunker have not left any legacy of business archives, buildings or other historical presence. The reports in this way describe a world which we have lost. Even if there is a Western flavour to such records, they are one of the few sources which historians can deploy to reconstruct that lost world.

Other banks no doubt have parallel collections of records, not just for the European theatre but also for markets much further afield. These collections were created wherever there was a regular traffic in overseas visits, interviews and surveys. Midland itself has other examples. Holden, notably, kept a diary of his visit to North America, a visit which was an important influence on his own thinking and also an important influence on some of his transatlantic customers.[6] His chief lieutenant, Samuel Murray, kept a diary of his mission to Moscow in 1909, when the bank was in negotiations for a share of the Union Bank.[7] Wilfrid Crick, head of the bank's Intelligence Department, reported fully on a fact-finding visit to Germany in 1933. His report, describing a society already under extreme tension, greatly influenced McKenna and his colleagues in their standstill negotiations later in the 1930s.[8]

Elsewhere in the HSBC Group archives, the reports by the inspectors of the Hongkong and Shanghai Banking Corporation provide a channel of information about local conditions over and above the detailed work of auditing the branch offices throughout the Far East. Investigations of new locations for overseas branches also offer valuable comment and analysis on local conditions. The Mercantile Bank of India, for example, looked hard at the possibility of opening in Manchuria in the late 1920s and in East and West Africa and the Bahamas a generation later (Green and Kinsey, 1999, pp. 68, 117). The reports produced by such adventures – even if they did not lead to any banking results – add to the rich lateral seam of information characteristic of banking archives.

Some of the reports discussed here clearly have uses for a wide spectrum of historians and other researchers. In this special category of banking experience, these are 'travellers' tales' from the history of banking, in which bankers visit and report upon societies in crisis, or confusion, societies which are otherwise distant or obscured from historical view, or societies which simply have little surviving documentation and explanation. Clearly, archivists as well as historians should treat such caches of records of intelligence gathering as a priority, as their value and quality reaches far beyond the banking history community.

References

Cottrell, P. L., with Stone, C. J. (1992), 'Credits, and deposits to finance credits', in Cottrell, P. L., Lindgren, H. and Teichova, A. (eds), *European Industry and Banking between the Wars. A Review of Bank-industry relations*, Leicester: Leicester University Press, pp. 43–78.

Forbes, N. (2000), *Doing Business with the Nazis: Britain's Economic and Financial Relations with Germany, 1931–1939*, London: Frank Cass.

Green, E. (1985), 'Reginald McKenna', in Jeremy, D. J. (ed.), *Dictionary of Business Biography*, 4, London: Butterworth, pp. 33–7.

Green, E. and Kinsey, S. (1999), *The Paradise Bank. The Mercantile Bank of India, 1893–1984*, Aldershot: Ashgate.

Holmes, A. R. and Green, E. (1986), *Midland: 150 Years of Banking*, London: Batsford.

Roberts, R. (1995), 'A special place in contemporary economic literature: the rise and fall of the British bank review, 1914–1993', *Financial History Review*, 2, pp. 41–60.

Notes

1 In this chapter the bank is given the short title of Midland. In the period discussed in this chapter, its full names were London City and Midland Bank (1898–1918), London Joint City and Midland Bank (1918–23) and Midland Bank (1923–99).
2 The following paragraphs are based on Holmes and Green, 1986, pp. 133–41.
3 HSBC Group Archives (HSBC), Acc. 151/5. Bunker to Holden, May 1918.
4 *Midland Venture* (the magazine of the Midland Bank Staff Association), (October 1930), p. 432.
5 These reports are held in two series at HSBC Group Archives: Acc. 192/4 (Wurth's reports) and Acc. 284 (reports by Bunker and others).
6 HSBC, Acc. 150/2. 'Mr Holden's report on his visit to America', September–November 1904.
7 HSBC, Acc. 30/226. Diary of S. B. Murray's visit to Russia, September–October 1909.
8 HSBC, Acc 30/207. Report by W. F. Crick on his visit to Germany, September–October 1933.

CHAPTER 5

Croatian Banking During the 1926–36 Depression[1]

Ivo Bićanić and Željko Ivanković

Introduction

The current wisdom on economic transformation stresses the special role of the financial sector and monetary policy as a precondition for successful transformation and, ultimately, modern economic growth and economic convergence. Thus monetary policy is viewed as the main economic policy tool for achieving and maintaining macro-economic stability. The financial sector is given multiple roles and is seen as the sector which can accelerate transformation, institution building and the consolidation of a modern market economy. At the same time, it creates a favourable climate for investment and accumulation, in turn ensuring real economic convergence with developed economies.

The stress on the importance of the financial sector and monetary policy in this interpretation might sound extreme and could be disregarded were it not for its very important and influential backers. It has become a central part of the current 'transition package' of the international financial community. The economic conditions (as well as other conditions) which they can and do impose, together with the wide scope and influence of the international economy, makes this view more than academic; one should bear in mind that the international financial community has influential offices in every economy in transition.

Given this strong current emphasis on the financial sector and monetary policy, it seems worthwhile to look at its past track record. However, this chapter will not, as is often the case, look at the record in the period after the Second World War or through a cross-section of economies. Instead it will discuss the decade from 1926 to 1936 in the limited region of Croatia.

This period and area are especially interesting for purposes of comparison. The period involves multiple external shocks (the collapse of agricultural exports, the Great Depression) and internal shocks (the introduction of a dictatorship, the problem of 'peasant debt'); a stubborn adherence to a restrictive monetary policy and exchange rate stability in the changing environment of post-war boom, crises, depression and growth; and policies for restructuring the financial sector by establishing a state sector and tilting the playing field in its favour, selective bail-outs, rehabilitation and restructuring schemes. Furthermore, as there was a private banking sector, the reactions and behaviour of this sector can be examined. The limited area of Croatia (as opposed to the whole of Yugoslavia, of which it was part during the period) was chosen because the authors feel it is especially well suited for the purpose of the paper. At that time it had a relatively high level of monetization and financial sector development and it experienced an especially full restructuring of its financial sector. Of course, the authors are aware that monetary policy and financial sector restructuring in the decade 1926–36 are usually treated in a nationalist and 'conspiratorialist' framework; this approach has some validity but in this chapter it will be downplayed because the primary purpose is to discuss monetary issues.

This chapter is divided into four sections. The first gives an overview of monetary policy and financial sector developments during the period from 1926 to 1936. The second discusses their impact on the Croatian financial sector generally. The third discusses the fate of the largest bank in the country, the First Croatian Savings Bank. The final section attempts to offer some conclusions, while the Appendix explains the definition of 'Croatia' used here.

Monetary Policy and Real Sector Developments, 1926–36

One of the reasons for choosing to concentrate on the 1926–36 decade is the interesting interaction of a very active monetary policy with other major real sector developments. To understand these interactions in Croatia it is necessary to give a brief overview of economic development during the period.

Real sector developments began with the end of the post-war export boom in agricultural and raw materials, together with an end to the inflationary period of easy credit and signs that prices had started to fall. As a result of these developments, Yugoslav exports fell dramatically and even the excellent harvest of 1928 could not reverse this trend (Cuvaj, 1930). This period of crisis was followed by a brief upswing from 1929 to mid-1931 (Tomašević, 1938, p. 231). This upswing ended in 1931 but the reasons are controversial. The financial sector was facing a combination of internally and externally generated shocks. Some contemporary authors as well as the yearly reports of the Chamber of Commerce stressed the dominance of the

Table 5.1   Real sector developments in Yugoslavia: the value of total exports, agricultural exports, employment and wages, 1926–36

	Value of exports (billion dinars)	Trade balance (billion dinars)	Yearly average number of insured workers	Number of unemployment benefit recipients (December value)	Average wage of insured workers (dinars)
1926	7.818	+0.186	474 610		24.11
1927	6.400	− 0.886	511 493		25.04
1928	6.445	− 1.391	565 796		25.82
1929	7.922	+0.327	605 065		26.32
1930	6.780	− 0.180	631 181		26.56
1931	4.801	+0.001	609 190		26.19
1932	3.056	+0.196	535 917	14 809	24.58
1933	3.378	+0.495	520 980	19 964	23.22
1934	3.878	+0.305	543 559	17 787	22.24
1935	4.030	+0.331	564 287	19 619	21.65
1936	4.376	+0.299	616 209	19 328	21.68

Source: Statistical Yearbook of Yugoslavia, various years.

internal causes of the crisis – that is, monetary policy decisions, the peasant debt issue, price deflation and the contraction of demand and production (Lamer, 1939; Tomašević, 1938; Kadragić, 1936). Others saw external shocks, such as the fall of exports, the world economic crises, the fall of worker remittances and contraction of tourism, as dominant (Kosier, 1932; NBJ, 1934). The depression bottomed out in 1934 and stronger growth followed in 1936. However, in the decade from 1926 to 1936 growth did not emerge (Stajić, 1952). This whole period was a decade of under-performance even by the standards of the very low growth rates experienced during the interwar period. The initial research results also confirm this picture for Croatia (Stipetić, 2002).

At the same time, registered employment fell less and unemployment never reached dramatic proportions. This is understandable given the level of development and dominance of agriculture; at the time of the 1931 census, 76 per cent of the population was rural and agricultural exports dominated total export values. This initial downward trend was further depressed when the trade implosion of the Great Depression hit the Yugoslav economy in 1930. But as is clear, the Great Depression had less effect on the economy than the agricultural crises of the late 1920s.

The end of the export boom coincided with an important development in the monetary sector. At the beginning of the decade under consideration, there was a major shift in monetary policy. The shift had three aspects: first, the absolute priority of maintaining exchange rate stability; second, restrictive monetary policy aimed only at supporting the exchange rate, and third, a proactive policy of financial sector restructuring.

First, in 1926, the government took a policy initiative to underpin exchange rate stability through new legislation. The initiative was formally presented to the National Bank (then still the National Bank of the Kingdom of Serbs, Croats and Slovenes) in 1927. The bank expressed its reservations, pointing out that there was only an external equilibrium (created by exchange rate stability and balance-of-payments surplus) but not an internal one (NBJ, 1934, p. 185). Thus the legislative support of a fixed exchange rate was postponed but exchange rate stability remained a policy priority. As a result the exchange rate was *de facto* stable from 1926 onwards. The fixed exchange rate became legally binding only when a package of laws regulating the whole financial sector was passed in the first half of 1931 which started being implemented in the second half of 1931 (see NBJ, 1934, p. 186). These laws fixed the dinar at 0.0265 grams of gold, the exchange rate at 0.0912778 Swiss francs and determined the minimum money reserves at 25 per cent of gold and 10 per cent of convertible foreign currency reserves. They also defined all the necessary legislation required to implement institutionalized monetary stability. The fundamentals of this rigid system remained intact until the end of the period, when doubts about the fixed exchange rate emerged again in 1935. The pressures for relaxing the exchange rate were eventually accepted and in 1936 the currency was devalued. However, during the decade under consideration, there was exchange rate stability and a monetary policy which was designed around that stability. The basic data are provided in Table 5.2. Modern economic theory views such a course – exchange rate stability and an initial boom followed by a recession – a common and understandable sequence of events. This Exchange Rate Based Stabilization (ERBS) syndrome has been thoroughly documented for economies in transition at the end of the century (Sobolev, 2000).

In the early 1930s, a trade deficit and export implosion put exchange rate stability under attack. The central bank took measures to deal with the impending crisis, notably the restriction of capital outflows, increases in discount and Lombard rates, and the stoppage of new and partly used central bank loans (NBJ, 1934). It also introduced a 'prime' rate over the

Table 5.2   Monetary variables in Yugoslavia: the exchange rate, money supply and gold coverage, 1926–36

	Price index, 55 products, (1926 = 100)	Currency in circulation (million dinars)	Currency backing*	Zagreb bourse, average yearly exchange rate for 100 Francs
1926	100	5 812	n.a.	1 095.06
1927	102.6	5 743	n.a.	1 095.36
1928	106.6	5 528	n.a.	1 095.26
1929	100.6	5 818	n.a.	1 095.09
1930	86.6	5 397	n.a.	1 095.98
1931	72.9	5 172	40.05	1 098.36
1932	65.2	4 773	41.24	1 104.02
1933	64.4	4 327	44.05	1 098.36
1934	63.2	4 383	43.46	1 104.02
1935	65.9	4 900	35.80	1 426.25
1936	no data	5 409	30.07	1 320.81

* Comparable currency backing data was collected only after the 1931 legislation.
Source: Statistical Yearbook of Yugoslavia, various years.

official rate which increased over years. Finally the exchange rate was devalued in 1936, at the end of the decade under consideration.

Exchange rate stability as a policy priority meant that monetary authorities had little manoeuvring space regarding the money supply. Until legal stability in 1931 this was a self-imposed restriction and after 1931 one imposed by law. In comparative terms, the gold-backing coefficients built into the law were restrictive, so there was no option but that of a tight monetary policy (Kadragić, 1936). Even though the 1931 legislation required a 33.3 per cent gold backing the actual coverage was higher. This policy remained during the whole period and with it came high credit restrictions. The business community continually complained that tight credit and insufficient money supply resulted from badly chosen money-base coefficients and that this contributed to the depression (Cuvaj, 1930, 1931, 1932). They insisted that monetary policy further destabilized already volatile developments in the real sector which was subject to internal and external shocks. The eventual devaluation of 1936 led to money expansion.

The third policy was the policy of financial sector restructuring. From the mid-1920s, the central bank conducted a proactive policy of financial sector restructuring. Its goal was to build a financial sector comprised of several large banks with branch offices in the whole country. This implied that the existing structure dominated by numerous small small local banks, often with no branch offices, was considered obsolete. Even though this policy had already been adopted in the mid-1920s it was given a major boost under the dictatorship of 1929. Initially the dictatorship made major policy shifts towards state interventionism in the financial sector. The restructuring policy was upgraded as a priority and with this purpose in mind the state provided the capital for establishing three state banks. The Privilegovana agrarna banka (Privileged Agrarian Bank) was the largest of the three but still smaller than the largest private bank and was aimed at providing long-term finance to agriculture. The Državna hipotekarna banka (State Mortgage Bank) was smaller and aimed at providing mortgage loans to business and the urban population. The smallest of the three was the Zanatska banka (Craftsmen's Bank) aimed at providing long-term finance to the small-business sector. Together with the Post Office savings bank, which was established in 1923 and which started collecting savings in 1926, this made a formidable state banking sector.

Later monetary policies supported this restructuring objective. Two such policies stand out. The first concerned official policies favouring the nascent state sector. Until 1931, private and state banks faced a more or less level playing field. After that the institutional framework undisputably tilted the balance in favour of state banks and against private ones. This was especially important for Croatian banks and for Zagreb, as the largest private financial centre in the country. Private banks were regulated by the Ministry of Industry and Trade while the much more powerful Ministry of Finance regulated the state banks. State banks could get state guarantees not available to private banks and state institutions were required to keep their accounts in state banks (initially the State Mortgage Bank and later any of their choice of three). On the savings deposit market the Post Office savings institution enjoyed special tax and other benefits (Košak, 1936; Tomašević, 1938).

The second policy issue was the way 'peasant debt' was handled. During the boom years of the early and mid-1920s, credit was abundant and the agricultural sector acquired a large debt. With export reduction and price deflation during the crises of the late 1920s, peasant indebtedness further increased as did the burden of repayment. The private financial sector did not adapt its credit policy to the new circumstances and eventually arrears and defaults led the financial sector into a crisis (Ivšić, 1938). By the late 1920s, it was obvious that only drastic policy decisions could deal with the growing problem of peasant debt. The king appointed a three-member commission of distinguished private bankers in 1929 who proposed a moratorium on all debts and a general policy of bank rehabilitation. The proposal, by which the state would take over the debt and finance it through an international loan, was turned down. Instead a selected moratorium on peasant debt in private banking was chosen and a case-by-case rehabilitation scheme was introduced. The 'Zakon o zaštiti zemljoradnika' (Law on farmer protection) was passed on 19 April 1932 and represented the first step in the policy towards final settlement of the peasant debt problem.

The law stipulated a six-month postponement (until 20 October 1932) of court confiscations of peasant property in lieu of debt repayments while a more lasting solution was found. However, there were widespread objections to this solution. The law was extended for another two months and then in December it was extended indefinitely (in practice until the 1936 legislation which wrote off peasant debt). The law clearly defined who could benefit from the moratorium (by defining who was a peasant or farmer). It also offered protection to banks which got into financial difficulties due to the law and applied for protection.

The most important part of the 1932 law was its infamous Clause 5. This clause defined conditions under which banks could seek relief from difficulties caused by the implementation of the law. In effect, banks which had problems because of the moratorium of peasant debt repayment could seek state support. This support was to be recommended by the Ministerial Council on the proposal of the Minister of Trade and Industry and, to become valid, it was spelled out in the form of a special regulation. This regulation related to assets prior to the application for relief; it kept these assets in a separate account (thus these banks had 'new' and 'old' accounts); it defined the time frame and terms for the payment of bank obligations (including savings deposits); it defined the reorganization which was possible to increase the safety of depositors and bank creditors, and it placed the financial institution and its business under the control of a state-appointed commissioner. In brief, the bank applying for protection lost its business independence. The state-owned Privilegovana agrarna banka was exempted from the law (which meant that it could collect debt repayments) until 1934.

It must be noted that the law was passed in April 1932, after a major banking crisis. In the autumn of 1931 there was a confidence panic in Yugoslav banking, triggered by the collapse of the Österreichische Creditanstalt für Handel und Gewerbe in Vienna, resulting in a run on the banks.

Throughout the whole period fiscal policy was extremely conservative. In line with the current wisdom at that time, budgets were balanced and expenditures continually decreased in line with the falling state revenues which had resulted from the decade of crises. The yearly reports of the Chamber of Commerce and Trade continually complained about falling government consumption.

Croatian Banking, 1926–29

These policies and events had a profound influence on Croatian banking (the definition of 'Croatia' is given in the Appendix to this chapter). The period began with the undisputed dominance of Croatian banking in the whole Yugoslav economy and ended with the contraction of Croatian banking and the clear dominance by the state financial sector. This fate was determined not only by the banking sector's structure, business policy and the economic crises but also by government decisions and their influence (or more precisely lack of influence) on policy.

First, it must be noted that during the 1920s Croatia was the financial centre of the Yugoslav economy. It had the most developed banking sector with the largest share of savings deposits and net profits. The distribution is shown in Table 5.3; the start date of 1929 is used as it was the first year in

Table 5.3   The share of Croatian banking in Yugoslavian banking, 1929–36

	Percentage share of savings deposits in Croatian banks in private sector bank savings deposits in Yugoslavia	Percentage share of savings deposits in Croatian banks in private and state bank saving deposits in Yugoslavia	Percentage share of net profits of Croatian banks in private sector net profits in Yugoslavia	Percentage share of net profits of Croatian banks in private and state sector net profits in Yugoslavia
1929	44.23	41.72	45.29	37.19
1930	45.47	42.42	42.64	31.94
1931	49.30	48.75	33.14	21.20
1932	48.23	41.02	25.71	13.66
1933	46.83	38.04	65.94	45.65
1934	47.67	35.83	26.88	14.32
1935	48.06	24.94	61.63	37.01
1936	49.05	37.02	37.91	23.02

Source: Statistical Yearbook of Yugoslavia, various years. Croatia's share was calculated according to the explanation given in the Appendix while the aggregate value (state and private) is from the original source.

which data was collected for the *Statistical Yearbook*. Initially, Croatian banking accounted for almost half the savings deposits in private sector banking and two-thirds of all savings deposits. It also accounted for almost half the net profits of private banking and around a third of aggregate net profits. Furthermore, at the beginning of the period state banking was limited, certainly in comparison with private sector banking. In addition, all the major foreign-owned banks had their main offices in Croatia (Košak, 1936).

The structure of Croatian banking was marked by a very high level of concentration both in terms of size and spatial distribution. The largest bank in Croatia and the whole country, the Prva Hrvatska Štedionica (First Croatian Savings Bank), clearly dominated the entire financial community. Apart from this bank very few other Croatian banks had branch offices. In terms of numbers, typical banks had only a main office and were small local banks. This is clear from Table 5.4.

The second form of concentration was the dominance of Croatia's largest city, Zagreb, where the First Croatian Savings Bank had its head office. In

Table 5.4a   The size structure of Croatian banking, 1926–36

	Number of banks with head office in Croatia	Banks without any branch offices	Banks with branch offices (except First Croatian Savings Bank)	Largest bank (First Croatian Savings Bank)	Number of foreign banks*
1926	112	92	19	1	6
1927	122	105	16	1	6
1928	129	108	20	1	7
1929	122	99	22	1	7
1930	121	98	22	1	7
1931	22	9	12	1	7
1932	21	9	11	1	6
1933	15	8	6	1	4
1934	22	11	10	1	7
1935	22	12	9	1	6
1936	21	13	7	1	7

* Foreign banks are also included in 'Banks with branch offices'.
Source: Kompas-Yugoslavia, various years.

Table 5.4b The size structure of Croatian banking, 1926–36

	Total assets* (million dinars)	Banks without branch offices %	Banks with branch offices %	First Croatian Savings Bank %	Foreign-owned banks %	Total savings* (million dinars)	Banks without branch offices %	Banks with branch offices %	First Croatian Savings Bank %	Foreign-owned banks %
1926	6 264	11.08	56.23	32.69	29.58	3 671	8.68	54.33	36.99	14.10
1927	5 306	14.26	43.70	42.04	29.20	2 869	12.86	35.11	52.03	16.36
1928	7 735	11.42	57.92	30.66	46.27	3 884	11.06	49.70	39.24	33.96
1929	8 795	11.08	58.65	30.27	45.17	4 499	10.87	50.49	38.64	34.70
1930	9 398	16.35	51.58	32.07	40.64	5 298	18.81	44.30	36.89	29.76
1931	7 410	10.66	53.53	35.81	41.45	4 264	14.09	44.29	41.62	27.89
1932	5 435	13.39	46.92	39.70	33.26	3 054	15.57	34.84	49.59	18.98
1933	1 748*	40.49	59.51	–	56.42	0 971*	50.69	49.31	–	45.85
1934	5 591	13.96	45.75	40.29	34.63	2 890	18.14	34.78	47.07	20.49
1935	5 566	15.12	45.09	39.79	33.68	3 083	19.93	35.68	44.39	22.94
1936	5 113	19.47	38.94	41.59	38.69	2 824	25.17	27.56	47.27	25.35

* Data does not include the largest bank.
Source: Kompas-Yugoslavia, various years.

addition, most of the other larger banks and numerous small ones also operated from Zagreb. Foreign-owned banks also had their head offices in Zagreb, mostly as a result of old ties. For these reasons it could be claimed that Zagreb was the financial centre of the country at the beginning of the period.

Croatian banking did not emerge overnight and its roots go back to the mid-nineteenth century, when the famous First Croatian Savings Bank was established in 1846. This feature set it apart from the rest of Yugoslav banking in the first half of the twentieth century. But it was not the only characteristic which set Croatian banking apart. As in the other regions of Austro-Hungary which became part of Yugoslavia, its banking sector was more developed than in the rest of the newly formed country in the sense of having relatively more large banks with branch offices (as opposed to many small ones), banks which were independent (and for obvious reasons of size and location had weaker links with authorities) and a banking sector

Table 5.5a   The spatial distribution of Croatian banking: banks with branches in and/or outside Croatia, 1926–36

	First Croatian Savings Bank		Other banks with branch offices and head office in Croatia			Foreign-owned banks with head office in Croatia*		
	Bank structure		Number of banks	Bank structure		Number of banks	Bank structure	
	Offices in Croatia	Offices outside Croatia		Offices in Croatia	Offices outside Croatia		Offices in Croatia	Offices outside Croatia
1926	29	20	19	38	18	6	12	6
1927	28	20	18	33	20	6	14	10
1928	28	20	20	39	22	7	18	11
1929	30	21	22	38	33	7	18	10
1930	31	22	22	39	34	7	18	13
1931	31	22	12	31	25	7	18	12
1932	26	19	11	19	19	6	9	8
1933	no data		6	10	6	4	4	3
1934	25	18	10	19	18	7	10	7
1935	25	18	9	18	18	6	10	7
1936	24	15	7	14	10	7	10	7

* The number of foreign banks are also included among banks 'Other banks with branch offices and head office in Croatia'.

Source: Kompas-Yugoslavia, various years.

Table 5.5b   The spatial distribution of Croatian banking: the position of Zagreb in Croatian banking, 1928–34

	Number of large banks with head offices in Zagreb	Number of banks in Croatia	Value of deposits in larger Zagreb banks (million dinars)	Value of deposits in Croatia (million dinars)	Value of net profits of Zagreb banks (million dinars)	Value of net profits of Croatian banks (dinars)
1928	29		3 705		71.7	
1929	28	121	4 151	4 133	78.7	119 700
1930	28 (29)	120	4 605	4 681	74.9	119 300
1931	30	123	4 118	4 340	38.0	68 300
1932	30	122	3 185	3 265	28.3	28 990
1933	31	122	2 955	2 978	24.5	135 596
1934	31	121	2 955	2 569	21.3	26 957

Source: For Zagreb (columns 2, 4 and 6), *Mali statistički priručnik grada Zagreba*. For other columns, original data from *Statistical Yearbook of Yugoslavia*, various years. Croatia's share was calculated according to the explanation given in the Appendix (the numbers of banks in Tables 5.4a and 5.5a are slightly different due to a different source).

dominated by private banks (indeed no state banks had central offices in those regions). It shared with Slovenian banks the importance of the role of industrial financing and development.

In Croatia, banking was especially important. What set it apart from the rest of the country was that the population had a tradition of keeping their savings in deposit accounts (Lamer, 1939). It must also be noted that business in Yugoslavia, especially in its northern parts, traditionally financed itself through bank loans; indeed most of these loans were medium- and short-term loans which came to be used as long-term investment loans (Tomašević, 1939). This pattern put special pressure on banks and made them especially susceptible to changes in short-term savings deposits.

In the late 1920s and early 1930s, three events overturned the fortunes of Croatian banking. The 1929 crisis, the 1931 institutional restructuring and the 1932 policies regulating peasant debt completely changed the architecture of the financial sector at the expense of Croatian banking. In 1929, the three state banks were established creating a strong state banking sector. In 1931, institutional reforms, in addition to legalizing fixed exchange rates, also regulated the financial sector in a way which further tilted the playing field against private sector banks. Finally, after a run on

Table 5.6   The shift in savings deposits in Croatia, 1929–36

	Changes of savings deposits in Croatian banks (1929 = 100)	Changes of savings deposits in state banks (1929 = 100)	Change number of post office savings books in Zagreb branch office (1929 = 100)
1929	100	100	100
1930	113	133	106
1931	105	163	112
1932	79	212	123
1933	72	261	133
1934	62	317	138
1935	63	365	142
1936	63	305	145

Source: Columns 3 and 4 from original data in *Statistical Yearbook of Yugoslavia*, various years. Column 2 calculated from the same source according to the procedure from Appendix.

banks in the autumn of 1931, the provisional solution to peasant debt in 1932 dealt Croatian private sector banking a death blow from which it never recovered. This is most clearly visible in the changes in Croatian banking. The post-1932 data clearly shows the dramatic fall in the number of banks in Croatia and the fall in savings and profits.

The privileged position of the state financial sector enabled it to gain savings deposits after the 1931 run on the banks (Raffaeli, 1937). With the large private banks losing their independence and suffering from widely known financial difficulties, citizens' savings went into the Post Office Savings Bank or into savings deposits in the state banks. The value of Post Office savings at the Zagreb branch office is not known but the rise in the number of Post Office savings books issued during the whole period and the fall of savings in Croatian banks indicated a shift.

With no new capital – as mentioned citizens held their wealth in savings deposits – and having lost their independence, private sector banking in Croatia experienced a decline in profits which further undermined confidence.

The First Croatian Savings Bank

The fate of Croatian banking during the 1926–36 period is best seen by the changing fortunes of the First Croatian Savings Bank, the largest bank in

Croatia and Yugoslavia. This bank was not only the oldest in Croatia (established in 1846) but it was also by far the largest bank in the country, with branch offices in the whole of Croatia and in the neighbouring regions of Bosnia-Herzegovina, Serbia and Vojvodina. Its position in the financial sector is shown by the size of its savings deposits in relation to those in Croatian and the whole private sector banking. Its sheer dominance meant that any difficulty at that bank would have ripple effects in the whole of Croatia and beyond.

For the First Croatian Savings Bank the crucial event in the inter-war period occurred on 19 April 1932, the day the law on peasant protection was passed. The First Croatian Savings Bank was the first bank to seek protection under Clause 5 of the law and its application was processed on 21 April. The bank never recovered (and neither did private sector banking

Table 5.7:   The First Croatian Savings Bank, 1926–36

	Number of branch offices		Assets (billion dinars)	Saving deposits (billion dinars)	Shares %	
	In Croatia	Outside Croatia			Assets	Savings
1926	29	20	2.048	1.358	32.69	36.99
1927	28	20	2.230	1.493	42.04	52.03
1928	28	20	2.371	1.524	30.66	39.24
1929	30	21	2.662	1.738	30.27	38.64
1930	31	22	3.014	1.955	32.07	36.89
1931	31	22	2.653	1.775	35.81	41.62
1932	26	19	2.158	1.514	39.70	49.59
'new'			0.052	0.046		
'old'			2.106	1.469		
1933	no data					
1934	25	18	2.252	1.360	40.29	47.07
'new'			0.100	0.090		
'old'			2.152	1.270		
1935	25	18	2.215	1.368	39.79	44.39
'new'			0.185	0.164		
'old'			2.030	1.204		
1936	26	15	2.127	1.335	41.59	47.27
'new'			0.264	0.233		
'old'			1.863	1.102		

Source: Kompas-Yugoslavia, various years

generally) and the data shows that 'new' savings never increased sufficiently to enable it to operate even close to previous levels of influence.

Of course the law must also be viewed in the context of the 1931 run on banks and the tradition of financing investments through loans. Here the question of savings deposits was central because banks were extremely sensitive to changes in savings. As mentioned, savings accounts were the traditional form of keeping wealth and the First Croatian Savings Bank had collected the largest savings in the country and depended on them. Savings deposits in the First Croatian Savings Bank at the end of 1930 and before the panic were 1995 million dinars. By mid-1931, the total had further increased to 2175 million dinars. During the next six months, while the crisis continued, they fell by almost a fifth to 1775 million dinars and at the end of 1934 they were only 1270 million dinars. That represented a fall of over 900 million dinars or almost 60 per cent. On 20 February 1932 (two months before the law on peasant protection was passed), it was stated at the yearly shareholders' meeting of the First Croatian Savings Bank that 'the citizens of Zagreb have not calmed down' and that 'circumstances are very difficult and will become even more difficult if we do not take sombre stock of the situation, if there is not enough willpower and love in these hard times to protect the achievements of our people.'

Even so, the First Croatian Savings Bank weathered the crisis better than other banks. The changes in savings that it registered were not different from those in the rest of the country. According to the Chamber of Trade and Industry's yearly report for 1932, the savings deposits in private sector banking were growing very fast, from 8.5 billion dinars in 1928 to 10.5 billion by the end of 1929 and 12.5 billion by the end of 1931. These were yearly increases of a quarter, a fifth and a sixth respectively during the three-year period. By mid-1931, when the crisis began, savings deposits were estimated at around 14 billion dinars. Then, in a short period, they suddenly fell back to 1929 levels. The First Croatian Savings Bank, with about one-seventh of all savings deposits, weathered the storm better than other banks and increased its share of business.

With falling savings, the relative importance of loan repayments become more important. Among these, the president of the Zagreb Chamber of Trade and Industry noted in his 1932 yearly report that loans to farmers were 'to a large extent considered the safest activities of many financial institutions' (Cuvaj, 1933). The moratorium on peasant debt provided by the law made the portfolio of farmers' debts illiquid because the peasants had to a large extent stopped paying off any of their loans. Arrears were also reported in related industries such as milling and the wood industry. But cities and public authorities had also stopped repaying loans and hence the focal point of the downfall of the the First Croatian Savings Bank was its inability to maintain the repayment of loans when facing the aftermath of a run on savings.

Given such complex circumstances, together with the external shock of the Great Depression, the timing of the law was crucial. There are many interpretations of the timing of the law. Thus nationalist interpretations (which understandably abound in Croatia) argue that the government delayed the law until the difficulties of the First Croatian Savings Bank were such that it had to apply for protection when it was already too late. In this version, it is also argued that the main intention was to cripple Croatian banking at the expense of Serbian banks (Lamer, 1939). Marxists offer a similar argument but pose it in terms of the rivalry of nationalist capitalist factions in a new state, with the Croatian faction losing out to the Serbian one (Mirković, 1956). A third view places it in terms of policy efficiency and the percieved greater efficiency of policy in a centralized environment where the political and financial centres coincide (Kadragić, 1937). Another view carries the same argument further by pointing to the need of state capitalism and state-led growth which needs to dominate the financial sector through banking, preferably state-owned banking.

Nevertheless there is another aspect to the issue: the banks' failure to survive and adapt through a period of transition. If development and growth from a predominantly peasant agricultural economy with self-sustained production units to a industrial market economy is viewed as transition or transformation, then Croatia was at the time in a transition. It is difficult for financial institutions to find their bearings in a transition because it is always a 'first time' experience. The first signs of a crisis may be visible before they arrive on a bank's doorstep but, if the bank is not prudent, its reaction will be late in coming.

Conclusion

The chapter concentrates on the decade of 1926–36, when monetary policy was the only proactive economic policy on a national level in Yugoslavia. During the whole period, policy concentrated on maintaining a fixed exchange rate and a restrictive monetary policy, and restructuring the financial sector. All three goals in the monetary sector were achieved but this did not generate any positive developments in the real sector. Exports did not increase, employment did not rise and growth was not generated. Even though the economy was subjected to external shocks, the primary policy targets were defined in terms of internally generated issues. Furthermore, the defined monetary policy was unable to cushion these shocks; indeed, as many contemporaries stressed, it increased their impact.

The monetary policies chosen in Yugoslavia, especially those aimed at restructuring, had a profound effect on private sector banking. Regionally, the assymetric effects of policy ultimately shifted the financial centre of the country to the political capital. This is perhaps best seen in Croatia, the region with the most developed banking sector and one of the most developed parts of the country. The consolidation of financial sector legislation in 1931, the decision in 1926 which tilted conditions in favour of state banking from 1929, dealing with the peasant debt in 1932, and banking rehabilitation schemes implemented from 1932 together dealt a death-blow to Croatian banking and to private sector banking generally. The policies also crippled the largest bank in the country, the First Croatian Savings Bank. Croatian banking never recovered from the effects of these policies. So, although the objective of restructuring the financial sector was met, real sector effects did not develop. The regional inequalities created by these policies certainly fuelled many tensions, in the economy as well as in politics.

In this way, an 'overload' of monetary policy, in spite of achieving its goals, could not deal with the period of crisis from 1926 to 1936. A new set of policy priorities was eventually established by 1936 in which monetary policy supported a state-dominated, proactive growth policy. This, together with an industrialization plan which to a great extent resembled those of the late 1940s and 1950s, was to generate above-average growth rates.

Appendix: Defining Croatia

The authors use the term 'Croatia' to refer to the territory of the present Republic of Croatia, except for the part which was under Italian rule during the inter-war period (the Istrian peninsular with the port of Rijeka, the town of Zadar and a number of islands). During the whole period from 1926 to 1936, Croatia was an integral part of Yugoslavia (first the Kingdom of Serbs, Croats and Slovenes and from 1929 the Kingdom of Yugoslavia). But it never existed as a territorial unit. At the beginning of the period Yugoslavia was territorially divided in 33 administrative counties (*srezovi*) and Croatia was divided among nine of them. From 1929 to 1939, Yugoslavia was divided into nine banovinas and the city of Belgrade. The boundaries of these territorial units deliberately did not coincide with any historical, national or economic units (except in one case). Thus Croatia was divided among four banovinas – the whole of the Sava banovina, a large part of the Coastal banovina and small parts of the Danube and Zeta banovinas. As a result there is no primary data on the financial sector for Croatia for the period. Similarly there is no data in secondary sources; recalculations have been made only for demographic statistics (Wertheimer-Baletić, 2001) and more recently for initial efforts to estimate Gross Domestic Product (Stipetić, 2002).

As a result the authors have had to make their own calculations. The major restriction was data. The official statistics for the period prior to 1929 were published in an almanac whose format varied, the data was sparse and not published in desegregated form. The first reliable official statistical source is the *Statistical Yearbook of the Kingdom of Yugoslavia*, published with minor alterations from 1929. This was not a yearly publication and sometimes appeared bi-annually. The authors base their calculation of Croatian values on these sources and other sources are used only to supplement them.

Since Croatia was divided among four banovinas (Sava, Danube, Zeta and Coastal) the main difficulty was how to determine the 'Croatian' share in each. The chosen criteria was the share of population derived from the 1931 population census. That is, it was decided that the Croatian share in other variables was the same as that of Croatian population. The share of the Croatian population could easily be derived since the census data was published on a local level and the boundaries of these units do not differ significantly from current borders. The 1931 census data show that the whole population of Sava banovina lived in Croatia, that 64 per cent of the population of the Coastal banovina lived in Croatia and that 5 per cent of the Zeta and Danube banovinas lived in Croatia. Thus, in aggregate, the respective weights of the Sava, Danube, Zeta and Coastal banovinas were 1.0, 0.05, 0.05 and 0.64 respectively. Of course this procedure assumes homogeneity within the banovinas. While this is not a problem with the Sava banovina (the whole of which is in Croatia) or the Danube banovina (where rough calculations show the Croatian part is close to the average) it may be a problem with the Coastal and Zeta banovinas. In both cases, this weighting probably underestimated Croatian values because the Croatian areas were significantly more developed (as, for example, the Dalmatian coast versus the hinterland and Dubrovnik versus Montenegro). Obviously further research would produce better estimates but given the magnitude involved and the scope of this chapter the authors feel the chosen procedure satisfactory for monetary aggregates.

References

Cuvaj, A. (ed.) (1930), 'Izvještaj Komore za trgovinu, obrt i industriju u Zagrebu za godinu 1929', *Zaklada narodnih novina*, Zagreb.

Cuvaj, A. (ed.) (1931), 'Izvještaj Komore za trgovinu, obrt i industriju u Zagrebu za godinu 1930', *Zaklada narodnih novina*, Zagreb.

Cuvaj, A. (ed.) (1932), 'Izvještaj Komore za trgovinu, obrt i industriju u Zagrebu za godinu 1931', *Zaklada narodnih novina*, Zagreb.

Cuvaj, A. (ed.) (1933), 'Izvještaj Komore za trgovinu, obrt i industriju u Zagrebu za godinu 1932', *Zaklada narodnih novina*, Zagreb.

Cuvaj, A. (ed.) (1934), 'Izvještaj Komore za trgovinu, obrt i industriju u Zagrebu za godinu 1933', *Zaklada narodnih novina*, Zagreb.

Ivšić, M. (1938), 'Pedesetogodišnjica predstavnika Hrvatskog bankarstva', *Ekonomist*, 4, pp. 359–62.

Kadragić, A. (1936), 'Najnoviji zakoni o bankama', *Ekonomist*, 2, pp. 18–25.

Kadragić, A. (1937), 'Posljedice naše deflacione politike', *Ekonomist*, 3, 12, pp. 511–18.

Kosier, Lj. St. (1932), 'Godisnje bilance nasih velikih novcanih zavoda', *Bankarstvo*, 9, 5–6, pp. 218–20.

Košak, V. (1936), 'O inozemnom kapitalu u našim bankama', *Ekonomist*, 2, 9, pp. 361–9.

Lamer, M. (1939), 'O položaju Hrvatskog bankarstva, *Ekonomist*, 5, 1, pp. 126–8.

Mirković, M. (1956), 'Ekonomska povijest Jugoslavije', *Informator*, Zagreb.

(NBJ) Narodna Banka Jugoslavija (1934), *Narodna Banka 1884–1934, Zavod za izradu novćanica*, Belgrade.

Raffaeli, I. (1937), 'Stanje našega novćarstva', *Ekonomist*, 3, 1, pp. 216–24.

Rozenberg, V. and Kostić, J. (1940), *Tko finansira jugoslovensku privredu*, Belgrade: Balkanska štampa.

Sobolev, Y. (2000), 'Exchange-rate based stabilization policies: a model of financial fragility', International Monetary Fund Working Paper, 00/122, Washington DC: International Monetary Fund.

Stajić, S. (1952), *Narodni dohodak Jugoslavije 1923–1941*, Belgrade: Radnićka štampa.

Stipetić, V. (2002), 'Stupanj i dinamika gospodarskog razvoja Hrvatske', in Družić, I. (ed.) *Zbornik u podovu 80 godišnjice Jakova sirotkovića*, Zagreb: Golden Marketing.

Tomašević, J. (1939), *Novac I kredit*, Zagreb: author's publication.

Wertheimer-Baletić (2001), *Demografska povijest Hrvatske*, Zagreb: HAZU.

Notes

1   The research for this article was financed by a research grant from the Croatian National Bank. The authors would like to thank Ms Danijela Medak for her research assistance.

PART III
Banking in Civil War and Its Aftermath

CHAPTER 6

The Republic Besieged? British Banks and the Spanish Civil War, 1936–39[1]

Tom Buchanan

Introduction

It has long been assumed that the British banks should be counted amongst the enemies of the Spanish Republic during the civil war. On 31 October 1936, for instance, the Secretary General of the Spanish Ministry of State complained to the British chargé d'affaires in Madrid about the deterioration of relations between their two countries. 'Business and especially banking circles,' he went on, 'were unfriendly and unnecessarily denied credits and other facilities.'[2] In May 1937, the Spanish Ambassador in London complained to Foreign Secretary Anthony Eden that commercial relations were being 'aggravated by the attitude of certain British banking elements who have improperly retained funds remitted by the Bank of Spain'.[3] Many historians have subsequently endorsed this interpretation. Angel Viñas, the leading historian of the financing of the civil war, criticizes the role of specific British and US banks under the heading of 'Bancos anglosajones contra la República' (Viñas, 1979, p. 218). Enrique Moradiellos, an expert on British government policy during the conflict, has argued that the Republic's dealings with British banks were 'subject to such numerous obstructions and acts of sabotage' that they influenced its decision to make exclusive use of the Soviet banking network, and may even have been a factor in the fateful decision to deposit the Republic's gold reserves in the Soviet Union (Moradiellos, 1996, p. 96).[4]

These images of the perfidious role of the British banks fit comfortably with the concept of an international anti-Republican front (including businesses as well as governments) that is now increasingly found in the historical literature on the Spanish civil war. Robert Whealey, referring above all to the role of British and US oil companies, has written that Franco enjoyed the 'moral support of international capitalism' and 'drew aid and succour from capitalist companies' (Whealey, 1977, pp. 146–7). Helen Graham, in a major re-evaluation of the latter stages of the civil war, attributes the Republican defeat in large measure to the policies of 'Western *capitalist* democracy' in imposing a 'crippling economic embargo' (author's italics). The refusal of the Western democracies to provide the credits that would have allowed the Republic to feed its population, she argues, undermined the Republic's legitimacy in the eyes of its own citizens (Graham, 1996, pp. 193–5). Graham thus moves the focus of the debate over why the Republic lost the war away from the question of arms supplies (and hence the role of Germany, Italy and the USSR), and towards the responsibilities of international finance and the Western democracies (Britain, France and the US).[5]

Given this new emphasis on economic factors, and the various assumptions that underlie them, it is noteworthy that no attempt has yet been made to examine the Spanish civil war from the perspective of the British banks. Economic relations between Britain and Spain during the civil war have been studied through the archives of the British and Spanish governments, or the Bank of Spain rather than through the archives of individual banks and companies (Edwards, 1979, pp. 64–100; Little, 1985, passim; Viñas, 1984, p. 283).[6] This oversight forms part of a wider neglect of the history of business as an actor in the international relations of the 1930s. Donald Cameron Watt has recently observed *a propos* the vast literature on appeasement that remarkably little is known in any detail of the role of transnational businesses: 'whole pages in our historical atlas of the period [are] filled only with medieval-style maps of Africa', illustrated with 'grotesques' of leading financiers to fill the gaps in our knowledge.[7] This paper is an attempt to fill a particular gap in the understanding of the role of British banks during the Spanish civil war. On the basis of the limited archival evidence available, the paper examines how bankers perceived the civil war and how they responded to it. A complex picture emerges. Bankers were, on the whole, no friends of the Republic, but nor were they, with notable exceptions, willing to take risks to help Franco's rebels. For most of them the war did not represent an ideological crusade or a chance for profit, but rather an unwelcome disruption to settled patterns of business, and the imposition of severe political and diplomatic constraints on their freedom of action. Above all, whatever the outcome, bankers saw little immediate prospect of a return to pre-civil war normality.

Contexts

In the period before the civil war, Britain was the dominant factor both in trade with Spain and in internal investment, although this represented a relatively small proportion of overall British trade and foreign investments

(Edwards, 1979, pp. 65–7). Spain was not particularly attractive to British banks due to the limited commercial opportunities and its history of social and political unrest. The British financier R. H. Brand, when considering establishing a branch of Lloyds Bank in Spain during the First World War went so far as to comment that the 'greatest difficulties in the way of Englishmen doing business in Spain spring from the character of the Spaniards themselves'.[8] Accordingly, few British banks chose to retain offices in Spain. For instance, only one of the constituent banks of the future NatWest operated branches in Spain, between 1917 and 1924, and these were all closed due to deteriorating economic conditions and strikes by bank clerks in Madrid.[9] Those banks that did maintain a formal presence tended to be those which took an interest in Spain as part of wider extra-European trade. These included the Bank of British West Africa, with branches in the Canary Islands, and the Bank of London and South America, which in July 1936 was taking over the Spanish operations of the troubled Anglo South-American Bank (García Ruiz, 2001).

   Civil war broke out in Spain in July 1936 following a failed military *coup* against the elected government of the Second Republic. The result was immediate and widespread disruption to trade. Eventually, the confusion of the early weeks of the conflict settled into a prolonged division of Spain into separate zones under the control of the Republican government and of the Nationalist rebels. This division of Spain, and the *de facto* emergence of two economies, raised complex questions of political legitimacy, and even the prospect of legal liabilities, for British banks. For example, the gold reserves of the Bank of Spain were retained by the Republic but most of the Bank's directors joined the Nationalist side. The Bank of Spain kept an account in the London office of Martins Bank, and when the London manager of the Bank of Spain was sacked by the Spanish government in January 1937 a bitter struggle ensued between Republicans and Nationalists over the right to deposits worth £242 000. Martins Bank – with the support of the Bank of England – refused to pay out to either side and the matter was lodged with the courts until the end of the civil war.[10] Similarly, the prospect of legal action by the Spanish Embassy dissuaded the British company Bradburys from producing bank notes for the rebels, and the contract was completed in Germany.[11] Banks considering taking business from Spain had to weigh very carefully the prospects for victory of their prospective customers, and the possible damage to their own long-term interests. Thus, when the Basque government sought to lodge gold and securities with a number of London banks as the Nationalist forces were completing their conquest of the Basque Country, the Bank of England was forced to issue a warning that such banks would become liable to litigation.[12]

More generally, British trade and investment in Spain was affected by the framework provided by British government policy and international agreements during the civil war. Primarily, this related to the embargo on arms supply to both sides under the 'Non-Intervention Agreement' signed by 27 states in August–September 1936. The agreement was administered by the London-based Non-Intervention Committee, and was flagrantly ignored by leading signatories such as Germany, Italy, the USSR and (to a degree) France. However, the scheme was closely observed by Britain and this placed an obligation on British banks not only to avoid involvement in arms dealing, but also to report any suspicious activity to the government. Thus, in late August 1936, following Britain's unilateral ban on arms sales to Spain on 15 August, the manager of Barclays Bank (France) felt compelled to report a number of arms-related transactions, the eventual destination of which was likely to be Spain, to the British embassy. The official response was that there was no reason not to do business, and, tellingly, the War Office commented that 'such transactions provide information which is frequently of use'.[13] In a separate case, in early September 1936, the manager of the Westminster Bank called at the Foreign Office to ask whether, following the recent arrival of a new Spanish naval attaché, there was any objection to the bank keeping open an account for the Naval Commission. He went on to reveal that under the former naval attaché this account had 'suddenly swollen to large proportions' and had clearly been used to attempt to buy arms for the rebels from Germany and elsewhere. In turn, it was assumed that the new attaché wished to buy arms for the Republic. The Foreign Office replied that while it could not interfere it would like to hear of further payments in connection with arms, and the bank was happy to oblige.[14] The fact that the bank felt compelled to report its suspicions only when a pro-Republican attaché had taken over perhaps gives an indication of where its sympathies lay.

Aside from the question of arms, it was less clear how the Non-Intervention Agreement would impinge on commercial relations between Britain and the two economic zones in Spain. In October 1936, the Treasury, at the instigation of the Foreign Office, asked the Bank of England what steps it had taken since the outbreak of civil war to 'discourage lending to Spain'. The response was that the bank 'had taken no step of this kind because, so far as we knew, nobody in London had been proposing to lend money to Spain'.[15] In early 1937, Wilson Smith of the Treasury commented that it was 'almost inconceivable' that either side could raise significant funds in Britain.[16] After the civil war there was certainly a belief in the Treasury that 'we generally discouraged British financial help to Franco',[17] although clearly not sufficiently to discourage Kleinworts from extending a very significant loan in 1937 (see below, p. 95). The issue of financial assistance was investigated thoroughly in early 1937 when it was raised in the Non-Intervention Committee. The British government had been pressing Germany and Italy for a ban on foreign volunteers in Spain, and felt that an extension of the Non-Intervention Agreement to cover financial assistance would be a suitable 'window-dressing and a sop' in return, so long as credits and loans made in the 'normal course of bona fide commercial business' were not included. These discussions were inconclusive as Germany and Italy were primarily concerned with choking off the export and sale of the Spanish government's gold reserves for arms purchases rather than preventing the small quantity of private loans. Moreover, the Treasury and Bank of England concurred that 'watertight control is technically impossible'. Accordingly, the proposals would be 'futile' as credits could simply be passed through countries not party to the Non-Intervention Agreement such as the US.[18]

British trade with Spain was vulnerable in 1936 precisely because, somewhat ironically, the months immediately prior to the civil war had seen a move towards more settled trading conditions. In January 1936, Britain and Spain had signed an 'Anglo-Spanish Payments Agreement', in response to Spain's shortage of foreign exchange. Under the agreement payments for imported goods were made into central Clearing Offices in Madrid and London, and then used to settle outstanding debts in chronological order. On the outbreak of the civil war this system initially made trade with the rebel zone almost impossible, as all payments had to be made through the office in Madrid and, thus, to the Republic. No issue was more vexatious for British traders, who faced the choice between paying twice for their imports or breaking the law. One leading company importing sherry from Cadiz was said to be remitting sterling direct to its trading partners. A Bank of England official minuted the reported comments of a senior partner in this firm: '"I am not going to stop paying my Spanish friends for sending me sherry. I know that I am breaking the law; but it is a damned silly law anyhow."'[19] Acute problems were also caused for the banks that specialized in trade with the rebel-controlled areas. For instance, the well-preserved archive of the Bank of British West Africa deals with little other than the problems endured by traders. The immediate problem was solved with the suspension of the Payments Agreement in December 1936, which allowed direct payments to be made for imports so long as the sterling was primarily used to buy British goods. For the remainder of the war, pragmatic measures were taken for the handling of trade with both zones in Spain.

Therefore, the political and diplomatic context for banking during the civil war was one that was not conducive to business. For a bank to support either side financially would be a gamble, with little prospect of sympathy or assistance from the British government. Non-Intervention complicated matters because the definition of 'intervention' was constantly being redefined, and for the banks this necessitated a policy of caution and constant deferral to the British government.

The Impact on Banking in Britain

Both the Republican and Nationalist war economies were assembled on an *ad hoc* basis, and both had significant strengths and weaknesses (Viñas, 1984; Hubbard, 1953, pp. 380–406). The Republicans retained the gold reserves and much of Spain's industrial capacity, while the Nationalists controlled much of the country's agricultural and mineral resources. The Republican gold was, to some degree, balanced by the extravagant credit that the Nationalists received from Italy and Germany, repayment of which was largely deferred until after the war. Even so, both sides looked for assistance to independent financial institutions. For the Republicans, the main task was to convert their gold reserves into foreign currency that could be utilized to purchase arms, while the Nationalists sought credits to cover the import of goods unavailable from Germany and Italy. The general verdict amongst historians has been that the Republic was unfairly treated by Western banks, while the Nationalists received considerable assistance.

Central to the criticism of British banks has been the role of the Midland Bank. Angel Viñas identifies the Midland as a 'very well documented' example of a bank that 'sabotaged the transfer of funds urgently required by Republican agents and diplomats' (Vinas, 1984, pp. 268–9). The principal evidence concerns attempts in late October 1936 to send $3 million via the Midland to Félix Gordón Ordás, the Spanish ambassador in Mexico. The bank delayed the transfer, in part because the official order was in the name of 'Ordax' rather than 'Ordas'. The Republican ministers and agents were outraged. Foreign Minister Julio Alvarez del Vayo told Gordón on 20 October that 'sabotage and boycott are making the financial situation extraordinarily difficult', and on 30 October the Minister of Marine and Air proposed to tell Gordón that 'the foreign banking sabotage, amongst which the role of the Midland Bank stands out, has reached unimaginable limits'

(Vinas, 1979, pp. 221, note 39). Gordón himself, in his memoirs, said that the Midland had played an 'ignoble game' on him and was guilty of a 'masterpiece of perfidy' (Gordón, 1965, pp. 71–2). Viñas also describes how, at the same time, the Midland failed to transfer funds from France to New York due to political objections from the correspondent banks in the US (Vinas, 1979, p. 223). The transfer to Gordón was eventually made in November by the Banque Commercial pour l'Europe du Nord, a Soviet financial institution based in Paris.[20]

The failure of these transactions was clearly a blow to the Republican war effort at a time when, with Franco's forces nearing Madrid, the Spanish government was fighting for its life. The deleterious impact on Anglo-Spanish relations is clear from the comment by the Secretary General of the Spanish Ministry of State cited above (see p. 87). The story of the Midland Bank's alleged perfidy has been repeated, unaltered, in Gerald Howson's recent book on arms dealing during the civil war (Howson, 1998, pp. 169–70). However, as it stands, this account is unsatisfactory. Viñas depicts it as a case of politically motivated sabotage, alluding to the role of the chairman of the Midland Bank, Reginald McKenna, who he claims was a friend of the Francoist financier Juan Ventosa. However, there is no evidence that McKenna played any role. Moreover, neither Howson nor Viñas consulted the records of the Midland Bank. Although the archival evidence is very limited, what there is is revealing. At the bank's Management Committee on 29 October, it was reported that a US bank had expressed its unwillingness to make a payment of 75 million francs, while the Midland was having difficulty in identifying the beneficiary for 69 million francs. Accordingly, '*it was decided to endeavour to get out of making any payment* and return the amount we have received in francs'. Counsel's opinion was taken on the wording of a telegram to explain the bank's actions in returning the money (for the credit of the Bank of Spain).[21]

This episode can be contextualized with reference to two other incidents involving the Midland Bank. First, on the previous day (28 October 1936) the Management Committee had discussed a letter from the so-called 'Bank of Spain' in the rebel capital Burgos, asking permission to open a sterling current account in its name with the Midland. The committee noted that 'our only account with the Bank of Spain is with the central office at Madrid', and in the absence of instructions from Madrid it was agreed not to make any reply. Thus, just at the point when the Midland was accused of perfidy and sabotage, the bank was adopting a very proper stance towards the Republic. Secondly, in November 1936 a report reached the British embassy in Paris from a Nationalist agent that the Midland was acting on behalf of a British aircraft manufacturer that was considering making a sale to the Spanish government. The money had been deposited by the Spanish ambassador with the Paris branch of the Chase Bank. The Midland was, it was reported, 'refusing to get ... involved in the transaction unless the Chase Bank will give them a certificate to the effect that everything is straight and above board'.[22] The Foreign Office instructed the Embassy to keep in contact with the agent to monitor the proposed deal. In this case the exposure of the bank to potential illegality was clear and its caution fully justified. In the absence of more substantial archival evidence, it seems appropriate to view the actions of the Midland Bank, including the farcical delay over Ordas' name, not as politically motivated sabotage, but rather as the response of an inherently cautious institution to its involvement in a transaction that might well cause it serious embarrassment. The question that needs to be answered, therefore, is not so much why the bank withdrew its cooperation, but rather why it became so deeply involved in the first place?

The experience of the Midland should also be viewed in the context of that of Barclays Bank in the early months of the civil war.[23] Barclays had a branch in Gibraltar, which was very swiftly approached by a group of US and Canadian banks with a view to opening credits for the export of olives from rebel-held Seville. On 14 August 1936, the manager of the branch sent a telegram to Head Office to ask advice on opening sight credits in dollars for this purpose. He continued:

> I was also sounded yesterday tentatively ... might be prepared facilitate sales Seville pesetas against sterling up to £50 000 or advance same amount sterling to Spanish customers against British government security for purpose of aiding military revolt (stop) replied did not think we can agree (stop) application was not pressed but we presume this your policy in view of necessity of maintaining neutral attitude present conflict (stop) views of myself refusal ... (stop) Gibraltar government also have issued decree ordering neutrality words and deeds in present situation.

On 17 August, the branch reported that the Madrid government had decreed that all transactions in rebel-held towns would be considered contraband:

> This decree presumably will not affect our operations in Gibraltar with Spaniards under such credits as are in question but presumably Madrid government would be strongly opposed to such credits being opened especially as they liable to provide military with foreign exchange (stop) It is not clear how far we should consider such

> political factors but we must bear in mind our balances in Spain
> (stop) Unfortunately whatever lines we take we might experience
> difficulties later according to which party wins.

Thus caution, conditioned by regard to legal propriety and political wisdom, was also characteristic of Barclays' policy. So, too, was deferral to the wishes of the British government and the Non-Intervention policy. When the bank's general manager consulted with the Foreign Office on 10 September over an approach to finance the purchase of aeroplanes in the US for export to Spain, mentioning a sum of £100 000, he was informed that this was 'quite out of harmony' with government policy. The enquirers were then told that the bank was not interested.[24]

The one British bank that threw itself wholeheartedly into supporting the Nationalist cause was the merchant bank Kleinworts, for whom the civil war presented the opportunity for 'intrigue and [John] Buchan-like exploits' (Wake, 1997, p. 249). Kleinworts had been involved in Spain for some years prior to the civil war and had a close relationship with the financial expert José Mayorga. Through Mayorga they came into contact with the dubious Majorcan financier Juan March, who had made his fortune in tobacco smuggling and who became their leading Spanish client (Stafford, 1999, pp. 84–90). March was a prominent right-winger who strongly supported the military rebellion. Kleinworts came to play a leading role in the international financing of the Nationalist movement, beginning with the channelling of funds to hire the plane that would fly General Franco from the Canary Islands to North Africa at the start of the rebellion. During the civil war, Kleinworts advanced loans worth £1 860 000 to the Nationalist government, with security provided by the international bonds and the personal gold and jewellery of Nationalist supporters in London. One member of the bank's staff later recalled the queues of Spanish aristocrats that would form to make deposits: 'it was astonishing – all the jewels and gold that came in …' (Wake, 1997, p. 254). Although the guarantor of the credits was Juan March, it only became apparent later that the loans themselves were actually March's own money. As José Mayorga's son put it: 'Everybody thought it was Kleinworts' money, it looked that way … but it was Juan March's money.' In fact, the true source was already known to the British government: in October 1939, a Treasury official notifed the Bank of England that he was informed that 'the money really comes from Juan March'.[25]

When the civil war ended, Juan March tired of this game and in October 1939 told Kleinworts to call in the loan. The result was financial and diplomatic embarrassment both for the Franco regime and for a British government that was now itself at war. The Spanish government was unable to repay the loan, and the Spanish ambassador put intense pressure on the Foreign Office to persuade the Bank of England to take it over as a sign of Britain's goodwill. Meanwhile, the Treasury dreaded the sale of a large amount of British government stock during wartime. Treasury officials fulminated against Kleinworts for making such a large advance without 'the knowledge or consent of this Department', adding that 'if such consent had been asked in the first place it would almost certainly have been refused on financial grounds'.[26] Eventually Barings took over the loan on behalf of the Bank of England.[27] However, Kleinworts maintained a financial interest in Spain. Indeed, the company's historian regrets that Ernest Kleinwort's 'excessive caution' on a visit to Spain in 1947 (when he feared that the Franco regime might not last) cost his company 'valuable business' (Wake, 1997, p. 328). The experience of Kleinworts shows what could be achieved by British banks during the civil war when the tacit legal and diplomatic constraints (as well, one might add, as political and moral scruples) were disregarded. However, the evidence indicates that the bank was very much acting alone, and that its actions reflected its unique and longstanding involvement with Juan March and other Spanish financiers.

The Experience of British Banks in Spain

At first sight, the experiences of British banking staff in Republican and in rebel Spain would appear to be very different. Most bankers would have welcomed – and, indeed, felt reassured by – the military rebellion. For instance, the staff of the Bank of British West Africa in the Canaries had faced personal danger during anti-foreigner riots in September 1933 (Little, 1985, p. 154), and now took satisfaction in the assertion of authority and the jailing of militants. For those based in government territory, conversely, the outbreak of the civil war and the temporary collapse of law and order brought very real dangers to their safety. However, over time the experiences of British banking staff in both zones of Spain became increasingly similar, as all foreign banking activity struggled to cope with public hostility and political interference.

The impact of the civil war was faced most starkly in the Republican zone, especially in Barcelona where the collapse of central government authority ushered in a period of revolutionary chaos. During this period all foreign residents faced the danger of assassination, and foreign-owned businesses were placed under control of workers' committees. Only one British senior member of staff was left at the Anglo-South American Bank in Barcelona by the end of August, the British manager and sub-manager having both left.[28] The physical dangers were very real: a British bank manager in Valencia was held up by a youth of 17 who promptly shot himself in the foot.[29] British interests were vulnerable to the threat of expropriation, and this danger remained even when government authority began to be restored in the autumn of 1936. In reality, however, the banks remained closely controlled and subject to arbitrary demands. A detailed report on the impact of the civil war on British interests in Spanish government territory noted that the Barcelona branch of the Anglo-South American Bank had been obliged by order of the Generalitat (the Catalan government) to 'pay from its own funds [a] cheque for 7000 pesetas to a firm whose overdraft facility has lapsed'. The Royal Bank of Canada had been obliged by the Barcelona branch of the Bank of Spain to deposit 8 million pesetas worth of Treasury Bonds. It had also been compelled by the Generalitat to 'honour against its will certain cheques drawn by Workers' Committees'.[30]

Disconcerting as these reports were, however, it should be noted that other accounts emphasized the relative stability of the situation in Barcelona. On 24 November 1936, Consul-General King, frequently an alarmist commentator, reported that the managers of the Royal Bank of Canada and the Anglo-South American Bank had both opted to stay as the control of the workers' committees was 'largely nominal' and, despite 'minor unpleasant incidents', they still felt able to manage their offices. Although the Catalan government had taken decree powers to force open safe deposit boxes in search for gold deposits, King noted that only twelve out of 700 boxes at the Royal Bank had been forced, and of 300 boxes at the Anglo-South American only five (all belonging to Spaniards) had been forced. Gold had been seized from the safe deposit boxes of the Barcelona Traction, Light and Power Company (which was 75 per cent British-owned) and payment made in pesetas.[31] The physical dangers began to recede in 1937, although British bank managers found themselves trapped in their offices on 4 May when street fighting broke out in Barcelona between Anarchists and the authorities.[32] Even though these clashes resulted in a consolidation of central government authority, Republican Spain remained a difficult and uncongenial environment for bankers until the end of the civil war.

By contrast, British banking staff in the rebel zone warmly welcomed the rebellion, as it apparently marked an end to a prolonged period of social and political tension. The best surviving evidence for these attitudes is in the correspondence from the two branches of the Bank of British West Africa in the Canary Islands, where the rebellion had quickly triumphed. On 3 August 1936, the manager of the Tenerife branch, J. B. Shipley, complained to his head office that the *Times* had wrongly described the rebellion as a 'Monarchist rising. It is nothing of the sort, but a gallant attempt to save civilisation.' Confidence in Franco's victory was running high and 'please God it will be soon. If he should fail there would be a massacre of all decent people.' He wished that British supporters of the Republic could come to experience the 'Spanish Marxists savages [*sic*]'.[33] Months later he was still complaining at the use of the term 'rebels' by the BBC, which in his view rightly annoyed those who were fighting 'against the bolshevization of their country'. This resentment was, he claimed, shared by all British businessmen who had been in contact with Marxism over the last five years and 'suffered therefrom'.[34] Alan H. Selley, manager of the Las Palmas branch, shared many of these sentiments, albeit in a muted form. On 30 July, he wrote that 'the feeling here is one of optimism and from all accounts the movement is progressing satisfactory [*sic*] on the mainland. There will certainly be a long period of re-organisation, but the situation on these Islands should be greatly improved.'[35] Even so, his wife and young son were evacuated and he moved from his country house into town. In late September he looked forward keenly to the anticipated fall of Madrid: then 'the constructive life of the country, at present suspended, can be resumed and more intensely since the menace of Communism, which has been hanging over the country for so long, will no longer exist'.[36]

This transparent sense of relief and enthusiasm was tempered from an early stage by concern over the economic impact of the civil war, especially as the rapid military success in the islands was not repeated elsewhere in Spain. Problems were exacerbated by the distinctive nature of the Canary Islands' trade, whereby fruit was exported to Britain and commodities imported. So long as the Payments Agreement was in force, trade was almost impossible, and the BBWA branches repeatedly called for it to be suspended or circumvented. However, even the suspension of the agreement in December 1936 brought little relief, as the Nationalist authorities asserted their control over the islands' trade and took 70 per cent of all sterling earned. Thus, British bankers in rebel territory experienced increasing control over their activities, and mounting frustration as they sought to reclaim the pre-civil war debts of foreign clients (in some cases not settled until some years after 1939). Moreover, they had to deal with mounting political hostility. In October 1936, the BBWA branches successfully resisted, with the support of the British consul, demands from the authorities for them to make donations for the purchase of aeroplanes.[37]

In December 1936, J. E. Shipley admitted to the presence of anti-British feeling, which he attributed to Britain's stance over the Clearing Agreement 'contrasting with the conduct of Germany'.[38] In May 1937, Arthur Pack, the Commercial Secretary at the British Embassy, complained to Nationalist authorities about a press notice on the Canary Islands stigmatizing those who had dealings with foreign banks as 'bad Spaniards'. Joaquin Bau, president of the Nationalist Commission of Industry and Commerce, promised that the notice would be withdrawn, but Pack noted that the Spanish memory was 'not to be depended on'.[39] Eventually, in the course of 1937, the BBWA branches in the Canary Islands were closed down by Head Office.

The suspension of the BBWA's activities in the Canary Islands from 30 September 1937 was partly a testimony to the immediate difficulties caused by the war. However, there was also evidence of a wider gloom amongst those engaged in trade with Spain, that the war would bring a fundamental dislocation to their livelihood. An inspector sent from the BBWA Head Office observed on his return home from the Canaries that 'The future does not look to be good for foreigners, with Communism [business] would be wiped out at once; with Fascism it will be on a much reduced basis as they will have to set their house in order and to do so they must restrict the export of funds.' The only consolation, he added, was that the Nationalists would, in victory, have to turn to Britain for help with reconstruction.[40]

This view was one that was also widely held within British government, where the power of 'sterling diplomacy' became something of an official mantra. However, it is important to note that this belief in the power of sterling flew in the face of evidence of mounting anti-British sentiment, a switch to Spanish barter trade with Germany, and lasting damage to existing British commercial interests in Spain. René MacColl, a British journalist who entered Madrid with Franco's forces in 1939, warned that Britain faced a difficult task ahead. In Spain there was a 'sullen resentment' against the democracies and businessmen should not think that they could 'stroll back' to their old relationships. He added that 'airy talk of "they will have to come to us for a loan and then everything will be settled" means nothing'.[41]

Conclusion

Angel Viñas has written that 'the hostility of international financial circles which obstructed the Republic's foreign financial and commercial transactions' should be compared to the 'enormous goodwill' that international financiers showed to the Nationalists (Viñas, 1984, pp. 266, 268–9).[42] It is, however, questionable whether either part of this equation can be supported by research in British banking and governmental archives. Indeed, much of the criticism of the role of the British banks rests on rather slender archival evidence. The reaction of almost all British banks to the civil war was one of extreme caution. There was certainly little sympathy for the Republic, and a willing complicity with the British government in its policy of Non-Intervention. There is, however, no reliable evidence of any conspiracy against the Republic. Nor was there any manifest desire to invest in a Franco victory. It should be noted that the main exception to this rule – Kleinworts – was, in effect, simply recycling Spanish money in extending its loan. As the civil war came to an end in the spring of 1939, British banks looked forward not to business opportunities in Franco's 'New Spain', but rather to the slow process of clearing the large backlog of debt accumulated before July 1936.

References

Edwards, J. (1979), *The British Government and the Spanish civil war*, Basingstoke: Macmillan.

García Ruiz, J. L. (2001), 'La banca extranjera en España tras la Restauracion, 1874–1936', in Sudria, Carlos and Tirado, Daniel A. (eds), *Peseta y Protección, Comercio exterior, moneda y crecimiento economico en la Espana de la Restauración*, Barcelona: publisher not known.

Gordón Ordás, F. (1965), *Mi politica fuera de España*, Mexico City: publisher not known.

Graham, H. (1996) 'War, Modernity and Reform: The premiership of Juan Negrín, 1937–39', in Preston, P. and Mackenzie, A. L. (eds), *The Republic besieged: civil war in Spain, 1936–1939*, Edinburgh: Edinburgh University Press.

Howson, G. (1998), *Arms for Spain: The Untold Story of the Spanish civil war*, London: John Murray.

Hubbard, J. R. (1953), 'How Franco financed his war', *The Journal of Modern History*, 25, 4.

Little, D. (1985), *Malevolent Neutrality: The United States, Great Britain and the Origins of the Spanish civil war*, Ithaca, NY: Cornell University Press.

Moradiellos, E. (1996), *La perfidia de Albión: El gobierno británico y la guerra civil española*, Madrid: Siglo Veintiuno Editores.

Stafford, D. (1999), *Roosevelt and Churchill: Men of Secrets*, London: Little, Brown.

Tortella, T. (1995), 'Printing Spanish bank notes in England, 1850–1938', in Hewitt, V. (ed.), *The Banker's Art: Studies in Paper Money*, Dorchester: British Museum Press.

Viñas, A. (1979), *El oro de Moscú: Alfa y omega de un mito franquista*, Barcelona: Ediciones Grijalbo.

Viñas, A. (1984), 'The financing of the Spanish civil war', in Preston, Paul (ed.), *Revolution and War in Spain*, London: Methuen.

Wake, J. (1997), *Kleinwort Benson: The history of two families in banking*, Oxford: Oxford University Press.

Whealey, R. (1977), 'How Franco financed his war – reconsidered', *Journal of Contemporary History*, 12.

Notes

1 I am grateful to the EABH for inviting me to speak at the conference on 'Crisis and renewal in twentieth century banking', and to the following archivists for kindly assisting my research : Edwin Green (HSBC), Teresa Tortella (Banco de España), Jessie Campbell (Barclays), Philip Winterbottom (Royal Bank of Scotland), John Orbell (ING Barings). I would also like to thank David Boardman for his advice on published sources.

2 University of Aberdeen, Forbes of Boyndlie papers, Ms 2740, Box 40. Ogilvie-Forbes to Foreign Office, 31 October 1936. For the specific issue referred to see below, p. 93.

3 Public Record Office, Kew (PRO), FO 371/21383/W9628. Azcarate to Eden, 11 May 1937; for the episode referred to see below, p. 89.

4 Moradiellos gave the most forceful expression of this view in a BBC documentary: 'The hidden hostility of the British government towards the Republic could be seen in financial matters. It rejected all pleas for credit from the Republic. Moreover, it obstructed a financial operation on the part of the Republic to buy arms in America through Barclays Bank ... The British didn't do the same in the case of Nationalist purchases and financial transactions through the Westminster Bank' ('Beside Franco in Spain', 18 September 1991).

5 Whealey goes as far as to argue that these countries should not be referred to as the 'democratic' powers but as the 'sterling-dollar countries' (Whealey, 1977, p. 146).

6 To my knowledge, no historians have to date used the archives of the Bank of England relating to the civil war.

7 *Times Literary Supplement*, 22 December 2000, p. 9. It should be noted that Neil Forbes' important new book on this theme, *Doing business with the Nazis: Britain's economic and financial relations with Germany, 1931–1939* (London: Cass, 2000), has been published since this paper was prepared and presented.

8 Bodleian Library, Oxford, MS Brand, file 8. R. H. Brand to Sir Arthur Hardinge, Madrid, 2 December 1916.

9   This was the London, County and Westminster Bank. The Spanish branches were transferred to a subsidiary in 1920 which, in 1923, became the Westminster Foreign Bank Ltd (information supplied by Philip Winterbottom, Royal Bank of Scotland).

10 Barclays archives. Minutes of the standing committee of Martins Bank, 20 January 1937; 8 December 1937.

11 PRO, FO 371/21382/W805. Sir Henry Chilton to Foreign Office, 11 January 1937. See also Tortella (1995), p. 91.

12 Bank of England archives (BoE), OV 61/3/23. C. F. Cobbold to the Governor, 17 June 1937; see also the Barclays Bank Head Office circular of 24 May 1937 urging all branches to be on the lookout for any use of the bank's services in this connection (copy in Barclays archives). On 31 May 1937, the Accepting Houses Committee circulated a letter from José de Lizaso of the Spanish Embassy, in which he complained that 'agents hostile' to the Spanish government had spread falsehoods about the Basque government's confiscation of bank deposits. Lizaso appealed to the banks' 'sense of fairness' to contradict this view (ING Bank NV, London, Barings Archive, file 200703).

13 PRO, FO 371 20573, W9712/9549/41. Lloyd Thomas to Horace Seymour, 25 August 1936; 20573, W10590/9549/41, Captain W. P. Barclay to P. Leigh-Smith. Barclays (France) had already consulted with the *chef de cabinet* of the Socialist Finance Minister Vincent Auriol, who told them that both transactions were 'quite in order' and that he would help if there was any trouble.

14 PRO, FO371 20576/W11131/9549/41. Minute by Montagu Pollock. I was unable to find any reference to this episode in the minutes of Westminster Bank (RBS archive, London).

15 BoE, OV 61/2. Memorandum by C. A. Gunston, 13 October 1937.

16 BoE, OV 61/2. Paper by Wilson Smith, January 1937.

17 PRO, T 160 992/F17177. Marginal note by 'JS' on Treasury memorandum of 26 September 1939 by Sir Richard Hopkins, 29 September 1939.

18 BoE, OV 61/2. Paper by Wilson Smith, January 1937.

19 BoE, OV 61/26, item 27. Memorandum by L. A. Crick, 24 September 1936.

20 Bank of Spain archive. Letter from Bank of Spain, 6 November 1936.

21 HSBC Group Archives, London. Midland Bank management committee minutes, 29 October 1936 (author's italics).

22 PRO, FO 371/20587/W17249. Victor Perowne to C. J. Norton, Foreign Office, 27 November 1936.

23 The following references are taken from the Barclays Bank archives.

24 PRO, FO 371/20576/W11308. Minute by W. Roberts, 11 September 1936. Enrique Moradiellos presents this as an example of the British government's prejudice against the Republic, on the grounds that this money was to be used to purchase aircraft for the Republic. However, it is not clear that this inference is correct as the Foreign Office documents do not state for whom the aircraft were intended. The bank's archives show that Barclays was also being approached by rebel sympathizers at this time (Moradiellos, 1995, p. 95).

25 PRO, T 160 992/F17177. S. D. Waley to C. F. Cobbold, 14 October 1939.

26 PRO, T 160 992/F17177. R. V. Hopkins to R. A. Butler, Under Secretary of State, Foreign Office, 20 October 1939.

27 For a limited record of these transactions see ING Bank NV, London, Barings Archive, file 202353.

28 *British Documents on Foreign Affairs* (BDFA), Series F, vol. 27, p. 22.

29 BoE, OV 61/2. Memorandum by L. A. Crick, 5 August 1936.

30 BDFA, Series F, Vol. 27, p. 105.

31 BoE, OV 61/2. Consul-General King to Eden, 24 November 1936.

32 BDFA, Series F, vol. 27, pp. 111–2.

33 Guildhall Library, London (GL), Bank of British West Africa papers (BBWA), MS 28722/1. J. E. Shipley to D. Paterson, 31 July 1936.

34 PRO, FO 371/21382/W63. D. W. Paterson to Under-Secretary of State, enclosing Shipley's letter of 15 December 1936, 30 December 1936.

35 GL Ms 28722/1. A. Selley to D. Paterson, 30 July 1936.

36 GL Ms 28722/329. Shipley to Sir E. Roy Wilson, September 1936.

37 PRO, FO 371 20583, W14302/9549/41. Consul Patteson to Foreign Office, 23 October 1936; 20584, W15098/9549/41. Patteson to Foreign Office, 3 November 1936.

38 PRO, FO 371/21382/W63. D. W. Paterson to Under-Secretary of State, enclosing Shipley's letter of 15 December 1936, 30 December 1936.

39 PRO, FO 371/21383/W10542. Memorandum by A. Pack, 27 May 1937.

40 GL MS 28722/3. Letter to General Manager, BBWA, from Head Office Inspector, 6 October 1936.

41 Imperial War Museum, London, René MacColl papers, undated typescript on 'Britain and the New Spain'.

42 Angel Viñas, in Paul Preston, *Revolution and War in Spain*, London: Methuen, pp. 266 and 268–9.

CHAPTER 7

Spanish Banking After the Civil War: A Halting Reconstruction Under Fascism[1]

Gabriel Tortella and José L. García-Ruiz

Introduction

How serious was the destruction suffered during the Spanish civil war? There is some dispute among scholars about the extent of the devastation. Many researchers have found that 'economic' destruction, that is, the destruction of physical capital equipment, was less extensive than the Franco regime reported, whereas the main damage may have been inflicted upon human capital and other less tangible assets, such as organization and the transportation system (Núñez, 2001; Ros Hombravella, 1973; Catalán, 1995, pp. 41–59). The Franco regime was interested in exaggerating the physical damage caused by the war in order to justify the very low living standards prevailing during the post-war years. This was a period which – unfortunately for the average Spaniard – coincided with the Second World War and with the most extreme autarkic (self-sufficient) policies of the Franco regime. As a result of the war in Europe and Spain's alliance or proximity to the Axis powers, the country was deprived of the bulk of capital imports that were needed for reconstruction.

Regarding casualties, the most reliable estimates show that those of the Spanish civil war were rather on the low side compared to those of the main combatants in the Second World War: deaths were around 1.5 per cent of the population, with a substantial fraction of them due to repression after the war.[2] As to agriculture, the leading specialist Barciela has stated that 'the war, contrary to what was stated by the Francoist propaganda, had no catastrophic effects on agriculture'. According to this author, the fall in wheat output during the war and thereafter was due to grievous mistakes in economic policy, not to physical destruction (Barciela, 1987, p. 258). At factories and mines as well, the destruction was not very serious, except in cases when factories were located inside towns and cities. It was the centres of cities and the military installations that were bombarded rather than the outskirts, where most of the industries were located. An indication of the relatively small damage suffered by factories is the surprising fact that, according to Tafunell, business profits during the war never fell below 50 per cent of their 1930 level.[3]

Estimates by Catalán suggest that destruction of dwellings in Spain was relatively small when compared with France, Italy and Greece during the Second World War. In 1940, the official in charge of rehabilitation of destroyed areas said that the total value of the claims that were being considered by his department was about 1 per cent of all urban wealth in Spain – 'a not very alarming quantity', he added. The amounts devoted to reconstruction of destroyed dwellings was a paltry 35 million pesetas at a time when the book value of the Bank of Spain's buildings was 98.4 million pesetas. These rather modest figures contrast with those cited by Van der Wee for other European countries after the Second World War: 40 per cent of buildings in Germany, 30 per cent in the United Kingdom and 20 per cent in France.[4]

The more serious losses due to the Spanish civil war affected the transportation network. It is estimated that 30 per cent of locomotives were destroyed; in rolling stock, the loss was 60 per cent of passenger carriages and 40 per cent of freight wagons. About 22 per cent of shipping capacity was lost. Roads were badly damaged, and the car and truck stocks were severely damaged. The Spanish network, however, was not more severely damaged that those of the combatants in the Second World War (Catalán, 1995, pp. 44–5).[5]

Even if the physical destruction of productive assets was less than the Franco regime repeatedly stated, the disruption of production due to the war was undeniable. This was due to the loss of less tangible assets such as human capital, organization, transportation and distribution networks. Because of these and other factors, post-war reconstruction in Spain turned out to be an amazingly slow process. It is well known and well documented that Spain took almost 15 years (not including the three civil war years) to recover the pre-war levels of *per capita* output.[6] Table 7.1 shows a comparison of the lengths of the reconstruction processes in different European nations after the Second World War. In fact, the real figures for Spain should be higher, since the civil war ended in 1939, not in 1945. Consequently, Spain's recovery of GNP levels really took 15 years and the recovery of industrial output levels took 12 years.

An internal report by the Bank of Spain, written in February 1946, stated repeatedly that 'we have not yet reached the level of 1935 either in agrarian or in industrial production'. Agrarian production was 'scarcely 80 per cent that of 1935'. Scarcity of coal and electricity had caused low levels of output

Table 7.1   Duration of the post-war reconstruction period in several European countries

	GNP per capita			Industrial output per capita		
	Maximum before 1939	Year maximum level recovered after 1945	Years elapsed since 1945	Maximum before 1939	Year maximum level recovered after 1945	Years elapsed since 1945
Germany	1938	1948	3	1938	1949	4
Austria	1929	1950	5	1937	1949	4
Belgium	1929	1949	4	1929	1955	10
Denmark	1938	1946	1	1938	1947	2
Spain*	1934	1954	9	1930	1952	7
Finland	1937	1948	3	1938	1947	2
France	1929	1948	3	1929	1951	6
Greece	1937	1949	4	1938	1950	5
Italy	1930	1950	5	1938	1949	4
Norway	1938	1946	1	1938	1947	2
Holland	1929	1948	3	1929	1949	4
Portugal	1938	1945	0			
UK	1938	1945	0	1937	1947	2
Sweden	1938	1945	0	1938	1945	0

*Series from Alcaide, 1976.
Source: Catalán, 1995, p. 27.

in iron and steel, less than half the figure of 1929. Something similar could be said about cement: 'In spite of the reconstruction needs of the cities, of enlarging and improving the transport system and of all the military works, the cement industry has not been able to surpass the output figures of 15 years ago.' This low level of cement output is an indicator of the low pace of reconstruction. Meanwhile, as 'nominal wages have not increased at the same pace as prices ... the real wage of a workman in 1946 stands at between 55 and 60 per cent of that of the year 1936. His possibilities of consumption and his standard of living have been reduced to little more than half of what it was then.'[7]

Compared to most European combatants in the Second World War such as France, Italy or even Germany – the country where destruction and disruption were even more pervasive – Spanish reconstruction after the civil war proceeded at a snail's pace. In 1949, even for a European visitor from war-ravaged France, Madrid seemed a bleak city to visit. High officials of Crédit Lyonnais and Paribas on business trips were appalled by the situation they witnessed: Madrid had daily power and water cuts, and food was so scarce that hunger affected productivity, which they estimated was reduced to 50–60 per cent of normal. A visit to the countryside did not reveal a better situation. Their assessment of the Instituto Nacional de Industria (INI) was not unlike what is said here below.[8] Contemporary analysts and present-day students are in total agreement about the remarkable retardation of Spain's recovery. The question remains: why was there such a slow pace of recovery? To what extent were the banks responsible for this halting performance?

The Economic Policy of Early Francoism

During the post-civil war years, the economic policies in Franco's Spain were very close to those of its German and Italian allies (Tortella and Houpt, 2000, pp. 136–43). It has been maintained by some later-day Franco apologists that autarky was really not in the Franco programme, but only imposed by the circumstances of the Second World War. This is misleading: well before the end of the civil war, that is, almost a year before the outbreak of the Second World War, Franco announced that an autarkic Spain could achieve full-scale economic well-being (Preston, 1993, pp. 197–8).[9]

Agriculture was the area where these comprehensive nationalistic policies were first implemented. The body entrusted with the carrying-out of these policies was the Servicio Nacional del Trigo. The Servicio was created by the Francoist Junta during the war, in August 1937. Originally it was destined to exercise its control over the wheat market only (hence its name), but it soon widened its purview to all grains and legumes, thereby extending its scope over the largest share of agricultural output. The basic idea behind the Servicio was that Spain could and should be self-sufficient in food. However, prices were established on the low side and consequently there was a general decline of agricultural output. Those years were remembered in Spain as the 'hungry forties' (*los años del hambre*).[10]

Industrial policies were even more imbued by principles of state intervention, economic isolation and autarky. Self-sufficiency was the aim pursued by two laws issued on 24 October and 24 November 1939, which were accompanied by some other ancillary measures. The Spanish authorities blamed the private sector for industrial stagnation. They decided to create another state agency, the Instituto Nacional de Industria (INI), which was established by a law of 25 September 1941 and was modelled upon the Italian IRI (Istituto per la Ricostruzione Industriale), which had been created in 1933. The INI's effort was gigantic, but one must ask whether it was not also misguided and wasteful. The INI production was an end in itself regardless of cost (comparative, opportunity, or otherwise); contrary to its avowed aims, the INI also colluded with private firms and thereby reduced competition within the industrial sector. All in all, the INI contributed to keep prices high and Spanish industry non-competitive (Donges, 1976; Schwartz and González, 1978; Martín Aceña and Comín, 1991; Ballestero, 1993).

The Bank of Spain was critical of these policies. An early report stated that 'the exaggeration of autarkic tendencies fostered the belief that the economic reconstruction of Spain could be the work of Spaniards alone. This, which was perhaps possible, made reconstruction slower, more difficult, and more expensive.' On the other hand, the same report characterized Spanish public finances as follows: 'The synthesis of the evolution of Spanish public finances after the war can be summarized in a single phrase: excessive public expenditure, not justified by economic necessity or by political necessity.'[11]

When the war ended, the Spanish budget was saddled with a heavy burden of war debt. Both sides in the conflict had had recourse to credit from the Bank of Spain. The Spanish central bank, like many other institutions, was divided during the war. In the first months of the conflict, a numerous group of the Bank's board met in Burgos (the capital of the Franco side) and reorganized themselves as the Francoist Bank of Spain. Madrid retained the central offices and vaults, however, and the main stock of precious metals. Most of this stock was sent to Russia by the Republican authorities in order to prevent it from falling into rebel hands and as a guarantee of the loans they might receive from the Soviet Union, their main ally at the time. In fact, the Russians never returned this stock, as they considered that their credits to the Spanish Republic, mostly weapons and military personnel, exceeded the value of the precious metals deposited with them.[12] On top of this, in order to pay for the remaining expenditure of the war, the Republicans requisitioned valuables and jewellery from the other banks and from civilians. Finally, they had recourse to funds not only from the Bank of Spain but also from government agencies and local bodies such as provincial and municipal governments (Tortella and García Ruiz, 1999, pp. 87–9, 183–7; Sánchez Asiaín, 1992, pp. 77–88, 170–5. See also Banco de España, 1974, pp. 265–334).

The Franco side was therefore deprived of the cash stocks of the Bank of Spain. It only had the small amount that was deposited in the bank's branches in the cities which were in its territory. It had access to the valuables and jewels deposited in commercial banks and it also imposed campaigns of 'donations' from private citizens. All this was insufficient to finance the war effort. The Franco government had ample recourse to foreign credit, not only from Germany and Italy but also from allied countries. An unusual source of credit for the Franco government was the oil company Texaco which, in an unprecedented decision in that business sector, sold Franco unlimited supplies of oil on credit (Tortella, et al., 1986). Furthermore, the nationalist government had full access to the credit of the Bank of Spain: 'During the three years of 1936 to 1939 war expenditures [on the Franco side] were financed with loans from the Bank of Spain, to the tune of ten thousand and one hundred million [10 100 million, sic] pesetas.'[13] This figure of state indebtedness with the Bank of Spain was enormous for a country whose total internal debt in 1935 had been 19.8 million pesetas, even though inflation made the burden a little less heavy. Although the Francoist state repudiated the debts of the Republic, the weight of obligation was very heavy and encumbered the structure of the state budget for many years.

Table 7.2 shows some selected items of the expenditure side of the Spanish budget. The table shows some surprising facts. The most startling one is that, in spite of all the reconstruction rhetoric of the new government, the development heading in the state budget actually shrank in relative terms in

Table 7.2   Selected items of expenditure and ratios in the Spanish budget, 1931–60 (percentages)

	1931–35 average	1941	1945	1950	1955	1960
1. Defence	15.8	35.2	43.0	32.3	28.1	18.8
2. Education	6.1	4.2	4.7	5.7	6.2	6.2
3. Public Health	0.6	0.6	0.9	1.3	1.0	0.8
4. Social Security	7.9	4.5	5.7	8.1	5.0	5.2
5. Housing	0.9	0.7	1.2	1.6	3.4	12.9
6. Development	21.7	14.3	13.3	16.5	21.5	25.4
7. Other	47.0	40.5	31.2	34.5	34.8	30.7
8. GFCF/Expenditure (%)	7.7	7.2	7.1	7.8	12.6	10.1
9. Expenditure/national income (%)	13.2	17.3	17.9	10.3	10.2	14.1
10. Deficit/national income (%)	0.9	4.7	8.1	0.9	− 0.3	0.7

Lines 1–7, relative to total budget expenditure; Line 8 also relative to total expenditure.
Source: Fiscal data have been calculated from Comín in Carreras (1989a). National Income from Alcaide (1976).

comparison with pre-war times from 22 per cent to 14 per cent, a really substantive drop. The shrinkage was not only relative: development expenditure also fell in absolute terms, if we allow for inflation, until 1944. The 'housing' heading also deserves some comment. After the wartime destruction, one would expect an increase in housing expenditure but the reality was disappointing. The relative share of housing within total budget expenditure in the immediate post-war years hovered at around the same level as in the pre-war years. One must take into account that the pre-war years were depression years, so the levels of house building must have been low. Examining the year-by-year figures of the 1930s and 1940s (not shown in Table 7.2 for reasons of space) this becomes obvious. In fact, the pre-war average conceals wide divergences. In the 1931–33 period, housing expenditure was only 0.5 per cent of total expenditure, while in 1934–35 it was 1.4 per cent. Hence the paucity of the housing effort of the post-war Franco governments becomes more glaring when compared with the immediate pre-war years. In absolute deflated terms, the 1935 housing investment figure (65 million in pesetas of that year) was only surpassed in 1944.

If we switch to the analysis in economic terms of budget expenditure, line 8 of Table 7.2 shows investment on Gross Fixed Capital Formation (GFCF). Not surprisingly, in view of what has been said in previous paragraphs, the share of GFCF fell in the post-war years, with the exceptions of 1943 and 1944. The reason for the exception is far from encouraging, however. As Carreras has shown, this was an accounting 'legerdemain': railway companies were nationalized in 1942, and in 1943 and 1944 the Ministry of Public Works paid the bulk of the compensation to their former shareholders; this was no real increase in fixed capital formation, just a change of hands (Carreras, 1989b, p. 23).[14]

What kind of effort did the government undertake then? It was certainly not towards improving education, where the fall was even more unmistakable than in development and housing. Education expenditure (line 2), which had been on the increase in absolute and relative terms in pre-war years, fell in those same terms in the post-war period. Within total expenditure, education stood at 6.1 per cent on average before the war; the proportion was well below that after the war, fluctuating around 4.2 per cent in 1941–45. In real deflated terms, expenditure in education, measured in 1935 constant pesetas, was below the 1931–35 average every year in this period.

This simple review goes a long way towards explaining the tardiness of recovery in post-war Spain: in plain words, the government made no serious effort at reconstruction. On the contrary, it reduced investment in rebuilding infrastructure and also in capital formation, both physical and human. As a consequence, the stock of human capital slumped precipitously during the 1940s, while population went back from the cities to the farms, thus slowing down the recovery effort.[15]

The declines in development, housing, and education spending were compensated with large increases in military spending. Here the jump in relative and absolute terms was substantial. The share of defence within the budget more than doubled, although the trend fluctuated and – naturally enough – declined at the end of the Second World War. On average, if the pre-war share (for 1931–35) was 15.8 per cent, the post-war share (for 1941–45) was 39.8 per cent. This was a quantum jump. In real terms, on average, the volume of military expenditure almost tripled from pre-war to post-war years.

The policy of deep state involvement in industry and in agriculture, together with the pressing deficit caused by war debt and military expenditure, required heavy outlays. Hence the state needed wide discretionary borrowing and spending powers, alongside a very weak and subordinate central bank. The trend towards limiting the independence of the Bank of Spain had started with the Banking Law of 1931, part of an international tendency generated by the Great Depression and the Second World War. The Banking Law of 1931 had greatly increased the control the government had over the Bank of Spain. This was achieved by the appointment by the Ministry of Finance of three board members, and by increasing the power the ministry had over the bank's policies, especially the setting of interest rates.

Banking legislation after the Spanish civil war followed this same interventionist trend. The attitude of the new Spanish rulers towards banking was contradictory. The Franco coalition was a conglomerate of fascists, monarchists and conservatives whose economic opinions were often conflicting. As to the banks, the falangists' programme demanded nationalization. They were strong in the official union organization (Organización Sindical) and in the Labour Ministry. The other groups took a less extreme view. A cautiously liberal economist, Luis Olariaga, wrote that strong state intervention in the Spanish banking sector was not justified, because Spanish banks had been able to sail through the Great Depression virtually unscathed. Even totalitarian governments such as those of Germany or Italy – although they put the superior reins of monetary and credit policy in the hands of the state – did not rule over the day-to-day operations of their central or commercial banks (Olariaga Pujana, 1989, pp. 222, 226).[16] In the end what predominated was conservative interventionism. Banks were not nationalized, but they were subjected to state control. In fact this control turned out to be erratic and arbitrary. It was stronger in the immediate post-war years and became more lenient, especially as regards the big banks, thereafter.

The main legislation affecting banks in this period can be summarized as follows. During the civil war, the Franco government had decreed the so-called *statu quo bancario* or *numerus clausus*, whereby no new banks or even new bank branches were allowed. This was confirmed by a peacetime decree (7 May 1940) which prohibited even moving branches to new locations. Later, a limit was put to the distribution of dividends (in the decree of 31 December 1941). The purpose of this measure was twofold: first, to make bank equity less attractive to investors, thereby making public debt bonds a competitive alternative; and second, to encourage banks to invest more and at the same time to avoid public awareness of their high profits. In the end all these high-handed measures were circumvented. *Numerus clausus* worked to the advantage of the big banks, which obtained permits to absorb smaller banks and open new branches with relative ease. They also made their shares more attractive by offering frequent splits.[17] Later, two important laws were issued, one on 13 March 1942 specifically regulating the Bank of Spain, and then the general Banking Law of 31 December 1946.

At the end of the civil war the situation of the Bank of Spain was very confusing. Its balance sheet included debts and credits incurred in both the Franco and the Republican camps. Rates of inflation had differed widely in both zones. The unification of the different currencies in circulation posed serious problems. In the end the solution, according to a plan drawn up by the Minister of Finance (and former councillor of the Bank of Spain) José Larraz, was to declare null and void all Republican banknotes issued after the beginning of the war, and to recognize Republican bank deposits (that is, deposits in banks and bank branches that were in the Republican zone at the end of the war). The deposits were subject to depreciation coefficients graduated by date; depreciation was higher the older the deposit. This posed accounting problems for all banks, but especially for the Bank of Spain, which had large credits against the Republican state. These debts were repudiated by the Franco government (see above, p. 109), but this could not be done by a simple cancellation. The main objective of the law of 1942 was to lay down guidelines for drawing up the bank's balance sheet. This had become pressing because up to then the bank's balance sheet, without the state's approval, was not official. This meant that no report to shareholders was possible. As a consequnce, dividends could not be distributed. This became a pressing problem: shareholders complained and some of them claimed to be in 'a really distressing situation'.[18]

The 1942 law was draconian. The bank's assets were considerably reduced as a consequence of the application of the principles enumerated above. Republican banknotes and loans made to the Republic were nullified and Republican deposits were considerably reduced. The bank's assets, at 51.2 per cent of their previous levels, greatly diminished.[19] A large part of the bank's profits was appropriated by the state and applied to reducing the remaining state's debt towards the bank, which was still enormous. Furthermore, the control of the state over the bank was firmly tightened. The governor was to be appointed by the state without any participation by the bank, and he was to be flanked by two 'technical adjuncts' who in fact displaced the traditional vice-governors. These still remained, but in a limited capacity. The bank, therefore, was to be ruled by the government. As the governor said in announcing the law: 'No matter how great the sacrifices imposed on the bank due to the present circumstances, the bank's opinion is to express its total agreement with the government's viewpoint.' This was far from true but nobody dared contradict him. Four months earlier, a joint committee of the bank had written a report saying that 'the immediate cause of the bad state of the balance sheet were the legislative measures the National Government had been forced to take since the beginning of the civil war and to the end of 1939 in matters of banknotes, [and] freezing and unfreezing of bank and non-bank credits and debits'. They were complaining that the Republican state's debts with the bank had been wiped out, while the deposits made with the bank in the Republican zone, although submitted to reduction, were still active. The report was suppressed.[20] The application of the 1942 law implied a takeover of the bank by the state, and was resisted by the board members who represented the shareholders. There was a bitter debate, but the governor made clear that 'after the Law of March 13, the government [of the bank] must be exercised by the Governor, assisted by the two Adjuncts ... it is the Governor, which is tantamount to saying the government, who controls the direction of the Bank and of credit policy'. The other members protested, but there was nothing else they could do.[21]

The purpose of this legal takeover of the bank by the government was to increase the loans by the bank to the government. The resistance of the board members was motivated by a document of instructions issued by the governor, which gave rules on the bank's credit policy and stated that these were convenient 'to the general interest in the present circumstances'. Its first rule stated that 'the applications for credit with State or Treasury bonds as collateral will be granted without any limitation'. By contrast, credits with private bonds as collateral and personal credits were suspended. This explicit policy only reinforced what the bank had been doing since the beginning of the war, that is lending almost exclusively to the state.

Table 7.3 shows the radical change in the operations of the Bank of Spain after the civil war. It can be readily appreciated that the increase in the proportion of operations devoted to public sector after the civil war was enormous; it was now 3.5 times more than before. The increase did not necessitate the 1942 law, but this measure no doubt reinforced the power of the state and served to quell the protests of the representatives of the shareholders on the Bank's board, who made themselves heard periodically, although to little avail.

State control over the banking sector was enshrined in the Banking Law of 31 December 1946.[22] There were a series of features in this law which subordinated monetary policy to nationalist agrarian and industrial policies. Spain was one of the few European countries which had never been subjected to the discipline of the gold standard, and this was confirmed in 1946, when the link between fiduciary circulation and the metallic reserves in the Bank of Spain was definitively broken. The bank's monopoly of note issuing was renewed and the control of the state over the bank reinforced through the direct nomination by the cabinet of the bank's governor, deputy governor and five members of the bank's council. The 'technical adjuncts' disappeared, but the strongest of them, Luis Sáez de Ibarra, was made vice-governor. The Ministry of Finance's powers over the bank's policies were also extended, including the use of a veto. This extension was already part of the 1942 law. The 1946 Banking Law (Chapter II) also confirmed the ultimate control of the state over commercial banks as relating to the establishment of new firms, expansion, and relocation, and also to the setting of ceilings to deposit interest rates.[23] One of the openly stated aims of

Table 7.3   Distribution of the Bank of Spain's assets, 1931–60 (percentages)

	Foreign Sector	Private Sector	Public Sector
Average 1931–35	39.2	39.8	21.0
1941	0.1	24.5	75.4
1948	0.6	26.3	73.1
1950	− 1.1	38.1	63.0
1955	− 2.7	45.3	57.3
1960	28.4	29.9	41.7

Source: 1941, calculated from Banco de España, Mms 1931–35 and 1948–60; Martín
     Aceña in Carreras (1989a).

this policy was to assure that rates remained low, so as to encourage private investment and to permit the state to borrow at low prices.

The falangists were disappointed with the 1946 Banking Law because neither the Bank of Spain nor the specialized official banks were nationalized and because in dealing with commercial banks the law was a renewed version of the 1921 Banking Law. Furthermore, the Sindicato Nacional del Crédito (created in 1941 as part of the Organización Sindical) was abolished and replaced by the Consejo Superior Bancario (a semi-private organisation originating in the 1921 Law in which the big banks were conspicuously represented).[24] Moreover, in many respects commercial banks remained less regulated in Spain than they were in some neighboring democratic countries. During the debate on the law the banks were backed by the Ministry of Finance and the mostly liberal members of the *Cortes*.[25] An exception to such loose legal framework was the Agricultural Finance Law of 17 July 1946 that made it compulsory for commercial banks to invest up to 5 per cent of their deposits in agricultural loans at a fixed low-interest rate and without commissions. Afterwards, the falangists managed to include within this limit the finance of fishing (Caja Central del Crédito Marítimo y Pesquero, 1949) and housing (Instituto de Crédito a la Reconstrucción Nacional, 1952). The banks and the Ministry of Finance were opposed to this kind of intervention, which they considered as inflationist and high-handed; the resources devoted by the banks to these ends were always far below the ceiling.[26]

Finally, the 1946 Banking Law confirmed that exchange rate policies were taken out of the hands of the Bank of Spain and placed with a Foreign Currency Institute (Instituto Español de Moneda Extranjera, IEME), which in fact was a dependency of the Ministry of Industry and Commerce. This permitted the government to exercise strict control over exchange rates, which became a key policy instrument (Martínez Ruiz). Combined with quantitative controls over foreign trade (tariff rates became redundant), exchange rate controls and multiple exchange rate systems almost totally sealed the Spanish economy from international markets at the government's will. Insulation from foreign market 'contamination' was of course essential for the autarkic policies of the early years of Franco's regime.

The Banks' Response

Banks adapted as well as they could to the hostile post-war atmosphere. Spanish banks had followed a rather individual path relative to other banking systems in Western Europe in the 1930s. They had been able to weather the depression without any serious collective upheaval (Tortella, 1999, pp. 174–6). Their trauma, obviously, had been the civil war. The war affected the banks' activities and profits: many of them suffered serious losses, and those who did not saw their profits seriously diminished (Sánchez Asiaín, 1992, pp. 178–80). At the end of the war they found themselves constrained by the restrictive legislation (making Spain a model of a 'repressed banking system') and by the painful process of 'monetary unfreezing' (*desbloqueo*). Nevertheless they had two great advantages: inflation made the burden of debt much more bearable, and the interventionist straitjacket protected them from competition, both domestic and foreign. Related to the repression of competition was the restrictive legislation affecting stock exchanges, which turned the banking sector into almost the monopolist of credit for industrial firms.

In these circumstances it was wise for banks to invest in industry and public debt, and this is what they did during this period. Investing in public debt had an added advantage, because it could be readily used as collateral for loans from the Bank of Spain.[27] In turn the Bank of Spain was expressly authorized by the 1946 Banking Law to acquire public debt bonds, something it had been forbidden to do since the beginning of the twentieth century. We have also seen that the instructions from the governor were to lend freely on public debt bonds as collateral. In any case, banks had not been constrained to purchase public debt by the 1946 Banking Law, but they could be induced to do so with a carrot-and-stick policy. The carrot was the possibility of obtaining automatic loans from the central bank by pledging public debt bonds. There were several sticks: in the first place, by controlling interest rates the Ministry of Finance could make public debt bonds more attractive than ordinary loans. In the second place, there were outright public pressures. Sáez de Ibarra, who was at the time the president of the Consejo Superior Bancario and vice-governor of the Bank of Spain, advised in a circular letter to bankers (6 November 1947) that they should be 'faithful to the Spanish banking tradition of having a strong mass of public state and Treasury bonds as a guarantee of their deposits and passive balances'. He recommended a proportion of nothing less than between 45 and 50 per cent of the 'creditor' balances (that is, deposits). And then came the warning: 'The Bank of Spain will take into very special consideration, in its policy of support to Spanish banks which may need it in the future, the circumstance of having or not having followed the suggestions contained in this letter in a faithful way.' This was not Sáez de Ibarra's last injunction. Three years later he announced that the Bank of Spain was going to revise its classification of banks for rediscount according to the criteria announced previously. And he added: 'If a sufficient number of public debt bonds [to fulfil the quotas] cannot be found in the market, the banks concerned can address themselves directly to the Bank of Spain.'[28] As a result the holdings of public debt by the banking sector evolved as is shown in Table 7.4.

Most large Spanish banks invested in industrial securities, and had been doing so since a modern commercial banking sector had begun to take shape in Spain at the beginning of the twentieth century. Scholars have debated whether this practice made Spanish banks comparable to German 'universal' banks (Martín Aceña and Pons, 1994). It is true that, after reaching a maximum in the pre-war period, the share of industrial equity within total assets of commercial banks declined from 19.5 in 1930 to 9 in 1950 and 5 in 1970.[29] This does not mean that the banks' stake in industry diminished, just that their total assets increased faster than their industrial holdings. In fact, Spanish banks invested heavily in basic industries in the post-war period. By the 1950s, the five or six big banks certainly included industrial groups in their portfolios, a fact which some economists denounced as proof of monopolistic factors (Sierra, 1951, 1953; Velarde Fuertes, 1953, 1955; Muñoz Linares, 1955; Tamames, 1961, 1967, 1977; Muñoz, 1969). While there is little doubt that the big banks and their industrial groups constituted a tight oligopoly – which among other things reached internal agreements to avoid competition in interest rates and in other fields – it is also true that these agreements often failed to achieve their purposes.[30]

Table 7.4 Public debt in circulation held by Spanish banks, 1920–59

Date	Public debt portfolio/Total public debt (%)	Loans from Bank of Spain pledging public debt/Total public debt (%)	Date	Public debt portfolio/Total public debt (%)	Loans from Bank of Spain pledging public debt/Total public debt (%)
1920	7.7 (a)	4.5	1945		3.7
1925	7.7 (a)	9.1	1950	31.1	17.3
1930	11.9	6.5	1955	37.9	14.4
1934	14.4	5.6	1959	43.8	23.3 (b)
1941	26.0	4.9			

(a) 1922 (b) 1958

Source: Ministerio de Hacienda. Dirección General de Banca, Bolsa e Inversiones (1961), pp. 5–8.

The contribution of the big banks to reconstruction – and in particular to growth through the building up of an industrial infrastructure – has been underlined by several writers. There is little doubt that these mixed banks played a Cameronian or Gerschenkronian role in the decades bestriding the civil war.[31] As we have pointed out, if in the post-war years they operated in a repressed atmosphere, they also enjoyed considerable protection. However, they came out of the war considerably diminished; they could not have made the same impact on the economy which they would have achieved with a larger relative size. Table 7.5 offers Goldsmith's Financial Interrelations Ratio (FIR) or ratio of bank assets to national income for Spain in the middle decades of the twentieth century. In the Goldsmith ratio, a FIR of 1 marks the threshold to financial maturity of a banking system. The table shows that Spain was reaching this threshold just in the pre-war years, and did not attain it again until some thirty years later.

Table 7.6 offers another glimpse of the contribution of Spanish banks during these years. It shows the share of total business securities issued that were acquired by commercial banks. This proportion was steadily declining,

Table 7.5   Financial interrelations ratio (bank assets : national income) in Spain, 1915–68

Year	FIR	Year	FIR	Year	FIR
1915	0.38	1931	0.98	1953	0.62
1916	0.36	1932	0.96	1954	0.66
1917	0.33	1933	1.01	1955	0.76
1918	0.40	1934	0.97	1956	0.81
1919	0.42			1957	0.78
1920	0.55	1942	0.43	1958	0.77
1921	0.75	1943	0.44	1959	0.79
1922	0.77	1944	0.44	1960	0.88
1923	0.78	1945	0.50	1961	0.90
1924	0.74	1946	0.45	1962	0.91
1925	0.70	1947	0.49	1963	0.90
1926	0.76	1948	0.50	1964	0.94
1927	0.81	1949	0.53	1965	0.98
1928	0.88	1950	0.62	1966	0.93
1929	0.97	1951	0.52	1967	0.98
1930	1.02	1952	0.58	1968	1.17

Source: Bank assets from Carreras (1989b), columns 1164 and 1641 (Series by Martín Aceña and Alcaide).

Table 7.6   Private portfolio investments by commercial banks in Spain,
1943–59 (million current pesetas)

Year	(1) Yearly increase of securities purchases by commercial banks	(2) Yearly issues of securities by firms	(3) Ratio [1/2]%
1943	274	1 244	22.0
1944	255	1 171	21.8
1945	491	1 756	28.0
1946	629	5 022	12.5
1947	591	2 992	19.8
1948	683	4 316	15.8
1949	412	3 481	11.8
1950	333	3 608	9.20
1951	787	7 383	10.7
1952	1 175	4 077	28.8
1953	934	6 985	13.4
1954	1 368	9 920	13.8
1955	1 156	11 543	10.0
1956	1 520	13 989	10.9
1957	2 602	19 712	13.2
1958	2 052	19 423	10.6
1959	2 187	21 993	9.90

Source: Ministerio de Hacienda, Dirección General de Banca, Bolsa e Inversiones
(1961), p. 17.

from highs near 25 per cent in the early 1940s to figures around 10 per cent 15 years later. This means, of course, that the contribution of banks to private capital formation was relatively higher during the early post-war years.[32]

Conclusions

One of the most original, if unfortunate, features of Spanish twentieth century economic history is the long gap in its national income series from the mid-1930s to the mid-1950s. While a part of this slump must be attributed to the civil war, this is only part of the explanation, since this dismal performance contrasts with those of its neighbours, including France, Italy and the United Kingdom, which recovered from the much more serious damage suffered during the Second World War at a much faster pace.

From the evidence we have reviewed here, politics and misguided economic policies were the main culprits of the retardation during the 1940s. Spain had the wrong set of allies, while state intervention and outsize military expenditure became unsurmountable obstacles to recovery, let alone economic growth.

In this situation the banking sector could not take a leading role. The state pressured and repressed the banks in order to obtain funds from them to spend on its priorities, especially military build-up and heavy industry. The banks emerged from the war in a weakened state, having shrunk in size not only in absolute terms but even in relation to the very low levels of national income. In this condition the sector could not be expected to perform miracles. The banks accommodated themselves to the situation, adapted to the guidelines of the all-powerful state, and feebly tried to steer the course of policy towards less strict interventionism and also towards less economic isolationism. Many years later, with the reform and the Stabilisation Plan of 1959, a decisive step was made in this direction. But it had needed fully twenty years since the end of the civil war to reach that point.

Abbreviations

ABE: *Archivo del Banco de España*, Bank of Spain Archive, Madrid
ACH: *Archivo Central de Hacienda*, Ministry of Finance Central Archive, Madrid
ACL: *Archive Crédit Lyonnais*, Paris
AP: *Archive Paribas*, Paris
BBdE: *Biblioteca del Banco de España*, Bank of Spain Library, Madrid
BdE: *Banco de España*, Bank of Spain, Madrid
CA: *Actas del Consejo de Administración*, Board Meeting Reports
Leg.: *Legajo*, bundle, packet, or dossier.
Mm: *Memorias de las Juntas de Accionistas*, Reports to Shareholder Meetings

References

Alcaide, J. (1976), 'Una revisión urgente de la serie de renta nacional española en el siglo XX', in Ministerio de Hacienda *Datos básicos para la historia financiera de España (1850–1975)*, Madrid: Instituto de Estudios Fiscales.

Álvarez Lázaro, P. (ed.) (2001), *Cien Años de Educación en España. En Torno a la Creación del Ministerio de Instrucción Pública y Bellas Artes*, [Madrid]: Ministerio de Educación, Cultura y Deporte.

Alvarez Llano, R. and Andreu, J. M. (1982), *Una historia de la banca privada en España. Revista Situación*, 3.

Ballestero, A. (1993), *Juan Antonio Suanzes, 1891–1977. La política industrial de la postguerra*, León: LID.

[Banco de España] (1974), *Los Billetes del Banco de España, 1782–1974*, Madrid: Banco de España.

Barciela, C. (1981), *La Financiación del Servicio Nacional del Trigo, 1937–1971*, Madrid: Servicio de Estudios del Banco de España.

Barciela, C. (1987), 'Crecimiento y cambio en la agricultura española desde la Guerra Civil' in Nadal, J., Carreras, A. and Sudriá, C. (eds), *La Economía Española en el siglo XX. Una perspectiva histórica*, Barcelona: Ariel, pp. 258–79.

Carreras, A. (1985), 'Gasto nacional bruto y formación de capital en España, 1849–1958: primer ensayo de estimación' in Martín Aceña, P. and Prados de la Escosura, L. (eds), *La Nueva Historia Económica en España*, Madrid: Tecnos, pp. 17–51.

Carreras, A. (ed.) (1989a): *Estadísticas Históricas de España, siglos XIX–XX*, Madrid: Fundación Banco Exterior.

Carreras, A. (1989b), 'Depresión económica y cambio estructural durante el decenio bélico (1936–1945)' in García Delgado, J. L. (ed.), *El Primer Franquismo. España durante la Segunda Guerra Mundial*, Madrid: Siglo XXI.

Catalán, J. (1995), *La Economía Española y la Segunda Guerra Mundial*, Barcelona: Ariel.

Cipolla, C. M. (ed.) (1976), *The Fontana Economic History of Europe. Contemporary Economies*, Glasgow: Collins.

Comín, F., Martín Aceña, P., Muñoz Rubio, M., and Vidal Olivares, J. (1998) *150 Años de Historia de los Ferrocarriles Españoles*, Madrid: Anaya.

Consejo de Economía Nacional (1965): *La Renta Nacional de España, 1940–1964*, Madrid: Consejo de Economía Nacional.

Consejo Superior Bancario, *Anuario Estadístico de la Banca Privada*.

Dirección General de Regiones Devastadas y Reparaciones (1940), *Datos sobre la Reconstrucción de España*, Madrid.

Donges, J. B. (1976), *La Industrialización en España. Políticas, Logros, Perspectivas*, Barcelona: Oikos Tau.

Jackson, G. (1976), *La República Española y la Guerra Civil, 1931–1939*, Barcelona: Crítica.

Juliá, S. (ed.) (1999), *Víctimas de la Guerra Civil*, Madrid: Temas de Hoy.

Maddison, A. (1976), 'Economic policy and performance in Europe, 1913–1970', in Cipolla, C. M. (ed.), *The Fontana Economic History of Europe. Contemporary Economies*, 2, Glasgow: Collins, pp. 442–508.

Martín Aceña, P. and Comín, F. (1991), *I.N.I.. 50 años de Industrialización de España*, Madrid: Espasa Calpe.

Martín Aceña, P. and Pons, M. A. (1994), 'Spanish banking after the civil war, 1940–1962', *Financial History Review*, 1, pp. 121–38.

Martínez Ruiz, E. (2000), 'El control de cambios en la España franquista: el Instituto Español de Moneda Extranjera, 1939–1973', unpublished doctoral thesis, Universidad de Alcalá, Madrid.

Ministerio de Hacienda, Dirección General de Banca, Bolsa e Inversiones (1961), *Memorándum del Ministerio de Hacienda sobre el Sistema Bancario y Crediticio*, Madrid: Ministerio de Hacienda.

Mitchell, B. R. (1976a), *European Historical Statistics, 1750–1970*, New York: Columbia University Press.

Mitchell, B. R. (1976b), 'Statistical appendix, 1920–1970,' in Cipolla, C. M. (ed.), pp. 625–755.

Muñoz, J. (1969), *El Poder de la Banca en España*, Algorta, Vizcaya: Zero.

Muñoz Linares, C. (1955), 'El pliopolio en algunos sectores del sistema económico español', *Revista de Economía Política*, 6, 1, pp. 3–66.

Muñoz Rubio, M. (2001), 'La contribución del ferrocarril al desarrollo económico entre 1950–2000: una primera estimación', typescript.

Núñez, C. E. (2001), 'El Ministerio de Educación y la economía española cien años después', in Álvarez Lázaro, P. (ed.) *Cien Años de Educación en España*, [Madrid]: Ministerio de Educación, Cultura y Deporte, pp. 27–52.

Olariaga Pujana, L. (1946), *La Ordenación Bancaria en España*, Madrid: Sucesores de Rivadeneyra.

Olariaga Pujana, L. (1989), *Escritos Varios. Advertencias, Incitaciones y Reformas*, Madrid: Fundación FIES.

Paris Eguilaz, H. (1939), *El Estado y la Economía. Política Económica Totalitaria*, Madrid: Ediciones F.E.

Paris Eguilaz, H. (1947), *El Problema de la Reforma Bancaria en España: Consideración sobre la Ley de Ordenación Bancaria de 31 de diciembre de 1946*, Madrid: Author.

Pohl, M., Tortella, T. and Van der Wee, H. (eds) (2001), *A Century of Banking Consolidation in Europe. The History and Archives of Mergers and Acquisitions*, Aldershot, UK: Ashgate.

Pons, M. A. (1999), 'Capture or agreement? Why Spanish banking was regulated under the Franco regime, 1939–75', *Financial History Review*, 6, pp. 25–46.

Prados de la Escosura, L. (1995), 'Spain's gross domestic product, 1850–1993: quantitative conjectures', working paper, Universidad Carlos III, Madrid.

Prados de la Escosura, L. and Sanz, J. C. (1996), 'Growth and macro-economic performance in Spain, 1939–93', in Crafts, N. F. R. and Toniolo, G. (eds), *Economic Growth in Europe since 1945*, Cambridge: Cambridge University Press, pp. 355–87.

Preston, P. (1993): *Franco*, London: Fontana Press.

Rein, R. (1993), *The Franco-Perón Alliance. Relations Between Spain and Argentina, 1973–75. Its Causes and Course, 1946–1955*, Pittsburgh & London: Pittsburgh University Press.

Ridruejo, E. (1954a), 'El sistema bancario español', in *Los bancos en la postguerra, vuelta a la normalidad?*, Madrid: Consejo Superior Bancario.

Ridruejo, E. (1954b), 'El sistema bancario español', *Moneda y Crédito*, 51, pp. 35–81.

Ros Hombravella, J. et al. (1973): *Capitalismo español: De la autarquía a la estabilización. I (1939–1950); II (1950–1959)*, Madrid: Edicusa.

Sáez de Ibarra, L. (1954), 'La regulación de la banca española', *Moneda y Crédito*, 51, pp. 15–33.

Sánchez Asiaín, J. Á. (1992), *La Banca Española en la Guerra Civil, 1936–1939*, inaugural lecture, Madrid: Academia de la Historia.

Sardá, J. (1970), 'El Banco de España (1931–1962)', in Banco de España, *El Banco de España. Una Historia Económica*, Madrid: Banco de España, pp. 419–79.

Schwartz, P. and Gonzalez, M. J. (1978), *Una Historia del Instituto Nacional de Industria (1941–1976)*, Madrid: Tecnos.

Sierra, Fermín de la (1951), 'La concentración económica de la banca privada española', *Revista de Estudios Políticos*, 59, pp. 57–94.

Sierra, Fermín de la (1953), *La Concentración Económica en las Industrias Básicas Españolas*, Madrid: Instituto de Estudios Políticos.

Sylla, R., Tilly, R. and Tortella, G. (1999), *The State, the Financial System, and Economic Modernization*, Cambridge, UK: Cambridge University Press.

Tafunell, X. (1998), 'Los beneficios empresariales en España, 1880–1981. Estimación de un índice anual del excedente de la gran empresa', *Revista de Historia Económica*, 16, 3, pp. 707–46.

Tamames, R. (1961), *La Lucha contra los Monopolios*, Madrid: Tecnos.

Tamames, R. (1967), *Los Monopolios en España*, Madrid: ZYX.

Tamames, R. (1977), *La Oligarquía Financiera en España*, Barcelona: Editorial Planeta.

Tortella, G. (1999), 'The role of banks and government in Spanish economic development, 1850–1935', in Sylla, R., Tilly, R. and Tortella, G. (eds), *The State, the Financial System, and Economic Modernization*, Cambridge, UK: Cambridge University Press, pp. 158–81.

Tortella, G. (2000), *The Development of Modern Spain. An Economic History of the Nineteenth and Twentieth Centuries*, Cambridge, MA: Harvard University Press.

Tortella, G. (2001), 'Bank mergers and consolidation in Spanish history', in Pohl, M., Tortella, T. and Van der Wee, H. (eds), *A Century of Banking Consolidation in Europe*, Aldershot, UK: Ashgate, pp. 18–49.

Tortella, G. and García Ruiz, J. L. (1999), *Una Historia de los Bancos Central e Hispano Americano (1900–2000). Un Siglo de Gran Banca en España*, typescript.

Tortella, G. and Houpt, S. (2000), 'Economic policies in twentieth century Spain', in Teichova, A., Matis, H. and Pátek, J. (eds), *Economic Change and the National Question in the Twentieth Century*, Cambridge: Cambridge University Press.

Tortella, G. and Palafox, J. (1984), 'Banking and industry in Spain, 1918–1936', *Journal of European Economic History*, 13, 2, pp. 81–111.

Tortella, G., Cabrera, M. and Coll, S. (1986), *Historia de CAMPSA. Los Primeros Veinte Años, 1927–1947*, typescript.

Van der Wee, H. (1986), *Prosperity and Upheaval. The World Economy 1945–1980*, Berkeley & Los Angeles: University of California Press.

Velarde Fuertes, J. (1953), 'Sobre la decadencia económica de España', *De Economía*, 25–6, pp. 495–549.

Velarde Fuertes, J. (1955), 'Consideraciones sobre algunas actividades monopolísticas en el mercado papelero español', *Revista de Economía Política*, 6, 3, pp. 29–125.

Villalonga Villalba, I. (1961), 'La banca española en lo que va de siglo', *Arbor*, pp. 92–111.

Notes

1   We express our thanks to: Teresa Tortella and her aides at the ABE; personnel at the BBdE; Pierre de Longuemar of the AP; Roger Nougaret of the ACL; Agustín Torreblanca of the ACH; Clara Eugenia Núñez for her help in compiling the reference list; Inmaculada López Martínez for her helpful comments; and the Spanish Ministry of Education whose grant SEC97–1407 financed part of our research.

2   On Spanish figures, see Jackson, 1976, p. 14, and Juliá, 1999, p. 410. For other countries, approximate percentages were as follows: USSR: 13 per cent; Yugoslavia: 10 per cent; Greece: 8 per cent; Germany: 5.5 per cent; France: 1.3 per cent; Italy: .6 per cent. Calculated from Maddison, 1976, p. 470, and Mitchell, 1976a and 1976b.

3   The series was as follows: 1930: 100; 1935: 83.2; 1936: 50.7; 1937: 50.9; 1938: 76.4; 1939: 87.9. Tafunell, 1998, p. 731.

4   Dirección General de Regiones Devastadas y Reparaciones, 1940, p. 13; Ros Hombravella, 1973, vol. 1, pp. 167–8, cite an even lower estimate of 0.5 per cent made in 1945; Catalán, 1995, p. 45; BdE, RS 1942, balance sheet, p. 72; Van der Wee, 1986, Ch. 1.

5   On railroad destruction see Comín et al., 1998, II, Ch. 7.

6   See Consejo de Economía Nacional, 1965; Ros Hombravella, 1973; Alcaide, 1976; Carreras, 1985, 1989a, 1989b; Prados de la Escosura, 1995; Prados de la Escosura and Sanz, 1996.

7   BBdE, D-6421, 'Informe sobre la situación económica española, Febrero de 1946', pp. 12–13, 17, 20–1. These statements are borne out by recent statistical work. See Maluquer de Motes in Carreras, 1989a, pp. 512–13. For post-war wages see also Paris Eguilaz, 1947, p. 181.

8   ACL, DEEF, Paquet 73.242–2. AP, Conteneur 63, Dossier 14, folder 'Correspondance'.

9   The falangist economists were writing in the same vein at the same time. See Paris Eguilaz, 1939, p. 330. This rather long book was published in early January; it must have been written in the summer and autumn of 1938.

10 See Barciela, 1981. The isolation of the Franco regime after the war and its chronic commercial deficit aggravated the food situation, which was palliated in 1947–48 by a commercial agreement with Argentina, whose dictator, Juan Perón, sympathized ideologically with Franco. See Rein, 1993.

11 BBdE, D-6421, 'Informe sobre la situación económica española, Febrero de 1946', pp. 14–15.

12 BdE, Mm 1942; Sardá, 1970, pp. 429–37.

13 BBdE, D-6421, 'Informe sobre la situación económica española, Febrero de 1946', p. 4.

14 On railroad nationalization, see Comín et al., 1998, Ch. 8; on the dubious contribution of the nationalized railroads to the national economy in the Franco years, see Muñoz Rubio, 2001.

15 On the fall of human capital stock see Núñez, 2001, esp. Grap. 3; on the ruralization of the population in the post-war years, see Carreras, 1989b, pp. 28–9, and Nicolau in Carreras, 1989a, pp. 78–9.

16   This was published in 1946, but had been written in 1942 as a report to the Ministry of Finance. Olariaga had been appointed to the board of the Bank of Spain in 1940. Another anonymous report entitled *Normas restrictivas de las operaciones de la banca privada* insisted on the same issue. See both reports in ACH, Leg. 18,549.

17   A high economic official and vice-governor of the Bank of Spain admitted in writing that *numerus clausus* was loosely applied; see Sáez de Ibarra, 1954, p. 24. On mergers and absorptions at the time see Tortella, 2001.

18   BdE, CA, 3 and 7 August 1939, 4, 14, and 25 January, 16 December 1941, 21 January 1942.

19   BdE, Mm 1942, p. 66.

20   BdE, CA, 12 February and 24 March 1942.

21   BdE, CA, 12 June 1942.

22   For a summary of the 1946 law, Martin Aceña and Pons, 1994, pp. 123–4. For a longer description, Sardà, 1970, pp. 455–60. On the 1931 law, see Tortella and Palafox, 1984, pp. 101–3. For the general regulation framework of banks in the 1940s, see Pons, 1999.

23   In the previous years, the bankers had defended their separate status in the Spanish financial system against the saving banks and the official public banks. See ACH, Leg. 19,918, 19,939 and 29,579. For this reason, they gladly accepted a clearer definition of their functions and the creation of a strict register for private banks where very likely new foreign banks would be excluded.

24   The Consejo Superior Bancario also assumed the functions of the Comité Central de la Banca Española, a bankers' association created during the IWW.

25   On the opposition of the Ministry of Finance to the Sindicato Nacional del Crédito, see a report in ACH, Leg. 19,928. For the debate of the 1946 Banking Law in the Cortes, see ACH, Leg. 59,252. The disappointment of the falangists is clear in París Eguilaz (1947), whereas the satisfaction of the banks is obvious in Olariaga Pujana (1946) and Ridruejo (1954a). Olariaga was appointed chief economist of the Consejo Superior Bancario and Ridruejo was the CEO of the Banco Español de Crédito.

26   ACH, Legs. 17.527, 18.549, 19.959 and 19.965. In 1946 the falangists pressured for taking the operations of the public welfare institutes away from the commercial banks and awarded to the saving banks; later on, in 1951, they promoted the creation of a 'labour credit' network as a way 'to release the workers from the usury of the banks'. The Ministry of Finance aborted these measures. ACH, Leg. 19.959.

27   This is explained in Tortella (1999), pp. 169–74. There is a considerable literature about this in Spanish.

28   ACH, Legs 19,954 and 19,961.

29   Calculated from Álvarez Llano and Andreu (1982) and CSB, *Anuario estadístico de la banca privada*. See also Ridruejo (1954b).

30   The initiative of these agreements (*arreglos*) came from the big banks trying to impose ceilings upon passive interest rates and floors to loan rates, with a substantial differential between them. There were written agreements in 1941, 1949, 1952 (unofficially backed by the government) and 1960, but they were

observed in the breach. For this reason, since 1964 the whole range of rates was officially published. See ACH, Legs 19,928, 19,954, 19,962 and 29,579.

31 Villalonga (1961); for a brief statement, Tortella (2000), pp. 391–5.

32 Some big banks adapted particularly well to the post-war atmosphere (for example, Banco Central), whereas others prefered to continue its tradition of commercial banking (for example Banco Hispano Americano, the largest in the Spanish banking system, that relied on its associate Banco Urquijo for the industrial operations). See Tortella and García Ruiz (1999), especially Part Three. On Banco Central in the 1920s and 1930s, see also Tortella (1999), pp. 174–6.

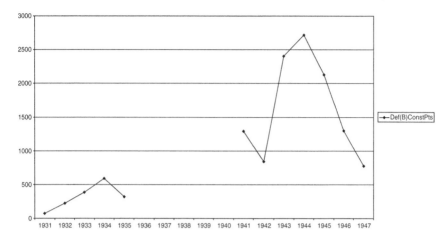

Figure 7.1   Spanish budget deficits, 1931–47 in million constant pesetas (calculated from Carreras, 1989a)

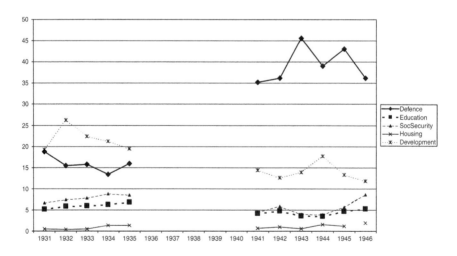

Figure 7.2   Spanish budget expenditure items, 1931–46 (%) (calculated from Carreras, 1989a)

CHAPTER 8

The Transition After the Civil War in Greece

Konstantinos Kostis

The title, at least at first glance, appears to define the subject of this chapter with a great deal of accuracy. In reality, however, it is not possible to be so precise. The changes which were observed in the Greek monetary and financial system during the civil war – even if we ignore what is called its 'first round', which took place during the Occupation – are impossible to understand without a sound knowledge of the changes which took place in the Greek credit sector from 1941–44. Even if we limit our study to the exact period of the civil war (1946–49), it is impossible to ignore the effects of the Marshall Plan upon the evolution of the Greek monetary and credit system. While its implementation coincided with the period of the civil war and the immediate post-civil war years, its goals were more or less independent with regard to Greek political situation. Consequently, the title of this chapter can be nothing more than a starting point. The effects of the civil war on the Greek monetary and banking field must be studied taking into account other factors which as a whole shaped the political and economic framework within which the Greek banking system was reformed.

In 1952, K. Varvaressos, an outstanding Greek economist and Governor of the Bank of Greece for many years, commented as follows on the performance of the Greek banking system prior to the Second World War: 'In Greece, prior to the war, the Banks did not have ... the ability to influence the monetary situation. From a monetary point of view, their role was a neutral one, accepting deposits and lending based on these deposits' (Varvaressos, 1952, p. 67). This was a viewpoint, once very widespread, which ignored the basic parameters of the functioning of the Greek banks. The absence of a capital market and the oligopolistic character of the Greek banking system, for example, had implications both for the way in which credit was handled in the economy and the cost of money.

The Greek banking system, prior to the Second World War, was made up of 35 banks. Two of these, the Agricultural Bank and the National Mortgage Bank, had an exclusive privilege over the exercise of agricultural and mortgage credit respectively. In the field of commercial banks, the National Bank of Greece dominated, and on the eve of the war more than 60 per cent of the credits and deposits of the commercial banks were concentrated in the National Bank. In one way or another, it was also in a position to control some other commercial banks and to maintain absolute control of the National Mortgage Bank. This was an exceptionally high concentration, which developed simultaneously with the cartelization of the market by the Hellenic Banks Association. A counterweight to the exceptional strength of the National Bank was the central bank of the country, the Bank of Greece. Theoretically its great distinction was to carry through a central banking policy on the British pattern. In reality, it exercised a broad range of commercial activities in order to be able to guarantee such profits as would allow its survival, but also to control the money market (Kostis, 1999). Thus, prior to the outbreak of the Second World War, in the Greek banking system there was an oligopolistic situation in which the central bank was a constituent factor as it did not hesitate to participate in the banking cartel. This organization had consequences both for the level of interest rates and for the amount of credit which was channelled into the market, while two banks – the Bank of Greece and the National Bank – played the role of lender of last resort.[1]

The delicate balances upon which this system was formed were overturned during the Occupation (Etmektsoglou-Cohen, 1995; Thomadakis, 1984). Hyper-inflation was the basic channel for transferring market power from the Greek population to the powers of the Axis. This was used to such an extent that, on the eve of liberation, the drachma had been abolished as a means of exchange and its place had been taken by the gold pound (Delivanis, 1946). A basic consequence of these developments was also the complete impoverishment of all the banks. By then they had ceased

Table 8.1   Notes in circulation, gold sovereign price, and cost of living indexes in Greece, 1941–44 (April 1941 = 1.0)

	Notes in circulation index	Gold sovereign price index	Cost of living index
April 1941	1.0	1.0	1.0
December 1942	15.7	127.7	156.5
December 1943	135.5	1319.2	1527.7
October 1944	8 276 320	1 633 540 989	2 305 984 911

Source: Bank of Greece, 1947, p. 25.

to be provided with deposits, the basic resource for their business, while all their assets (with the exception of premises) were reduced to nothing. Under these circumstances, the banks found themselves at the mercy of the central bank. Every economic activity, even the provision of the wages for bank personnel, could be covered only with loans from the Bank of Greece, which in its turn was obviously supported by the printing of money. In other words, the survival of the banks could no longer be anything but dependent upon decisions of a clearly political character.

As the central bank, the Bank of Greece had, for the first time in its short history, an exceptional advantage. All the financing of the economy depended on the exercising of its issue privilege and the development of other banks' activities also depended upon it. Among the managers of all the banks, the fear that the Bank of Greece would follow a competitive policy with regard to the commercial banks was obvious from the first days of liberation.[2] The significant increase in the staff of the central bank during the Occupation and also immediately after liberation led the Bank of Greece *de facto* to look for business in order to respond to its own wage obligations. This was one of the basic reasons why, immediately after the liberation, it avoided the financing of the country's economic activities through the other banks and moved decisively to cover directly the larger part of capital demand.

The successive attempts at monetary stabilization, first in 1944, for a second time in 1945 and once again in 1946 (Chatziiossif, 1992), were bound to fail in so far as the budget deficits of the Greek state allowed no flexibility

Table 8.2 Commercial bank deposits and notes in circulation in Greece, 1945–52 (million drachmas)

Year end	Total deposits	Note circulation	% deposits to note circulation
1938	23 500	9 453	
1945	8 600	104 082	8.3
1946	151 500	537 460	28.2
1947	398 200	973 600	40.9
1948	657 500	1 202 200	54.7
1949	1 153 300	1 858 600	62.1
1950	1 539 700	1 887 100	81.6
1951	2 118 100	2 198 500	96.3
1952	2 196 000	2 475 900	88.7

Source: Candilis, 1968, p. 71.

for covering the deficits other than by printing money. The persistent preference of the public for gold was not irrational under conditions of high inflationary pressures and the flight away from the drachma was a situation which resulted in the weakness in the creation of savings in drachmas (Varvaressos, 1952, p. 69). The final result was a complete inability of the banking institutions to attract significant resources in the form of deposits throughout the period at least until 1953. Bank deposits remained continually at very low levels. Their largest portion came from deposits of public sector organizations, which – and this point should be underlined – remained deposited in a privileged position at the National Bank, as was foreseen in the agreement for the transfer of the privilege of issue to the Bank of Greece in 1928.[3]

The complete failure to establish a stable monetary environment in the first year following liberation, together with the policy of the Bank of Greece during this period, resulted in the creation of the Currency Committee at the beginning of 1946. The committee was clearly a political instrument which had, at least in the beginning, under its total control the monetary circulation of the country. The Currency Committee was not a Greek invention but was created under the framework of the Tsouderos-Bevin agreement for providing Greece with economic and other aid, including a loan of £10 million for monetary stabilization. Members of the committee, which had its headquarters at the Bank of Greece, were the Minister of Coordination (who also chaired the Committee), the Minister of Economics, the Governor of the Bank of Greece and in addition one British and one American representative, who at least theoretically were appointed by the Greek government. The lifespan of the Currency Committee was originally set at 18 months, but it survived for 35 years. In that period it constituted the basic instrument of monetary policy of the Greek state, with the Bank of Greece serving as the tool for carrying out its decisions.

The Currency Committee was created only a few months before the outbreak of the civil war in a climate of great political intensity. It began from the basic idea that without monetary stability, any attempt to reconstruct the Greek economy would be in vain.[4] In addition, it had been established that the policy undertaken by the central bank had had results completely opposite to those which it was to pursue, while the British now demanded a greater voice in the administration of the significant funds which would be offered to the Greek economy, both in the form of loans and in the form of economic and technical aid.[5] In other words, the British attempted through the Currency Committee to impose a form of control on the Greek economy. It was no coincidence that, in exchange, they offered the abolition of the International Financial Committee which had been formed in 1898 after the bankruptcy of the Greek state. The IFC's role appeared anachronistic, if not useless, for the purposes of the Allies. As such, it would soon be shown that the direct control, which the British had achieved (given that the decision of the Currency Committee had to be unanimous), could not change the more general framework of the functioning of an economy. The committee was called upon to develop under conditions of war, even though it seemed that 1946 would be a better year than those which had come before.

The Currency Committee attempted to make some rules for the financing of the economy. In August 1946, it determined the financial framework of the remaining banks, even for their wage expenses. Although this choice at least allowed the commercial banks to find relief and to feel that they had a firmer base under them than they had in the past, the conditions of the financing of the economy had not changed significantly. The central bank offered loans to the commercial banks with an interest rate of 5 per cent; the latter however provided loans in cases of good short-term credit at 36–40 per cent. However, the beginning of the civil war created a completely different climate and, despite the improvement which appeared in 1946, the performance of the Greek economy in 1947 exhibited signs of worsening, with inevitable consequences for the functioning of the banks. Once again, the Bank of Greece increased its own share of the credit in order to meet its obligations, within the framework of the restrictive policy which had been imposed by the Currency Committee. The share of the resources which remained for the use of the commercial banks was thus significantly limited.

From this moment onward, the commercial banks would turn towards the only resource which was available in the Greek economy: the deposits of the public sector organizations. These accounts remained preferentially with the National Bank, which provided an interest rate of 1.5 per cent. Offering an interest rate many times greater than this – in violation of the law of course – the commercial banks began to pull these deposits from the National Bank. The National Bank was in turn forced to increase its interest rates in order not to lose these resources. The result of this competitive climate, which was created for the first time in the Greek market, was the immediate lowering of the credit interest rates to 18–22 per cent, approximately one-half of the previous rate (Galanis, 1960, p. 32).

At about the same time, Britain declared its inability to carry on the economic and military aid to Greece after 31 March 1947. The Americans began preparations to take Britain's place. This change of protector also altered, to a large degree, policies for the financing of the economy.

Experience up to that point demonstrated that the economic aid which the Allies had offered with 'largesse' to Greece had not been deployed or had only been deployed to a small degree for the purposes for which it was intended. The most obvious consequence was the weakness of the Greek economy in recovering to its pre-war levels of activity. The Allies placed a large part of the responsibility upon the Greek governments, which they frequently alleged to be corrupt and more often inefficient. Furthermore, the Americans were less discreet in their interventions in Greek political and economic life than the British. They were not prepared to accept that the dizzying amounts of aid – by Greek standards – should be managed solely by the Greek governments of the time.[6] Therefore the preparation for the distribution of American aid to the Greek economy did not and could not leave the institutional framework for monetary and credit policy unaffected.

With the legislative adjustment of the spring of 1948, the Currency Committee's sphere of authority was significantly enlarged (Fatouros, 1984, p. 436). The Currency Committee's now had the authority to determine the amount of credit to be available in the Greek economy, its distribution among productive sectors, and the terms under which each sector would be included. Furthermore, the authority to proceed with any kind of monitoring, either general or particular, was assigned to this committee. Using these new spheres of jurisdiction, the committee moved on to a) the differentiation of the credit interest rates, b) the determination of the highest limits of the credit per sector, c) the determination of the preconditions and the terms of financing for every banking transaction, and d) the regulation of the size of the minimum reserves of the commercial banks in the Bank of Greece.[7] Imitating the US exemple, Greece passed through a phase of quality and quantity control of its banking system.

Apart from the broadening of its jurisdiction, however, the Currency Committee also had to face ongoing problems, primarily those of the deposits of the public sector organizations. Recent developments had been uncomfortable, even for the National Bank, which saw itself losing a basic resource for the development of its activity. The government, for its part, refused to accept the eventuality that the National Bank of Greece, a basic tool of its policy, could accept blows such as this (HANBG, file 36). Thus in August of 1948, the Currency Committee proceeded to abolish credit interest rates higher than 5 per cent on public sector organization deposits (Bank of Greece, 1949, p. 102).[8] In this way, the only competitive factor in the Greek banking system was eliminated.[9]

In the same period that the monetary authorities intervened in order to restrain the competition between the commercial banks for the deposits of the public sector organizations, the Currency Committee reached a new decision concerning the minimum reserves the banks should keep in the Bank of Greece. The National Bank was required to maintain as minimum reserves within the Bank of Greece 15 per cent of the sight deposits while the rest of the banks were obliged to maintain 5 per cent (Zolotas, 1950, p. 95).[10] At least at first glance there is nothing odd about this measure, which had already been implemented rather unsuccessfully in Greece during the pre-war period. In any event the choice to implement it at that particular moment can only be explained by the obligation which the Bank of Greece took on to undertake a restrictive policy, precisely at the time at which its profits were relatively low. In this way, the Bank of Greece acquired those resources to extend its credit without increasing the monetary circulation.

From one point of view, the introduction of minimum reserves in the central bank appeared to be one more stage in the progressive increase of state control over the Greek banking system. But there was another aspect to the credit policy of the American mission in Greece. This was the limitation, in every possible way, of the competition between the banks and the absolute submission to the orders of the state and therefore also to the Allied powers. The economic efficiency of the system was ultimately of far less significance than the political consequences which the direction of bank credit would have had if it had been carried out in a different way from that to which the governments – but in reality the Allies – had given immediate priority. In a country which was still at war and of which a large segment of the population had migrated to the urban centres, the choices which would allow the political regime to survive were the top priority.

While the Americans were in a position to create a new institutional framework for more effective intervention in the management of the capital which they offered, this did not mean that the new institutional framework met their expectations. The Allies intervened further in the Greek banking system but the results remained disappointing. With the agreement of 12 November 1948 between the Greek government and the American Mission, the Central Loan Committee was created. This was a mechanism for the granting of long-term loans in the Greek economy, with the basic task of distributing credit between manufacturing enterprises. The distribution of these loans to industries would provide the banks with a commission of 2 per cent (Chalikias, 1976, pp. 28–9 and Tsoutrellis, 1963, p. 25).

The struggle between the banks to secure capital from American aid was difficult and became even more so from the moment at which these funds began to be limited due to the transfer of a large portion of American aid from the outlays for reconstruction to military outlays. The military success of the government ranks was very limited in 1948 and for this reason it was believed that it would be useful to strengthen further the financing of the war (Amen, 1978). Furthermore, the largest part of the economic segment of the American aid was earmarked for farmers and *de facto* it was to be managed through the Agricultural Bank. Initially the National Bank attempted to directly monopolize the management of industrial loans (HANBG, file 36), but the final result was painful for the bank. For reasons which are not completely clear but which we can link with royalist connections, it was the National Mortgage Bank, its offshoot, which took on this role, at least to begin with (Stathakis, 1989, pp. 142ff; HANBG, op. cit., 'Note on banking policy').

Soon, however, the pressure which was exercised by the commercial banks led to a change of this tactic and with the agreement of 15 May 1949 between the American and Greek governments, all the Greek banks were able to participate in the provision of reconstruction loans (Arliotis, 1979, p. 235; HANBG, op. cit., Minutes of the meeting of 7 June 1948). The official body for the management of those loans was the Central Loan Committee, while the banks would play only a mediating role and would not take any responsibility for the loans which they provided. The consequences were calamitous as the largest portion of the loans of this category were never repaid, as no one (with the exception of the Americans) had an immediate interest in seeing that this happened (Association of National Bank Employees, 1957, p. 11).

In 1949, the civil war came to an end. The following year, for the first time, all the economic indices of the country surpassed their pre-war levels. The only exceptions to this rule were the indices of the banking system, which continued to be very far from those of 1938. The problem appeared more severe in the area of deposits, even more so since, according to the agreements which had been signed, it appeared that the American aid would come to an end in 1952. While the GDP had reached and surpassed its pre-war level, bank savings were far from approaching this level. As a result, the financing of the Greek economy in 1950 was two-thirds covered by capital from the central bank and only one-third covered by the bank resources themselves (Gregory et al., 1951, p. 119). British and American experts stated the position in the following way:

> Much that is regrettable in the present state of Greek banking arises from causes which cannot be corrected by legislation: we refer in particular to the serious shortfall in savings which offers a constant temptation to offer unduly high rates of interest and other inducements to depositors, and on the other hand forces banks to

> discrimination among borrowers, which in its turn has obviously
> undesirable aspects. (Gregory et al., 1951, p. 115)

Whatever the case, an effective and rational use of domestic resources was now necessary. This concern was expressed particularly in the circles of the foreign experts who were operating in Greece. They saw that all their interventions in the economy had failed and that while they hoped to disengage themselves gradually from the financing of the Greek economy, exactly the opposite happened. Given the economic conditions, any curtailment whatsoever of aid to Greece would have a huge political cost (Stathakis, 1995, pp. 375–404). With this in mind, on behalf of the Greek government but clearly on the suggestion of the American Mission, the Federal Reserve System was requested to carry out a study of the Greek banking system.

The proposals made by the Johns Committee were not adopted in their entirety. In some cases they were translated by the Greek authorities in a different spirit than they had been constructed. They did, however, constitute the basis for the implementation of the banking system policy at least for the next decade. Thus the Currency Committee, whose existence should have terminated with the end of American aid in 1952, was essential for the normal functioning of the monetary and credit system. Its functions needed to be extended and its jurisdiction enlarged, so that in reality it had full control of monetary and credit policy. At the same time, it would have to acquire a series of instruments in order to be in a position to fully control the banks. Moreover, foreign experts proposed the transfer of deposits of the public sector organizations to the Bank of Greece from the National Bank, with the central bank obliged to cede these deposits to the other banks in order to increase their available funds.

Among many other issues, the same report also raised the issue of the cost of the banks' functioning. The experts estimated that the Greek banks functioned at high cost. They requested that research be undertaken on this issue and, if the answer was affirmative, then measures were to be taken to limit those costs. They raised the issue of the control of banking competition with the limitation of the bank's branches and of course with the prohibition of the creation of new banking enterprises. Finally the report referred to the issue of the use of industrial credit – that is, to what degree it should be used by the existing banking organizations or whether a new credit institution should be created.

The response of the state to the recommendations of the Johns Committee was expressed through its viewpoints on the issue of the Currency

Committee and the deposits of the public sector organizations.[11] At the same time, a policy of low interest rates was continued for this whole period, which nevertheless only slightly influenced the credit interest rates and it was clear that it did not facilitate the increasing of deposits in the banking sector. They believed that in this way they could contain the functioning costs of the banking institutions. In this vein, measures were taken which could not facilitate the more rational functioning of the Greek banking system. The fact that a government of the right, with an authoritarian profile, had a large parliamentary majority since 1952, greatly eased the implementation of this policy.

Thus in 1953, the decision was made to merge the National Bank of Greece and the Bank of Athens, the country's two largest commercial banks. The result was the creation of a commercial bank of monstrous proportions relative to those of the Greek market. The decision of the government to represent, through the Ministry of Finance, all the public sector organizations which made up the majority of the shareholders of the National Bank, made this new bank completely dependent upon the governments of the time (Kostopoulos, 1953). However, the competition limitation policy was not restricted in the merger of the two large commercial banks. More or less at the same time as the merger, the Greek ship owner S. Andreadis acquired the majority of shares in the third largest commercial bank, the Commercial Bank of Greece, and a few years later bought out the businesses in Greece of the British Ionian Bank (the fourth in size, which in turn had under its control the Popular Bank, the fifth in size).[12] Thus in 1957, the Greek banking system functioned within the framework of a duopolistic structure, the consequences of which could be easily seen. Always sticking to the same logic, the Greek state moved on to the creation of an organization specializing in industrial credit in order to fulfil its policy. However, given that this took away that part of the business that the commercial banks wanted, it was careful to limit the activities of the Agricultural Bank (which in the pre-war period was their primary competitor in the area of deposit accumulation) and to completely limit the competition in the field of the commercial banking business.

This phase in Greek banking history came to an end in 1956. It was in this year that the Currency Committee chose to change its policy on the issue of interest rates on deposits, and in place of low interest rates introduced courageous increases. Suddenly the rate of increase in bank deposits, which had already displayed an upward trend since 1953 with the tough measures of economic policy taken this year (Goudi, 1953; Eliades, 1954), surpassed all previous records and the commercial banks gradually began to free themselves from the guardianship of the central bank. Yet, despite the views of those who inspired the policy of the concentration of the Greek banking system, the influx of deposits into the banking system did not produce the parallel increase in lending which had been expected. The banking structure which had been created maintained an exceptionally high level of liquidity and high interest rates, justified through the payment of commissions and insurance fees. And of course interest rates outside the banking system continued to remain high.

It remains difficult to isolate the consequences which the civil war had for the Greek banking system. What can be established is that throughout the entire period of the civil war and the first post-war years, first the British and then the Americans – the latter in a more direct and less pretentious way – attempted to intervene in order to adjust the system to a more rational functioning and to achieve a more effective use of the aid which they extended for the reconstruction of the Greek economy. In the final analysis, their policy led to a long-term increase in the state presence in the financial sector but without that policy becoming more effective. In fact, they failed (McNeill, 1957) and the Greek economy could not take advantage of the significant flows of capital which it received. The reason for this was that the social and political environment moulded the American interventions to its own specifications.

References

Amen, M. M. (1978), *American Foreign Policy in Greece, 1944–1949*, Frankfurt: Peter Lang.

Arliotis, K. (1979), *The History of the National Mortgage Bank of Greece*, Athens: National Mortgage Bank of Greece (in Greek).

Association of the National Bank Employees (1957), *The Bank Problem and the Organisation of the Financing of Economic Development*, Athens: Parnassos (in Greek).

Bank of Greece (1947), *Report of the Governor on the balance sheet of the years 1941, 1944, 1945, 1946*, Athens: Bank of Greece (in Greek).

Bank of Greece (1978), *The First Fifty Years of the Bank of Greece*, Athens: Bank of Greece (in Greek).

Candilis, W. O. (1968), *The Economy of Greece, 1944–1966. Efforts for Stability and Development*, New York: Praeger.

Chalikias, D. (1976), *Possibilities and Problems of Credit Policy. The Greek Experience*, Athens: Bank of Greece (in Greek).

Chatziiossif, C. (1992), 'Economic stabilisation and political instability in Greece, 1944–1947', in Baerentzen, L., Iatridis, G. and Smith, P. (eds), *Studies on the civil war*, Athens: Olkos (in Greek)

Delivanis, D. I. (1946), *The Drachma from the Autumn of 1939 up to the Monetary Restructuring of 15 January and its First Results*, Athens: Papazissis (in Greek)

Eliades, E. (1954), 'Stabilization of the Greek economy and the 1953 devaluation of the drachma', *International Monetary Fund Staff Papers*, 4.

Etmektsoglou-Cohen, G. (1995), 'Axis exploitation of wartime Greece, 1941–1943', unpublished PhD dissertation, Emory University.

Fatouros, A. A. (1984), 'How a formal framework of penetration is constructed: the United States in Greece, 1947–1948', in Iatrides, J. O. (ed.), *Greece in the Decade, 1940–1950. A Nation in Crisis*, Athens: Themelio (in Greek)

Galanis, T. (1960), *Issues of Bank Policy*, Athens: publisher not known (in Greek).

Goudi, M. N. (1953), *The Readjustment of the Foreign Exchange Rates*, Athens: Papazissis (in Greek).

Gregory, T., Gunter, J. and Johns, D. (1951), 'Report and recommendations on certain aspects of the Greek banking system submitted to the Governor of the Bank of Greece, June 30 1950', *Bank of Greece Report of the Governor of the Bank on the Balance sheet of the Year 1950*, Athens: Bank of Greece.

Historical Archives of the Alpha Bank, Archives of the General Managers, Archives S. Kostopoulos, file 22, Correspondence with the monetary authorities for the future of the small banks (1944–45).

HANBG (Historical Archives of the National Bank of Greece), A1Σ32Y1, Occupation and Reconstruction, file 36.

Kasimatis, G. (1945), *The Economic Problem*, Athens: Sakkoulas (in Greek).

Kostis, K. (1997), *Co-operation and Competition. Seventy Years of the Hellenic Banks Association*, Athens: Alexandria (in Greek)

Kostis, K. (1999), 'Les ambiguités de la modernisation: la fondation de la Banque de Grèce (1927–1928), *Histoire, Economie et Société*, pp. 701–14.

Kostopoulos, S. (1953), *The Policy of the Merging of the Banks*, Athens: Alpha (in Greek).

McNeill, W. H. (1957), *Greece: American Aid in Action, 1947–1956*, New York: Twentieth Century Fund.

Stathakis, G. (1995), 'U.S. economic policies in post civil-war Greece, 1949–1953: stabilisation and monetary reform', *Journal of European Economic History*, 24, 2, pp. 375–404.

Thomadakis, S. (1984), 'Black market, inflation and violence in the economy of occupied Greece', in Iatrides, J. O. (ed.), *Greece in the Decade 1940–1950. A Nation in Crisis*, Athens: Themelio, pp. 117–144 (in Greek).

Tsoutrellis, E. (1963), *Industrial Credit and Credit Policy*, Athens: Bank of Greece (in Greek).

Varvaressos, K. (1952), *Report on the Economic Problem of Greece*, Athens: publisher not known (in Greek).

Zolotas, X. (1950), *Monetary Problems and the Greek Economy*, Athens: Papazissis (in Greek).

Notes

1   It should be added that after 1928 the Post Office Savings Bank was used primarily as a mechanism to attract funds for public works. Its importance increased after the bankruptcy of the Greek state in 1932.

2   This was something a group of bankers did not neglect to mention in a memorandum which they submitted to the Governor of the Bank of Greece, asking him 'to be a kind supporter and not (their) relentless competitor'. See the Historical Archives of the Alpha Bank, Archives of the General Managers, Archives S. Kostopoulos, file 22, Correspondence with the monetary authorities for the future of the small banks.

3   For exactly this reason, on 31 December 1946, from a deposit total within the banks and the Post Office Savings Bank, which amounted to 131 billion drachmas, 108 billion were to be found in the National Bank (Galanis, 1960, pp. 15, 18).

4   In reality, the Currency Committee was the result of the efforts of the state to place the area of credit under its control but, also, of the wishes of the English to have the first word in the monetary policy of the country. Before the creation of the Currency Committee, two other laws had tried to establish a state control over the credit system: Obligatory Law 675 of 18/19 November 1945 'concerning the control of credit' under Prime Minister P. Kannellopoulos and the Minister of the Economy G. Kasimatis, which was succeeded a little later by Obligatory Law 685 'concerning the control of credit' of the Sofoulis Government. Both foresaw the transfer of authority for the credit and monetary policy from Bank of Greece to a political body but at the end they did not come in operation (Kasimatis, 1945, pp. 193–7).

5   A few years later, the creation of the Currency Committee was justified formally by the American bankers, one of whom was a member of the Committee, in the following manner: 'In summary, the reasons for vesting control over monetary policy in the Currency Committee may be broadly stated as including: (1) the acknowledged necessity of removing the formulation of monetary and credit policy as far as practicable from Greek party politics; (2) the necessity of bringing to bear upon these problems the experience and objective advice of foreign experts; (3) the necessity by these means of establishing and maintaining

satisfactory relations with foreign Governments and Central Banks' (Gregory et al., 1951, p. 123).

6   This was a point which was underlined directly from the beginning by Porter, the Head of the American Mission, who stressed that 'the complete control of the funds which the United States will offer to Greece must belong to the Mission' (Fatouros, 1984, p. 427).

7   The broadened jurisdiction of the Currency Committee was granted with Law 588/1948 'Concerning credit control', which was put together with the cooperation of the government, the Currency Committee and the American Mission in Greece (Bank of Greece, 1978, pp. 313–14). Moreover, one of the first measures within the framework of the broadening of the jurisdiction of the committee was the increase in interest rates on credit to 12 per cent and of the top level of commissions to 4 per cent so that the total cost reached 16 per cent and was close to the market interest rate. However, the grants of the Bank of Greece to the commercial banks were made at 5 per cent and loans to the Agricultural Bank at an interest rate of only 2.5 per cent. On the other hand the Currency Committee, not wanting to overburden the cost of functioning of the banks, continued to hold down the interest rates of deposits low (Bank of Greece, 1978, pp. 315–17. See also Zolotas, 1950, pp. 86–8, and D. I. Chalikias, 1976, p. 36).

8   In any case, this decision did not prevent the outflow of the deposits of public sector organizations from the National Bank of Greece towards the other banks. It simply made it worse, as the violation of the decisions of the Currency Committee allowed the reduction of the deposits of the public sector organizations held by the National Bank of Greece from 72 per cent of their total in 1948 to 67 per cent in 1949 and 65 per cent in 1950 (Gregory et al., 1951, p. 137).

9   Moreover, in another decision of the Governmental Economic Council which dates from March 1948, the use of the funds available from the public sector organizations was forbidden for purposes other than dealing with their current obligations and needs without the approval of the Currency Committee and of the Governmental Economic Council (Bank of Greece, 1978).

10   In a later decision of 27 January 1949, the Currency Committee makes this percentage the same for all the banks at the level of 22 per cent for the sight deposits and term deposits of public sector organizations and 10 per cent for all the other categories of deposits.

11   With Law 1611 of 31 December 1950 'Concerning deposits of the public sector and insurance funds', it is determined that all this capital of organizations will be deposited from now on in the Bank of Greece which will use them for the funding of the economy through other banks. In Law 1665 'Concerning the functioning and control of the banks', the way in which all the existing banks and those to be founded would be monitored and controlled was regulated (Bank of Greece, 1978, p. 320).

12   The two banks, the Ionian and the Popular Banks, merged in 1957.

Figure 1   Estonia's 10 kroon note depicts Jacob Hurt (1839–94), who collected Estonian dialects and folklore during the 'National Awakening' of the nineteenth century.

Figure 2 The Lithuanian pilots Steponas Darius and Stasys Girėnas, who died in 1933 trying to fly from New York to Lithuania, on a 10 litu note of Lithuania.

Figure 3 The poet Franc Preseren on the 1000 tolar note of Slovenia. Portraits, often of men, are the dominant image on the front of banknotes in Central and Eastern Europe.

Figure 4a A view of the Ursuline Convent in Ljubljana (a) and as it appears, right of centre, on the back of the 10 tolar note (b). Urban buildings on the back of the banknotes are often associated with Christianity.

Figure 4b

Figure 5   A Latvian note bearing an oak tree emphasizes a rural identity.

Figure 6 The opera singer Ema Destinnová (1878–1930) is one of three women depicted on banknotes of the Czech Republic.

Figure 7 St Stephen (born circa 972–75), the first king of Hungary, is a symbol of strong rule on the 10 000 forint note.

Figure 8 The national poet of Estonia, Lydia Koidula (1843–86), examplifies the theme of cultural heroes on Estonian notes.

Figure 9a The folkmaid on the 5 lat coin of Latvia, 1929 (a), became a cherished symbol of independence and she features on the country's current 500 at banknote (b).

Figure 9b

Figure 10 Macedonian notes featuring images of Christianity and early heritage, in this case a peacock from the mosaic floor of a basilica.

PART IV

Post-war Reconstruction: The German and Far Eastern Experience

CHAPTER 9

The Transformation and Reconstruction of Banking in Germany, 1945–57

Martin L. Müller

If we look at research in banking policy during the period directly following the Second World War in Germany, it becomes apparent that a clear concentration has taken place both geographically and institutionally. Only the three Western occupation zones have been studied, whereas the Soviet zone has mainly been neglected. Institutionally, almost all studies have concentrated on the three big banks and the central bank – from the foundation of the Bank deutscher Länder up to its transformation into the Deutsche Bundesbank. Regional banks as well as cooperative banks and savings banks have mostly remained unexamined.

The most attention has certainly been devoted to the Bank deutscher Länder, whose creation is also directly linked to the currency reform of 20 June 1948 and thus to the introduction of the Deutsch mark (DM) (Buchheim, 1998, pp. 91–138; Buchheim, 1988, pp. 189–231; Wandel, 1980; Möller, 1976, pp. 433–83). Above all, during the last decade the banking policy of the Western Allies towards the three big banks has been repeatedly studied. We are in the fortunate position of having studies both from the perspectives of the military governments (Horstmann, 1991) and from the banks affected (Holtfrerich, 1995, pp. 357–521).

Without a doubt, the treatment of the big banks – named the 'Big Six' by the Americans – is especially fascinating. The Deutsche Bank, Dresdner Bank, Commerzbank and the Berliner Handels-Gesellschaft as well as the state-owned Reichs-Kredit-Gesellschaft and Bank der Deutschen Arbeit were the main focus of the investigations of the American Military Government, which saw 'an unusual' or 'excessive concentration of economic power' (OMGUS [Office of Military Government for Germany, United States], 1985, p. 13; OMGUS, 1986, p. 5) in these institutions. Discussions on the investigative reports arising from this have continued up to the most recent legal proceedings in the United States. The OMGUS

Reports on Deutsche Bank and Dresdner Bank are being republished in the United States (Simpson, 2001). Although these new editions are being published, historical research in the history of big banks during the Third Reich has advanced significantly in the mean time and our understanding of the OMGUS Reports has been revised in numerous respects. The contents of the OMGUS Reports must now be seen in the light of their authors' motivation.

Eastern Regions

The big banks were the object of systematic investigations but only in the areas of the three Western occupation zones, especially the American zone. By considering the Western zones, however, only a little more than half of the big banks' areas of business from the pre-war period are covered. Besides the area of the three Western zones – the later Federal Republic – one can see the three regions of the German Reich in its borders of 1937, in which the banks were each subject to other regulations. To begin with, there were the regions to the east of the Oder-Neisse line, in which the bank branches had already been eliminated at the beginning of 1945. As to the exact course of events in Silesia, Pomerania and East Prussia, there is still little information available. In most cases, the documents of these East German bank offices have been missing since 1945. For this reason, no in-depth look at the fate of German banks in the former regions to the East is possible.

Berlin

Although a detailed overall study of the banking policy in the Soviet occupation zone and in the early period of the GDR is still sorely missed, a short outline of developments in the Soviet occupation zone as well as in Berlin is worthwhile.

Berlin's special role in the banking sector was already clear during the capture of the city by the Soviet troops (Weber, 1957, pp. 171–212; Wolf, 1990, pp. 116–25). Even while fighting in Berlin continued, the Soviet commander of the city ordered the closing of all banks. After a short interlude from the middle of May until the beginning of June 1945, during which business operations of all banks were once again permitted, the Soviet commander decreed what is known as the 'abeyance ordinance' on 5 June 1945. This order decreed that only one bank in Berlin – namely the Berlin City Bank (Berliner Stadtbank), the successor institution of the Reichsbank – was permitted to execute cash transactions. All other banks were temporarily suspended. Their cash inventories were to be turned over to the Berlin City Bank.

The order remained in effect until 4 July, when American and British forces moved into the western sectors of Berlin, followed by the French on 12 August. The only exception to this radical solution was the deposit business of the Berlin Savings Bank. At the beginning of 1946, a cooperative bank was successfully established. All other banks in Berlin, which previously had numbered 500 bank branches, remained closed. The formal expropriation of most Berlin banks, the majority of which had had their headquarters in central Berlin and were thus in the Soviet sector, took place at the end of 1947. The assets located in the eastern sector were assumed by the Banking Commission of the Division of German Central Finances in the Soviet occupation zone.

However, the banks in 'abeyance' in the western sectors of Berlin were unable to dispose of old assets. Nothing changed in this respect, even when the city was divided into two currency areas in June 1948 through the two currency reforms in the West and the East. This was surprising when it is remembered that the consensus among the four Allies had long since fallen apart. In particular, the Berlin issue contributed to the escalation of the differences between the Western Allies and the Soviets, reaching its peak in the blockade of the city from June 1948 until May 1949. And yet the Western Allies maintained their significantly stricter banking policy for Berlin in comparison to the western zones. In the middle of 1950, the prohibition against reopening Berlin banks in the western sector was renewed and, concurrently, the use of the traditional company names was forbidden. Banks in the western portion of the city also remained 'dormant banks' and were later transferred to the Federal Republic or liquidated. The Cold War changed nothing in this procedure. Did this mean that Berlin, as the centre of the German universal bank system and as the centre of economic power in Germany, was to be punished? If so, then the Allies' policy has been successful up until today. Berlin is a long way away from being an important banking centre, even in the twenty-first century. In addition to Frankfurt, Düsseldorf, Munich and Hamburg are well ahead of Berlin.

The reconstruction of the banking industry in the western sectors started practically from scratch. The big banks set up new Berlin subsidiaries that survived beyond the reunification of Germany with their Berlin special status. Only after 1990 were they merged with their parent banks: entirely normal branches emerged from the Berlin subsidiaries. Nowhere else in German banking did the post-war period last so long as in Berlin.

The Soviet Occupation Zone/GDR

In contrast to the former regions to the east, initially there was hope for the continued existence of German banks in the Soviet zone. At the signing of the resolutions of the four victorious powers at the Potsdam Conference on 2 August 1945, the Soviet Union agreed that 'Germany is to be handled as one single economic unit' and committed itself to a joint policy, including the areas of currency and banking.[1] In fact, however, the Soviet Union had already extensively redesigned the banking industry in their occupation zone. By the time of the Potsdam Agreement, they had begun to set up a system of central economic administration, which included the banking sector (Schwarzer, 1999).

As in Berlin, all banks throughout the entire Soviet zone were already closed by the end of April or beginning of May 1945. The Red Army carried out the closure of all the bank offices according to a similar model. The following passage describes the process in the city of Görlitz at the extreme south-east end of the Soviet occupation zone:

> Special attention was paid without exception to the cash offices, including the Reichsbank, in Görlitz. The branch of the Deutsche Bank, as the largest office, received the first visit already on the day of invasion of the Red Army [8 May 1945]. A Major and his staff, as the leader of the committee responsible, asked to examine the bank premises for 'gold, foreign currency and personal assets', was shown the vault, made a few inconsequential random checks and, after closing and locking the vault, took the keys, which were to be returned after checks had been made. From that point on, the bank was under military guard ...[2]

After closing down the banks, the first action of the Soviet Military Administration (SMAD) in July 1945 was to transform the branches of the big banks without much ado into the newly established Land Banks in the five Länder of the Soviet zone. The Land Banks (later renamed Land Credit Banks) were public institutions and operated branches in almost every larger town. They were organized entirely according to the model of the dissolved big bank; their personnel – and boards of directors – were largely drawn from the staff of the previous big bank branches. In contrast to the western occupation zones, however, NSDAP membership meant exclusion from continued employment in the Land Banks, even for bank personnel in subordinate positions. Here, East German denazification was clearly more thorough than in the western zones.

The reasons for and objectives of the bank closures and reopening of the new banks remained a secret, even from many of the employees of the new

Land Banks. It was generally assumed that banking business would be operating again in a short period of time in the same way as the previous big and regional banks had operated. In August 1945, the former Deutsche Bank director of the Görlitz branch (by then head of the Saxon Land Bank, Görlitz branch), wrote to one of his former colleagues of his hopes for the future of banking in East Germany after the end of the occupation period: 'I would think that a new government would then re-establish the monetary system as it had historically become according to German circumstances. In my view, the one-bank system does not suit Germans, and even less an economy now in ruins to be rebuilt using all means.'[3]

This experienced branch manager's prediction turned out to be entirely wrong. The path into the planned economy and single-level banking system had been mapped out by those responsible for policy in the Soviet zone long before that, and it progressed in several phases. With the SMAD Order No. 66 in March 1946, all credit claims on the old banks were called on to the benefit of the Land and provincial administrations. In February 1947, five placement and giro banks with Land Central Bank character and a joint clearing office in Potsdam were created at the Länder level. They were combined a year later into the Deutsche Emissions- und Girobank. As part of the currency reform in the eastern zone, this leading institution received the new name 'Deutsche Notenbank' shortly after its establishment; it was granted the right to issue the new currency in the east, the 'Deutsche Mark der Deutschen Notenbank' (Ermer, 2000). Finally, in 1950, the Land Banks were also merged with the Deutsche Notenbank. Thus the restructuring into a one-level banking system, following the model of the State Bank of the USSR, was essentially completed. The Deutsche Notenbank, which was renamed State Bank of the GDR (Staatsbank der DDR) in 1968, was both the currency-issuing bank of the GDR as well as the credit-issuing institution for enterprises in the GDR. In the planned-economy system, the State Bank acted as a central steering agency. Under the supervision of the State Bank, there were other credit institutions which received special tasks, for example, the German Bank for Foreign Trade. Likewise, savings banks and cooperative banks were assigned special functions. Cities and municipalities were authorized by the SMAD to establish new savings banks, although these were not to be the legal successors of the savings banks closed in July 1945 (Mura, 1982, pp. 3–21). The range of tasks of the savings banks was extremely limited by the first orders of the year 1945. They were authorized to conduct deposit business (savings and giro accounts) and short-term lending business up to RM 5000. Municipal loans were forbidden from the beginning; mortgage business was first permitted once again in a limited volume at the end of 1946. On 1 January 1951, the Deutsche Notenbank transferred all savings and salary accounts to the savings banks; concurrently, they had to surrender all accounts of state bodies and institutions to the Notenbank. The banks for commerce and trade, such as were often founded as commercial credit cooperatives, were given the task of supplying smaller companies with banking services according to guidelines from the Deutsche Notenbank.

This short outline has described the development of the banking environment in the Soviet occupation zone in the early years of the GDR. While the basic structures and lines of development have been known for some time, a companion to studies of the banking policy of the Western Allies in their occupation zones (such as that provided by Theo Horstmann) has been sorely missed. Such a study would consider the extent to which the banking policy of the eastern zone was based on planning drafted in the Soviet Union and then simply imposed from April 1945 on. We also need to know how banking policy was shared and implemented by the Soviet Military Administration and German communists. What were their conflicts? Was there room for any negotiations? Many of these questions, which have been answered in detail for the western occupation zones – above all the American zone – are awaiting additional research.

Western Occupation Zones/Federal Republic of Germany

American banking policy 1944–48

American planning on how conquered Germany should be administered began long before the end of the war. The basis for post-war planning for the Western Allies for Germany was the directive CCS 551 (Combined Chiefs of Staff Directive for Military Government in Germany prior to Defeat or Surrender, 28 April 1944), which had been produced by the Supreme Headquarters Allied Expeditionary Forces (SHAEF). This instructed the Allied Forces that 'Wherever possible, you should use the existing administrative and economic apparatus in Germany.' CCS 551 applied only for the period between the invasion into Germany and German capitulation; however, on the basis of CCS 551, the *Handbook for Military Government in Germany* was worked out by the German unit at SHAEF. In the financial sector, to which banks also belonged, the *Handbook* stipulated that the task of the future military government was

> ... to take such temporary measures as will attempt to minimize the potential financial disorder and chaos that is likely to occur and thus

> assist the military forces in their operations and ease the burdens that
> will face the more permanent Allied Control Organization that will
> later deal with the problems of Germany … Banks should only be
> closed if necessary and then only long enough to introduce
> satisfactory control by Allied Military Government, to remove
> objectionable personnel, and to issue introductions for blocking of
> certain accounts … Banks, if closed, will be permitted to reopen as
> soon as possible. Control over the banking system will be exercised as
> much as possible through the Reichsbank and its branches.
> (Horstmann, 1991, pp. 22 ff.)

As these instructions show, the banking sector was recognized as having an
important role in maintaining economic order. Denazification was also
planned for the credit institutions. Nevertheless no mention was made in the
Handbook on the restructuring of the banking industry in Germany.
Therefore there was no shortage of opposition to the *Handbook* from the
political arena. The *Handbook*'s toughest opponent was US Treasury
Secretary Henry Morgenthau[4] and he succeeded in eliciting this criticism
from President Roosevelt:

> This so-called 'Handbook' is pretty bad … It gives me the
> impression that Germany is to be restored just as much as the
> Netherlands or Belgium and the people of Germany brought back as
> quickly as possible to the pre-war estate. Too many people here and
> in England hold the view that the German people as a whole are not
> responsible. The German people as a whole must have it driven home
> that the whole nation has been engaged in a lawless conspiration
> against decencies of modern civilization. (Horstmann, 1991, p.25)

In the end, that version of the *Handbook* was withdrawn, the provisions
were made stricter in part and the *Handbook* in its final version was
approved with British consent in December 1944. Morgenthau was not
satisfied with this partial success. He became the driving force in the Briefing
Book produced by the Treasury which carried the official title 'Program to
Prevent Germany from Starting a World War III' (FRUS) and which has
remained in the German collective consciousness until today as the
'Morgenthau Plan'. Morgenthau initially appeared to be able to push
through his concept of a demilitarized, de-industrialized and sub-divided
Germany. However his opponents among the leaders of the War
Department and State Department regained the upper hand after
Roosevelt's death. The decisive Directive of the Joint Chiefs of Staff
(JCS) 1067 for the American occupation policy was once again character-
ized by moderation. With regard to the German banks, the Military
Government was authorized 'to close banks, but only for a period long

enough for you to introduce satisfactory control, to remove Nazi and other undesirable personnel, and to issue instructions for the determination of accounts to be blocked'.

The Finance Division, whose personnel had to a large extent been recruited from Morgenthau's Treasury Department, was responsible for the implementation of the softened finance directive within the US Military Government. Many of these men were professed New Deal liberals and left-wing Keynesians, many of whom were also emigrants who had left Nazi Germany in time and were now returning in American uniform. The composition of Finance Division personnel guaranteed the parent authority in Washington a continued strong influence on the banking policy in occupied Germany. This helps to explain the toughness with which the Finance Division of the US Military Government pursued the decentraliza-tion of the German banking system in subsequent years and, also, its attempts to prosecute leading German bankers.

These two goals led the Finance Division to start investigations against several German banks in the summer of 1945. They were looking for documents which were to support the accusation raised by the Finance Division that the banks under investigation embodied an excessive concentration of economic power. Moreover, the conduct of the banks during the National Socialist period was to be critically investigated. Four 'Reports on the Investigations' of Deutsche Bank, Dresdner Bank, Commerzbank and the Reichs-Kredit-Gesellschaft were completed in 1946/47, copied in large numbers and distributed to the interested parties.[5] The results of these reports legitimized the break-up of the three big banks pursued by the American Military Government. They confirmed the views of many officials working in the OMGUS administration that the German industrial and banking world carried a large share of the responsibility for the Second World War. Here ideological prejudices, resulting in over-estimating the role of banks in the Third Reich, should not be overlooked (Scholtyseck, 2000, pp. 27–53).

This line of argument has been accepted as an article of faith by a number of historians up into the most recent past: politically, the basic thesis was clearly left-wing but its American origin placed it above reproach or made it difficult for conservatives to attack. It was not socialist advocates who expounded the maxim that only the decentralization of the economy and big banks would be capable of avoiding a renewed transition of Germany into the totalitarian camp, but rather it was leading officials of the American Military Government.

The armour with which Germany was to be equipped against all relapses was – in exaggeration – a Glass-Steagall Act (passed in the US in 1934) for the German banking industry. The universal bank (which of course was not a discovery of the Nazis but rather of the middle-class liberals of the nineteenth century) was to become a thing of the past. A line was to be drawn through the intermingling of currency banks and investment business; there was to be no mixing of principal bank, industrial shareholdings, supervisory board mandates and portfolio proxy rights; institutions active nationwide were to disappear from the map. Whereas a disentangling of the heavy and capital-intensive industries was stopped at the beginning of 1948 out of consideration for the reconstruction which had begun in German industry, the break-up of the big banks remained a central part of the American decentralization policy well beyond 1948. General Lucius Clay, the head of the US Military Government, described the decentralization of the big banks as 'the biggest single step taken with respect to the elimination of excessive economic power in Germany' (Holtfrerich, 1995, pp. 414–15).

The rest is well-known: the state-run Reichs-Kredit-Gesellschaft was liquidated and disappeared completely from the banking horizon. The three big branch banks – that is, Deutsche Bank, Dresdner Bank and Commerzbank – were dissolved in the three western occupation zones. In May 1947, the US Military Government issued Law No. 57, whereby the existing big banks in each Land of the American occupation zone were required to transform themselves into new, independent regional banks. The French Military Government followed the American law shortly afterwards, and the British Military Government joined in despite initial rejection of the American regulation on decentralization. Through their consistent reference back to the positive experience of the past, the British at least prevented execution of the original American plan to do away with the universal bank system. Faced with the fact that stock market trading and the capital markets were in complete and utter ruins, maintaining the universal bank system initially represented simply a theoretical concession by the Americans (Wandel, 1980, pp. 66 ff.). In the years 1947–48, no one in Germany dreamed of issuing stocks and bonds.

The Dissolution of the Big Banks

The dissolution of the big banks at the Land level was completed jointly in the three western zones. Deutsche Bank was divided into ten, Dresdner Bank into eleven, and Commerzbank into nine separate institutions whose names were not permitted to evoke the original banks. These new institutions were neither fish nor fowl. Neither the administrators nor the executive management of the subsequent banks were subject to control by the shareholders of the pre-war banks. The interests of depositors, creditors and owners had to forgo the protection of important provisions of German stock corporation law, such as the publication of annual financial statements. From the start, they were disqualified from transacting international business.

However, it quickly became clear that this state of affairs was untenable. After the founding of the Federal Republic of Germany, the big banks were able to re-emerge in two phases. In 1952, as a transitional arrangement, three successor institutions were created with business areas limited to the north, west and south of the country. In contrast to the previous partial institutions, these were once again joint stock corporations (AGs). After the Federal Republic had gained its full sovereignty in 1957, the legal precondition for the reunification of the three big banks was created, which then took place during the same year.

The New Central Bank System

Just as the American example with the Glass-Steagall Act was applied to the transformation of the German big banks, so too the US Federal Reserve system served as the model for the new central bank system in occupied Germany (Buchheim, 2001, pp. 1–30). The Americans did not want to permit a unified central bank for the whole of Germany. The Reichsbank was therefore to be dissolved. In its place, an independent central bank (Land Central Bank) and a banking supervisory authority were to be established in each Land. To coordinate the Land Central Banks, the Americans proposed the suggestion to the Finance Directorate of the Allied Control Council that a Länder Union Bank should be created which would operate monetary policy for all of Germany. This suggestion, however, failed to overcome the opposition of the Soviet representatives in the Control Council.

After the failure in finding a joint approach, the Americans pursued the formation of Land Central Banks in their zone. The necessary laws were announced in Bavaria, Hesse and Württemberg by the end of 1946. Whereas the French followed the American model shortly afterwards – as with the decentralization of the big banks – and set up Land Central Banks in Württemberg-Baden, Württemberg-Hohenzollern and Rhineland-Palatinate, the British held onto the centralized Reichsbank organization in their zone. In doing so, the British Military Government in Hamburg utilized the head office of the Reichsbank, which operated between the Länder as the zones' central bank.

The British were primarily interested in an efficiently functioning banking apparatus which could serve the financial settlements between the occupation zones. This pragmatism contrasted with the politically motivated, radical reform advocated by the Americans (Buchheim, 1998, p. 104). The resolution of the central bank issue finally came in the form of an Anglo-American compromise. The British declared their willingness to dissolve the bank head office in Hamburg, to liquidate the Reichsbank and to establish a Land Central Bank according to the American model in each Land of their zone. In return, the Americans agreed to the establishment of a central bank for the coordination of monetary policy for all of the eight Land Central Banks in both zones. With effect from 1 March 1948, the Bank deutscher Länder was established as the bank of the Land Central Banks under the laws of the American and British Military Governments (using the same text). In the same month, the Land Central Banks of the French zone joined the Bank deutscher Länder.

The Bank deutscher Länder had the tasks and authorities of a currency and issuing bank for the areas of three western occupation zones and, starting in May 1949, for the area of the newly-established Federal Republic of Germany. It was the higher institution in a two-level central banking system. Each Land Central Bank also filled the position of a central bank within its Land – without, however, the right to issue bank notes and coins. With the founding of the Bank deutscher Länder, the first tri-zone institution was simultaneously created. The Bank deutscher Länder was thus the oldest central public institution of the later Federal Republic.

The most urgent task of the newly founded Bank deutscher Länder was currency reform. The currency break urgently needed for the economy took a long time in coming, because currency reform had long been sought for all four of the occupation zones. After the Soviet Military Government had left the Allied Control Council on 20 March 1948, planning focused clearly on currency reform in the three western zones. A short time later, under Allied supervision and strict confidentiality, 22 laws, executive ordinances, proclamation sheets and instructions were formulated by German experts. On 20 June 1948 (the 'Kopfgeldausgabe' or allotment of money 'per head' day), the Currency Issue Act regulating the issue of bank notes and coins by the Bank deutscher Länder and the Currency Act came into effect, replacing the Reichsmark with the Deutsche Mark. The currency reform simultaneously meant the effective start of the banking business and an active monetary policy for the Bank deutscher Länder. It was through this currency reform that the possibility was first created for an effective and meaningful central bank policy.

Despite its successful start, the Bank deutscher Länder was to exist for less than a decade. After the Federal Republic of Germany gained sovereign independence in 1957, the central bank system created by the occupying powers – the Bank deutscher Länder and the Land Central Banks – was replaced by the Deutsche Bundesbank. It assumed all of their business and continued their policy uninterrupted. According to the law on the Deutsche Bundesbank, the new central institution could not be founded on abstract principles; to a large degree its foundation reflected the federal structure of the state, represented in the Central Bank Council. The new law also strengthened the position of the central Directorate. The Deutsche Bundesbank has been operating with these structures adapted in 1957 until today. In the age of the euro, however, the question now arises as to whether these structures are still up to date.

Reconstruction Loan Corporation (Kreditanstalt für Wiederaufbau)

Whereas the dissolution of the big banks and new regulation of the central bank system were primarily driven by the political interests of the USA from the war years, the emerging East–West conflict increasingly began to determine the Western Allies' Germany policy. At the beginning of 1948, Germans in the western zones could be sure that the reconstruction of Germany was the firm objective of the Western Allies. In place of the Morgenthau Plan came the Marshall Plan with a completely different political character. The main financial burden of the reconstruction assistance was covered by the US. In April 1948, President Truman signed the Foreign Assistance Act, which regulated American assistance for the European reconstruction programme. The disbursement office for the Marshall Plan funds for Germany was the Reconstruction Loan Corporation, newly established by law on 5 November 1948 (Pohl, 1973; Harries, 1998). This new public sector credit institution was given the task of issuing mid-term and long-term loans to industry for its reconstruction. In the first years of its existence, the Reconstruction Loan Corporation was especially involved with the execution of various emergency programmes, employment creation programmes, investment assistance and export financing. Upon completion of the immediate reconstruction, the Federal German government gave the bank the task of financing development assistance in 1961.

Savings Banks Sector

In contrast to the big banks and the Reichsbank, the Americans had no concrete political objectives for the reorganization of the German savings banks sector. At first glance, this may appear surprising, given that the savings banks handled approximately 30 per cent of the credit issued to the Deutsche Reich or 85.6 billion Reichsmarks. Thus, their share in wartime financing was nearly double the amount of the private sector banks, including the big banks (Boelcke, 1992, p. 112). Additionally, the savings banks enjoyed the ideological support of the Nazis, which they in turn attempted to transform into competitive advantages (Kopper, 1995, p. 90). Through the close interweaving of the municipalities and savings banks organization, the savings banks were the first banks brought into line in the National Socialist framework. Nazi mayors, regional directors and city administrators had already been setting the tone for policy in most of the savings banks in the first months of 1933. Despite this fact, which naturally was known to American intelligence, the actions of the occupying powers were limited to the temporary closure of savings banks at the end of the war and the arrest of the most strongly compromised savings banks officials. With the exception of these individual cases, the savings banks sector during the immediate post-war period was characterized primarily by continuing operations. The decisive break, that can be clearly identified for the big banks and the central bank system, cannot be identified for the savings banks. Their decentralized structure apparently let them appear to the Americans as unthreatening. Detailed investigations of the business activities of the savings banks analogous to the OMGUS Reports did not take place. This means that we now have only very inexact knowledge, for example, of the role of the savings banks in what is known as 'Aryanization', which as far as small Jewish businesses were concerned principally took place among savings banks' customers and not among those of the big banks.

After currency reform, the savings banks profited from tax advantages on saving. After the reduction of these advantage in 1968, the savings banks increasingly pushed into non-savings business and, by doing so, transformed themselves into full-service universal banks. Even today, the banking industry in Germany is, in comparison to its European neighbours, characterized by the public sector's strong position. In particular, the heavy intermingling between savings banks and their public guarantors (the municipalities and Länder) has recently led to objections from the European Competition Commissioner. The further development of the savings banks sector may thus be decided to a great extent in Brussels.

Conclusion

The development of the savings banks – as with the cooperative banks – was characterized by continuity during the post-war period. This continuity extends from the Weimar Republic through the Third Reich up to the Federal Republic. Independently of the political system, the savings banks have been expanded as the lending institutions of the man on the street and have been supported by the state. The drive for independent provision of credit to the lower classes through savings banks apparently found support among the most varied ideological positions.

This continuity did not apply to the big banks. To the American Military Government, the big banks appeared to be the root of the Nazi evil. Concurrently, their break-up was part of the American security policy for Germany. The objective was to remove the banking policy capacity which had made it possible for the Third Reich to finance militarization and war. But it is an irony of history that the Allies adopted measures in dissolving the big banks which the bank-hostile, anti-capitalistic Nazis had always demanded since Gottfried Feders' party programme and could only dream of after their defeat during the bank inquiry (Bank-Enquête) of 1933.

The British Military Government only agreed to the decentralization of the big banks against its will. It was completely rejected by the Germans in any case, by both economic and political institutions. Actually, the Americans were never able to push through ultimate decentralization. The cohesion of the individual bank groups remained in existence beneath the surface. The authority of important leading figures was undiminished. Faced with the lack of acceptance, the American policy towards big banks was doomed to fail from the beginning (Horstmann, 1991, pp. 297–308).

Regulations were revised as soon as the political possibilities for their revocation were given. The Big Banks Act of 1952, which still required the Allies' approval, was the decisive step for the big banks to move into the future without Allied supervision. In 1957, the German big bank system was re-established. Although they were formally new establishments, the three institutions always saw themselves in the continuity of their predecessor banks in Berlin. After an interregnum of the twelve-year post-war period, the expanded components of the German banking industry were re-established. The extent and dominance of this continuity can be understood by posing the question of how the German banking industry would look today if the American decentralization policy had been made permanent.

At the same time, the American central bank policy was a more sustainable success. Despite a certain amount of continuity from the

Reichsbank[6] through the Bank deutscher Länder to the Deutsche Bundesbank, a new beginning is recognizable here. The Bundesbank's federal anchoring and the independence of monetary policy are the two essential principles of today's central bank system which were missing in the Reichsbank. The success of the Allies' central bank policy was largely thanks to their achievement, in contrast to the big banks' policy of explaining its motives and objectives to the German side. The American demand for a decentralization of the central bank system was transformed into the Länder's demand for a federal structure such as in the Central Bank Council. The new beginning cannot be overlooked here and it is not without reason that the Deutsche Bundesbank has become one of the most respected institutions of the second parliamentary democracy in Germany.

As to the banking system in the second German post-war state, the GDR, the break with the instituted bank system was a more complete one. The one-level bank system according to the Soviet model had been adopted and was completely subjected to the requirements of a socialist planned economy. Nothing changed in this system until 1989. Shortly after the Berlin Wall came down, the GDR banking system was redesigned on the West German model. Already when the Monetary, Economic and Social Union took effect on 1 July 1990, there was only one banking system in the two German states. The post-war history of the German banking industry, 45 years after the end of the war, had thus come to a close.

References

Abeken, G. (1955), *Das Geld- und Bankenwesen in der sowjetischen Besatzungszone und im Sowjetsektor Berlins von 1945 bis 1954*, Bonn: Deutscher Bundes-Verlag.

Boelcke, W. A. (1992), 'Die Finanzpolitik des Dritten Reiches. Eine Darstellung in Grundzügen', in Bracher, K. D., Funke, M., Jacobsen, H.-A. (eds) (1992), *Deutschland 1933–1945. Neue Studien zur nationalsozialistischen Herrschaft*, Düsseldorf: Droste.

Buchheim, C. (1988), 'Die Währungsreform 1948 in Westdeutschland', *Vierteljahrshefte für Zeitgeschichte*, 2, 36, pp. 189–231.

Buchheim, C. (1998), 'Die Errichtung der Bank deutscher Länder und die Währungsreform in Westdeutschland', in Deutsche Bundesbank (ed.), *Fünfzig Jahre Deutsche Mark. Notenbank und Währung in Deutschland seit 1948*, Munich: C. H. Beck, pp. 91–138.

Buchheim, C. (2001), 'Die Unabhängigkeit der Bundesbank. Folge eines amerikanischen Oktrois?', *Vierteljahrshefte für Zeitgeschichte*, 1, 49, pp. 1–30.

Deckers, J. (1974), *Die Transformation des Bankensystems in der Sowjetischen Besatzungszone/DDR von 1945 bis 1952*, Berlin: Duncker & Humblot.

Ermer, M. (2000), *Von der Reichswährung zur Deutschen Mark der Deutschen Notenbank. Zum Binnenwährungstausch in der Sowjetische Besatzungszone Deutschlands (Juni/Juli 1948)*, Stuttgart: Franz Steiner.

Frenzel, P. (1989), *Die rote Mark. Perestroika für die DDR*, Herford: Busse & Seewald.

FRUS (Foreign Relations of the United States) (1972), *The Conference at Quebec, 1944*, Washington DC: FRUS.

Greiner, B. (1995), *Die Morgenthau-Legende: zur Geschichte eines umstrittenen Plans*, Hamburg: Hamburger Edition.

Harries, H. (1998), *Financing the Future. KfW – the German Bank with a Public Mission*, Frankfurt am Main: Fritz Knapp.

Hofmann, W. (ed.) (1949), *Handbuch des gesamten Kreditwesens*, 4th edn, Frankfurt am Main: Fritz Knapp

Holtfrerich, C.-L. (1995), 'The Deutsche Bank 1945–1957: War, Military Rule and Reconstruction', *The Deutsche Bank 1870–1995*, London: Weidenfeld & Nicolson, pp. 357–521.

Horstmann, T. (1986), 'Der OMGUS-Bericht über die Ermittlungen gegen die Deutsche Bank – zur Edition eines Dokuments der deutschen Bankengeschichte', *Bankhistorisches Archiv*, 1, 12, pp. 39–44.

Horstmann, T. (1991), *Die Alliierten und die deutschen Großbanken. Bankenpolitik nach dem Zweiten Weltkrieg in Westdeutschland*, Bonn: Bouvier.

Köhler, H. (1986), 'Längst widerlegte Beschuldigungen. Der OMGUS-Report hat lediglich für die Beurteilung der Besatzungszeit Quellenwert', *Die Zeit*, 28 February 1986.

Kopper, C. (1995), *Zwischen Marktwirtschaft und Dirigismus. Bankenpolitik im 'Dritten Reich' 1933–1945*, Bonn: Bouvier.

Möller, H. (1976), 'Die westdeutsche Währungsreform', in Deutsche Bundesbank (ed.), *Währung und Wirtschaft in Deutschland 1876–1975*, Frankfurt am Main: Fritz Knapp, pp. 433–83.

Mura, J. (1982), 'Zur Geschichte des Sparkassenwesens in der DDR seit 1945', *Bankhistorisches Archiv*, 1, 8, pp. 3–21.

OMGUS (Office of Military Government for Germany, United States) (1985), *Ermittlungen gegen die Deutsche Bank*, Nördlingen: Franz Greno.

OMGUS (1986), *Ermittlungen gegen die Dresdner Bank*, Nördlingen: Franz Greno.

Pohl, M. (1973), *Wiederaufbau. Kunst und Technik der Finanzierung 1947–1953. Die ersten Jahre der Kreditanstalt für Wiederaufbau*, Frankfurt am Main: Fritz Knapp.

Scholtyseck, J. (2000), 'Die USA. vs. "The Big Six". Der gescheiterte Bankenprozeß nach dem Zweiten Weltkrieg', *Bankhistorisches Archiv*, 1 (26), pp. 27–53.

Schwarzer, O. (1999), *Sozialistische Zentralplanwirtschaft in der SBZ/DDR. Ergebnisse eines ordnungspolitischen Experiments (1945–1989)*, Stuttgart: Franz Steiner.

Simpson, C. (ed.) (2001), *The War Crimes of the Deutsche Bank and the Dresdner Bank. The OMGUS Report*, New York: Holmes & Meier.

Thieme, H. J. (1998), 'Notenbank und Währung in der DDR', in Deutsche Bundesbank (ed.), *Fünfzig Jahre Deutsche Mark. Notenbank und Währung in Deutschland seit 1948*, Munich: C. H. Beck.

Wandel, E. (1980), *Die Entstehung der Bank deutscher Länder und die deutsche Währungsreform 1948. Die Rekonstruktion des westdeutschen Geld- und Währungssystems 1945–1949 unter Berücksichtigung der amerikanischen Besatzungspolitik*, Frankfurt am Main: Fritz Knapp.

Wandel, E. (1987), 'Der OMGUS-Bericht über die Ermittlung gegen die Deutsche Bank', *Bankhistorisches Archiv*, 1, 13, pp. 51–6.

Weber, H. (1957), *Der Bankplatz Berlin*, Cologne: Westdeutscher Verlag.

Wolf, H. (1990), 'Das Ende privater Banktätigkeit in Mitteldeutschland – dargestellt am Beispiel der Commerzbank', *Bankhistorisches Archiv*, 2,16.

Notes

1   On the banking industry in the Soviet zone, see Thieme, 1998, pp. 609–53; Frenzel 1989, pp. 19–29; Deckers, 1974; Abeken, 1955, pp. 61–74, 111–20.

2   Deutsche Bank Historical Archives (HADB), P10991. Report to the Board of Managing Directors of Deutsche Bank in Berlin by Heinrich Otte, 15 June 1945.

3   HADB, P5/311. Letter from Heinrich Otte to Kurt Olte, 29 August 1945.

4   On opposition to Morgenthau, see Greiner, 1995, pp. 162–76.

5   Subsequent to the publication of the German translation of the OMGUS Report on Deutsche Bank, a few reviewers have handled the report and its development history (for example Horstmann, 1986, pp. 39–44. In contrast, others were more critical of the OMGUS Report (Wandel, 1987, pp. 51–6; Köhler, 1986).

6   Not only the personnel, building and inventory had been assumed from the Reichsbank offices, but also its liabilities and assets as well as the drawable claims and reserves of Reichsbank notes. The Coordination Committee of the Land Central Banks in the American and French zones also linked directly to the Reichsbank head office in Speyer (Buchheim, 1998, pp. 106, 108).

CHAPTER 10

New Political Realities and the Post-war Re-establishment of Foreign Banks in East and South-East Asia

Frank H. H. King

Retreat and Return

In 1942, as the Japanese forces moved down the Malayan Peninsula, the bankers packed up their books, loaded their cars, and drove ahead of them into fortress Singapore. There, under siege, they set up mini-offices in their respective main branch buildings, with little sign of which branch or agency was at which counter. After all, their customers had fled with them. And while the soldiers battled, the bankers sat down to put the books in order. Soon they would be in Japanese hands and the Yokohama Specie Bank would be in charge, ready to liquidate the foreign banks but also aware of the importance of the books and prepared to retain and even maintain them.

The banks' experiences were not everywhere the same, although final scenes were similar. In Hong Kong, the Hongkong and Shanghai Banking Corporation (the Hongkong Bank) had been caught with unsigned and unissued banknotes totalling in value the sterling equivalent of over £7 million; these the bank's officers were forced to sign, thus creating the duress issue.[1] Rangoon office moved by train to Mandalay, later to be overrun once more. In Shanghai, there were recriminations in Mercantile Bank as their eccentric manager refused to cooperate. But in all cases the books were up to date. Indeed, during the war, attempts – partially successful – were made to smuggle out the books to enable, for example, Hongkong Bank's emergency London Head Office to reconstitute the accounts.

In the worst years of the 1930s depression, a Hongkong Bank staff member wrote complaining of salary prospects; the chief executive replied negatively, adding that if he really had the interests of shareholders at heart he would sell up the bank and deposit the proceeds at interest in the Post Office Savings Bank. Now with all branches lost east of India, questions again arose as to profitability, even solvency. The Hongkong Bank was unique in having its head office in the East, but the bank's chief executive,

Sir Arthur Morse, his books partially reconstituted, convinced the Treasury that the bank was viable. When China went off silver in 1936, all reserves had been centred in London and were thus available. With exchange banks the focus was on trade finance and consequently the war meant loss of income; assets were less affected. Then standard accounting procedures called for writing down to zero the value of buildings and no book loss would be reflected there.

Meanwhile, planning units, separate for each occupied territory, were established in London, with a membership which included exchange bankers. Fortunately the war ended suddenly and the banking plans, which bankers thought to be mostly without merit, were not implemented. Asian cities did not have to be recaptured street by street with consequent destruction. However Jesselton, capital of British North Borneo, was in ruins due to Australian bombing, the recapture of Manila had devastated the bank's building there, and elsewhere the returning Allies found buildings run-down, mines requiring rehabilitation, and factories unable to operate efficiently.[2] The banks would have an immediate role to play, if they could play it. And with the end of hostilities and with books in place and offices serviceable, the banks were apparently ready to reopen.

Initial Problems

There were formidable obstacles ahead, some financial, many political, even social, and all categories interacting. Overriding all these were the problems of staff. Bankers released from prisoner-of-war camps might walk gallantly to their front doors, demand and receive possession, but they were in no shape to continue. Even taking possession of bank property might be complicated.

In China, the British authorities had given instructions for property owners to await the arrival of Chinese officials, but senior bankers feared complications and took short-cuts. In Peiping (formerly Peking and now Beijing), when the prisoners of war were repatriated, one Hongkong banker, F. J. Knightly, stayed behind. The regional Japanese liaison officer proved to be Viscount H. Kano, an admirer of Churchill and former London manager of the Yokohama Specie Bank. He met all Knightly's demands, even to the extent of supplying coal for heating.

In Vietnam, officers had to return north to Haiphong and Hanoi where the managers requested the assistance of Ho Chi Minh during a personal interview. And, as the offices were repossessed, local staff, except for those who found black market operations (especially in Saigon) more rewarding, came in from their refuge in the country ready to assist. In Iloilo, the Philippines, the former manager's young houseboy, A. I. Rabuco, returned to be offered a position as office boy in the branch itself; later he would became an officer of the bank.

The management priority now turned to repatriation and replacement. London managers argued for the early release of their staff from military service or from government departments. This achieved, the task was one of getting them to the East. A few arrived on the staff of military governors, others reached India and then awaited scarce and diverse transportation to their first post-war assignments. Meanwhile, new junior staff were recruited. But 'juniors' in banking included three young colonels, who, working together in Singapore, were a new experience for an old-time manager! Parallel to this was the weeding-out of senior staff, some for purely health reasons, some because they appeared unprepared for the challenges of the new Far East.

Staff: First Comments

Pervading all post-war staff policy was the constant question of 'local officers'. Before the war any such discussion was dealt with abruptly.[3] The British or American banks argued that their clients chose to bank with them because they were British or American. There were Indian banks, while in Singapore there was the well-established Oversea Chinese Banking Corporation, and in China there were equally sound foreign-style banks. What made the Hongkong Bank different was its British executive staff, supplemented in French Indo-China not by Vietnamese but by Frenchmen recruited through the bank's Lyon agency – these alone could sign for the bank.

The argument against local staff, given the immediate shortage of qualified staff, was inadequate. The issue, even when placed on the 'back-burner', would not go away. Eventually it was recognized that the problem went beyond staff shortages. What was involved was the whole concept of management control based on a common culture, a common training and experience, and personal knowledge by the chief executive of each officer, flawed though that knowledge might be. Thus to break down the barrier to appointment of local officers meant also to challenge the control system. The forcing of the first issue led to the change in the second, making possible the growth and therefore the continued survival of the bank.

Place by Place

The immediate post-war history of the British banks, once an operating staff was in place, depended on the peculiar circumstance of each territory. Hong Kong was exceptional in the political role played by the Hongkong Bank's chief executive, Sir Arthur Morse. For the first time this bank's 'chief manager' was also chairman of the board. This provided the status which enabled the Governor to appoint him to the Colony's Executive Council; his position also led to membership on various business and charitable committees. The leading banker and a governor focused on economic recovery were a formidable team. Their approach may be summed up by quoting the instructions given to a Hongkong Bank officer on his secondment to the position of Exchange Control Officer. Governor Alexander Grantham is reported to have instructed him, 'I know nothing about exchange control. But when faced with a request, if it is good for Hong Kong, say "Yes", if it is not, say, "No!"'

At the other extreme was Japan, then under the control of the Supreme Commander, Allied Powers (SCAP) and with British banking sidelined. Banking for Allied forces in Kure began in 1947. The Yokohama branch was in business by 1948 but Osaka not until 1951. When permission to enter was eventually given, there were staff, physically rehabilitated after years in prisoner-of-war camps, who were still anxious not to serve in Japan.

Return to French and Dutch territories was affected by local political turmoil and/or additional controls which gave advantages, ranging from food rations to exchange control facilities, to French or Dutch overseas banks. In Vietnam, exchange control was operated by a French bank acting for the Bank of France. In the Philippines, there were no particular initial re-establishment problems. Indeed it seemed for a time that the Hongkong Bank might open additional branches, but actual banking operations were complicated by adjustment problems (to be considered below) and by a growing administrative centralization fostered by the implementation of trade controls.

China was a special case. Foreign banks had operated under conditions of extra-territoriality which finally ended in 1943. The Hongkong Bank then obtained a Chinese banking license and opened in Chungking, the wartime capital. Thus when peace came, this bank needed only licences for new branches, if any, but it had to accept national banking regulations and central bank control.

Initial Operations

Nowhere was reopening actually prohibited but operations began cautiously. To former customers, Morse in Hong Kong made small 'start-up' loans without security but based on their past performance. Perhaps more important were the decisions he had made during the war from London, where – sometimes without authorization from the company – he had initiated or at least approved financing of orders for equipment, thus 'jumping the queue' and giving Hong Kong's port and superstructure an early advantage. There were also innovative trade finance initiatives which enabled, for example, Japan and Australia to trade on a bilateral account basis through Hong Kong. Morse financed the import of racing horses into Hong Kong; a racing enthusiast himself, he saw this not only as a boost local morale but also as an economic stimulus.

A New Political Scene

One could argue that the foreign banks had not really understood the political changes which followed the First World War. China, pressured by rival European financial groups or consortiums and crippled by indemnities, had become nationalist and was in constant political revision or revolution. Yet the banks, pressured by bondholder groups, maintained their hopes, sought lending opportunities, and argued for the repayment of their loans as the Powers adjusted the terms under which the Boxer Indemnity (dating from 1901) was to be repaid. By 1937 it was in reality a dead issue, but in the 1940s the Hongkong Bank, among others, continued to press for debt reservicing. It was their duty, perhaps, to do so. The Communist revolution in China, by ending all such dreams, might have been deemed helpful as it forced a focus on new challenges in the context of new political realities.

In executing the old pre-1914 policies, the Hongkong Bank had in 1898 formed with Jardine Matheson the British and Chinese Corporation to focus British development efforts in China. The company, with its subsidiary Chinese Central Railways, existed after 1945. As with the China Consortium itself, however, it was so out of step with reality that it faded away long before the formal corporate dissolution. Indeed, the British and Chinese Corporation had been so long out of action that its presence provided no precedent for post-war bank subsidiaries. Perhaps only Sir Arthur Morse as chief executive, his legal adviser and possibly his London deputy were even aware of this heritage; its dissolution merely removed an irritant.

Thus the foreign banks, once open and tentatively undertaking modest banking business, began to recognize the problems of a new political environment. Even as the remote past dissolved, the initial return to a more recent status quo was soon challenged. In Hong Kong itself, Morse was demanding as late as December 1946 that the British government should issue an unequivocal statement that they intended to retain the territory, despite disruptive attempts by the local Kuomintang (KMT), the Chinese Nationalist Party. In northern Vietnam, the banks had to recognize the authority of local nationalist groups. All colonial rule was challenged, but in British territories at least the expectation was for continuity in financial and banking matters. In the emerging self-governing territories (for example, Singapore), the legislative councils were increasingly elected, but for the remaining functional representation, finance was the last to be localized. In Singapore as late as 1955, the Chartered Bank manager, known derisively as the 'member for the Tanglin Club', oversaw the banking and finance portfolio.[4] 'They have cast me as the last colonial,' he said smilingly of his fellow-legislators, 'and I mean to play the part to the end!' This situation was reinforced by the existence of the Sterling Area controls and through the reality of London-based currency boards.

In China, there could be careful optimism, although waiting for better days was a head office instruction. While the US-sponsored cease-fire and KMT-Communist negotiations held out prospects for a coalition government, the Nationalist Government accepted responsibility for the repayment of Shanghai Municipal and long-term debt obligations while failing, on the grounds of shortage of funds, to actually implement relevant agreements. Meanwhile, serious inflation forced an overworked Shanghai staff to spend a high percentage of their time calculating cost-of-living allowances and locating the physical cash to make payment. Thus the long-term political scene was uncertain but the short term seemed sufficiently encouraging to permit a return to banking. There existed, however, a set of special post-war problems.

Duress Issue and Moratoria

First, there were the consequences of occupation: the wartime debt and moratorium arguments. Secondly, there was the problem of the 'duress' Hong Kong banknotes, which during the war the Japanese had forced officers to sign and the banks to issue in disregard of the regulations and/or 'cover'. Until these problems were settled, the residents of Hong Kong were uncertain of their own currency, and throughout the region businesses were uncertain as to the extent to which payments made during the occupation were recognized and accepted. Consequently, banks did not know their real position. Moreover, the arguments became political. In the Philippines, for example, a legislative moratorium on pre-war debt was legislated entirely biased towards the Philippine debtors; the legislation was vetoed by President Truman but reinstated at the country's independence in 1946. Everywhere settlement was based on negotiation and the uncertainty continued for at least two or three years after the end of the war.

Controls

In this new post-war world, the banks were operating in an environment of economic controls, including commodity trading controls. Thailand's rice trade was financed by British banks against nationalist opposition. Sterling Area controls affected the disposition of dollar earnings from natural rubber sales. French and Dutch colonial trade was more closely monitored, although Anglo-Dutch plantations were financed in part by sterling overdrafts sanctioned by the Bank of England. At another level, trade in gold was subject to International Monetary Fund regulations, although at least one British bank was involved in financing the transit of 'virgin gold' through the Philippines.[5]

From all this Hong Kong felt it must shake free. As an entrepôt its earnings had to be freely disposable. And yet, a Hong Kong without exchange control would have afforded a leak for Sterling Area earnings and become a source of export US dollar income for China, then subject of UN and US embargoes. The solution was for exchange banks to deal only in official exchange, but with an open market developing in parallel permitting the purchase and sale of US dollars with Hong Kong funds so ordered as to prevent any leakage from the Sterling Area. The Open Market was a key factor in the economic development of Hong Kong and one positive example of the impact of government policy on economic development. However, the question of Chinese exports remained. Hong Kong's industrialization was in danger if only because its products were similar to mainland products because its raw materials might derive from there. The solution this time was the 'certificate of origin', another document, another new political consequence impacting on exchange banking.

Impact on Management: Head Office and Branches

These immediate post-war developments created a management problem, forcing a change in approach which would be key to confronting subsequent competition and permitting sound expansion. Sir Arthur Morse's involvement in Hong Kong's public affairs, together with his lack of experience as a foreign exchange dealer, led to a growth of the bank's inspectorate and to a more complex information system. Consequently there was a better informed use of executive power, despite the fact that significant managerial reorganization was not formalized for some twenty more years.

The shortage of funds, which resulted in seeking overdrafts in London, the amounts of which had to be negotiated with and approved by the Bank of England, forced the Hongkong Bank to coordinate the demands of its traditionally independent branch managers. Once defined as a collection of banks with a single capital, the Hongkong Bank had to keep a closer scrutiny on branch operations, again reinforcing the role of those working in what was becoming a true 'head office'. A pre-war chief executive might on occasion reach into a branch and give directions, but after 1945 post-war, this became a standard, although not an entirely accepted activity. Branch managers objected to head office interference, but the erosion of control through personal knowledge and relationships, once an inspectorate was involved, prepared the bank subsequently to monitor and control staff, including those who had not been brought up in the service.

Role of Foreign Banks

Although the sudden ending of the Second World War had avoided the anticipated destruction of Asian cities, the superstructure was nevertheless in decay. And although priority was given to restoration, especially the production of primary commodities important in international trade, there was realization that nothing long-term could be safely implemented without some degree of planning and without some serious capital investment. The exchange banks had long been criticized as being uninterested in 'economic development' as opposed to 'trade finance'. The latter might include advances to planters and infrastructure closely related to trade but the exchange banks were seen as being on the periphery.

These criticisms, renewed in the context of the need for development finance, placed the foreign or exchange banks under political pressure just at the time when lack of funds limited their ability even to finance the rehabilitation of, for example, long-term mining customers in the Philippines. In consequence, the exchange banks were on the defensive as being 'foreign' and ultimately they suffered discriminatory legislation while local 'modern-style' banks were encouraged.

Branches

With drawing on London controlled, an obvious additional source of funds could be found by the garnering of local savings through the establishment of a network of small branches. In the 1930s, a Chartered Bank manager accompanied K. P. Chen of the Shanghai Commercial Bank into the Chinese countryside and observed the attempts to make small farmers 'banking conscious'. He also observed that this personal approach was not possible for foreign banks, at least not while they were obviously and peculiarly 'foreign'. Post-war staff were insufficient for a major increase in branches, and, indeed, such a policy had little management support. Funds could be bought in, relying on the branch network of local banks and 'native-style' banks, at least until such funds became expensive and the market competitive.

But by the time this occurred, the foreign banks found themselves restricted with their branch networks, if existing, frozen in place. Thus even where the exchange banks, as in Malaya, had a geographically diverse network based on pre-war trade finance requirements, these were not always the optimum locations for general banking operations. To the extent that branches were viable only because they were the government's bankers, political changes would undermine this 'monopoly'.

Post-war branch banking history is a combination of rationalization and expansion depending on changes in the economy and banking consciousness of the local population, management policy and government controls. In the Philippines, for example, the Hongkong Bank had a main office in Manila, which needed relocating as the old financial centre shifted to the Makati district, and a branch in Iloilo, a port town no longer viable as such. In the latter case, trade finance could be handled in Manila since the port had silted up and a move to another out-port seemed appropriate. However, a large number of former US employees, civil and military, were receiving social security checks; the Hongkong Bank was prepared to handle them, providing a service and encouraging the deposit of funds which were needed in Manila.

In Thailand, on the contrary, foreign banks were restricted to Bangkok where even local branches were frozen. A request to change the location of main office was permitted only if it were done, in effect, overnight, closing in one location and opening in another the following day.

In China, the banks had problems re-staffing existing branches, but a decision was made and permission granted to open in the capital, Nanking (Nanjing), although without much expectation of success. The move was political. At the same time the branch in Chungking, the wartime capital, had lost its function and was closed.

In Hong Kong, there was no restriction to branch banking. There was, however, the view that major customers would insist on retaining their accounts in the Head Office branch and that, therefore, other offices would not be viable. The changes in the economy forced by China's civil war and by the business activities of 'refugee' capitalists provoked a change of attitude, and a major branch in Kowloon, the focus of new industrial activity, proved to be effective. Nevertheless, there was still no proliferation, although the pressure for change was overwhelming.

If banks were short of funds after 1945, so were the colonial-type governments as they faced the costly task of rehabilitation. In British Borneo, one territory, British North Borneo, had been governed by a private company, and another, Sarawak, by a 'White Rajah'. Both became British Crown Colonies. The third territory, the Sultanate of Brunei, had oil. Development-minded governors encouraged banking, and both the Hongkong Bank and the Chartered Bank entered successfully into a highly competitive drive to establish branches in the principal trading locations. In the process they became involved in the finance of tobacco products exported from Borneo and then smuggled into the southern Philippines, where Americans were known as 'blue seals'.

Political Change, Second Series

One could summarize foreign banking in the period from 1945 to 1950 as one of limited post-war readjustment, limited in the sense that banking attitudes, although subject to new economic and political forces, remained essentially pre-war but with the immediate problems created by the Japanese occupation mostly resolved. At this point a new set of political factors were either introduced or became relatively more significant in their impact. These may be described simply as 'nationalism' in its several forms.

In 1949, the Communist Party of China established a new government, the People's Republic, and foreign banks were subject to the minute scrutiny of regulators and courts, especially in the field of personnel. One consequence was that the banks were prevented from destroying any documents, archives were thus preserved and, in the case of the Hongkong Bank, were eventually, in the mid-1980s, allowed to be removed to Hong Kong and so to London.

The policies of the new government forced the banks to retain expensive staff, both local and foreign, even as income fell, requiring the transfer of foreign exchange into China – until the banks made clear there were limits to be applied in the immediate future, with foreign staff as potential hostages. The ability to close branches was subject to local officials and to local relations, isolating foreign staff for periods of several years. Although much of the China business moved to Hong Kong where foreign banks dealt with the local branch of the Bank of China, China remained a drain on resources and policy wavered between seeking to close down completely and retaining at least one office to hope for better days. The Chinese government in fact held the trump cards, in permitting the physical presence of a minimal foreign staff. For many banks one office, in Shanghai, remained open (at least until the Cultural Revolution when at one point only one foreign banker remained at liberty).

This final solution was not achieved without drawn-out negotiations, especially in regard to US dollar holdings of the Chinese banks. The Hongkong Bank's 'all for all' settlement included the loss of all their buildings, valued on the books at zero, for all *non-dollar* claims. From this nadir, foreign banks would recover with a change, during the early 1980s and beyond, of both political and economic policy.

In Japan, the participation of the banks in economic recovery, once SCAP policy had changed, was limited by their lack of adequate funds. Foreign banks presumably were aware of pre-war Japanese banking policies and had, in any case, determined that priority should be given to a balanced participation in South-East Asian finance, with a focus on Hong Kong. Despite pleas from their managers in Japan, the banks did not attempt the impossible. Once the Japanese banking system had been rehabilitated, the foreign banks continued for a time to supplement this system while it was being re-established and recognized overseas.

In Vietnam, business in the north was virtually at a standstill and the atmosphere had become hostile. Managers in Hanoi and Haiphong were advised in 1953 that, if the worst came to the worst, they should close down and leave – with as many business records as possible. In anticipation they sent daily records of current accounts and other key transactions to Saigon. Evacuation was not immediate, and in 1954 Head Office was writing to the effect that if the bank could do business in Hanoi, then it should stay and do it while being prepared to leave both Hanoi and Haiphong.

Elsewhere the Dutch had been unsuccessful in their attempt to re-establish themselves as effective rulers of the East Indies, and the Indonesian authorities soon became involved in a policy first of nationalization and then of '*confrontasi*' with the Federation of Malaya and with Singapore. In the immediate post-war period, the Dutch had been the problem. The

Hongkong Bank demanded equality of treatment with Dutch banks, a reasonable margin of profit and the ability to remit profits. Although the bank had made no profit in Java since 1926, by 1951 the Jakarta and Surabaya offices were showing a small net profit despite increasingly stringent bureaucratic controls. In 1953, the Java Bank was nationalized by the Indonesian authorities; in 1955, all agreements with the Netherlands were abrogated; in 1957, all Dutch citizens were expelled and their businesses taken over; and in 1960 came an end to diplomatic relations. Although these measures were directed chiefly at Dutch interests, the mood was for control, and it was anti-foreign. In 1958, the Hongkong Bank closed its Surabaya Office and, with *confrontasi* in 1963, all foreign banks began a withdrawal. After the 1965 *coup d'état*, the Hongkong Bank applied to reopen and by 1968 foreign banks were once again operating in Jakarta.

Nationalism: The Continuing Impact

If there were not everywhere revolution or *coups d'état*, the realities of nationalism were only too apparent, but it was not clear how exactly to respond. Often banking policies changed before the impact was acknowledged or became part of the 'culture' of the corporation. In pre-war times, the foreign exchange banks had made loans to businesses not directly connected with foreign trade, but these formed no part of general policy; they were *ad hoc* uses of locally garnered funds. Nor was the post-war staff trained to participate in industrial lending. And now there was both pressure to prove they 'belonged' and measures designed to insure that they did not.

In the first category were normal central banking controls impacting on the bank in the particular country only. Pre-war India and Japan had had central banks; there was the Central Bank of China, while elsewhere the exchange banks on occasion played public roles. After the war not every country founded a central bank. Singapore and Hong Kong held out, partly because the financial system could be regulated through a monetary authority incorporating the role of the colonial monetary boards or other official exchange mechanisms and partly because of the cost.[6] In Hong Kong, the Hongkong Bank, as the government's banker, had perforce undertaken quasi-central bank functions, while denying any responsibility other than that of a private corporation and a bank reporting to shareholders and constituents. The exchange banks, which before the war had been regulated by the terms of their charters and/or colonial supervision, now faced local control by newly established governments.

As an example, liquidity ratios and capital adequacy regulations were based on assets and liabilities within the particular country.[7] In meeting these requirements, the banks benefited from their policy of having written down property values to zero. Sitting on prime real estate (as the banks usually were), a realistic revaluation of these properties was often sufficient to meet central bank requirements. Then too, if the banks were not prepared to make investments on their own account, they could and did contribute to various development or agricultural banking schemes, including participation in World Bank loans.

Even such local enthusiasm was to prove insufficient in Burma. Briefly, pre-war Burma had no domestic banks, only the foreign exchange banks and the chettiars.[8] After 1945, the number of foreign firms dwindled in consequence of Burmese economic policies. Foreign banks were unwilling to base any expansion on the expectations of local businesses; given also the increasing chaos caused by nationalisation of land, neither were they willing to take up the opportunity in agricultural finance, a consequence of the forced departure of the chettiars. In this latter case, the government attempted provision of agricultural credit but had proved incompetent in managing its complexities. The Hongkong Bank complained that there was no suitable business, that the costs of opening were great, and that the Burmese had no banking tradition or experience. However, Burma appeared ready for economic development and by 1960, the Hongkong Bank, which had previously focused on the finance of the international rice trade, indicated support for an industrial bank. Burma's leaders had long expressed their hopes of existing without foreign banks, but held off the day. In 1963, the new military government took over the foreign banks and ended their participation in an increasingly controlled but potentially rich economy.

Restrictions

While newly independent governments complained about the foreign banks' lack of 'belonging', they passed measures hampering development of their business. These measures included exchange control, which limited access to foreign exchange free markets and limited the remission of profits – not surprising given the commonly held view that these banks were draining the country, exploiting the territory's resources and transferring the profits overseas. As already noted, branch banking was either restricted or forbidden. Finally, and perhaps the most serious (in Sri Lanka for example), was the prohibition against foreign banks accepting any new local accounts, coupled with pressure on new foreign enterprises to bank with a local institution.

One could argue that none of this was new. Canada in the late nineteenth century had objected to the overseas origins of the Bank of British North America. Australia closed its doors to new foreign-headquartered banks as soon as it was politically competent to do so – the Chartered Bank of India, Australia and China, never reached Australia and operated under restrictions in India. The East India Company had for a time successfully controlled the establishment of banks with overseas head offices; subsequent Indian governments would limit the business of such banks. Japan had sponsored the Yokohama Specie Bank to counter the influence of the foreign exchange banks, their apparent ultimate triumph being their role in the 'liquidation' of those institutions in Japanese-occupied Asia – 'apparent' because many of their experienced managers were sceptical. China, bound by the restrictions of the Treaty System and extra-territoriality, had countered by developing their own modern banking system, producing bankers of international repute. But the feeling, however varied in its expression, that the banking system should somehow 'belong' and be answerable locally was general.

Resolution

One solution to this conflict of view was, interestingly, to return to the concept of a foreign international bank being a collection of banks operating with a single capital, or, as an important variation, with a shared capital. In the simplest case, the branch, although but a branch, was a complete bank, its local actions under effective local control. Or, in more complex cases, the bank branch became locally incorporated, and – developing still further – locally incorporated with a majority of shares, directors, and so on, being local. In return for this, such a locally incorporated bank would be freed from the restrictions pertaining to a foreign bank. When in the mid-1950s the Hongkong Bank decided to follow its Hong Kong customers to the US, it could effectively do so only by establishing its own wholly-owned subsidiary, at first clumsily named 'The Hongkong and Shanghai Banking Corporation of California, Inc.' (or 'ink' for short).

These major changes developed over time. Their origins, nevertheless, can be found in fundamental concepts of national sovereignty which were so important to the newly independent countries of South-East Asia in the immediate post-war period.

Consequences

In considering the impact of these post-war measures, one should distinguish between the earlier legislation designed to assert independence and to avoid being subject to what many nationalists saw as 'neo-colonialism', and measures taken subsequently designed to assert normal controls on increasingly complex economies and financial systems, as for example, central banking in the Federation of Malaysia. Indeed, as foreign banks were seen as contributors to development plans, their association with colonialism was 'forgotten'. And the banks themselves, their staff, their corporate culture and their resources were themselves changing beyond recognition. As one retired staff member commented, 'Sadly I cannot even *understand* today's published balance sheet.' Another, on visiting the bank's new Hong Kong head office, toured the executive floor and turning to the chairman's office messenger, an elderly Chinese, said, 'Back in the 1930s, Tom, you and I, just the two of us, did all this together.'

The continued political pressures on foreign banks in East and South-East Asia encouraged a series of changes, an evolution, the relative success of which would eventually determine survival. Total flexibility was required, nowhere more obviously than in the area of staff. There remained, however, an element of chance. Banks whose principal business was in high-tax countries found significant expansion impossible; the Hongkong Bank had an ideal, friendly base from which to survey the changing scene and to determine its strategy insulated from immediate crisis. In its home base, moreover, control was minimal and entry dependent upon nationality. Exceptionally, when Chase Bank ceased its Hong Kong operations in 1949, concerned with the territory's future in view of the advance of the People's Liberation Army, the governor made clear they would never be permitted to re-enter. And they did not – until they bought a Dutch overseas bank with a Hong Kong licence.

The End of the Compradore, Staff Reforms, and Their Impact

The specific policies undertaken in reaction to political crises depend upon the bank's staff, the members of which obviously change over time. To complete this survey of banks in war recovery, rehabilitation, revolution, neo-colonialism, and sometimes radical nationalism, we should consider the evolution of staff policy and the consequent changes in management.

As the Second World War began the bank staff was divided into three components: (i) the expatriate officers or 'European staff', (ii) the clerical grades, Portuguese, and Burghers (local employees other than Chinese), who handled the 'books', and (iii) the Compradore's or chief shroff's staff who dealt with cash and routine office operations. After the war these categories were reinstituted, but already there were cracks, and political pressures would soon make the distinctions untenable. What were those pressures and how did the banks, or indeed foreign business firms in general, react?

Strikes and Profits

As usual, it was a combination of factors which disrupted early post-war staff relations. Even bank managers, who above all others should understand the consequences of inflation, were unable to adjust to the full impact of the inflation which war shortages had created. A Hongkong Bank officer, newly returned to Shanghai, was arguing heatedly with his rickshaw coolie over the fare; a passer-by had to assure him that the fare was reasonable. Pre-war Treaty Port residents then in North America and Europe wrote demanding the balance of their accounts, only to be told that, although unchanged since 1938, their balances were now inadequate to purchase the postage stamp required.

More important, returning managers, with their eyes on branch profits, had difficulty accepting the need to adjust salaries for local staff. This, combined with local political developments, virtually invited politically directed unions to initiate strikes. The foreign staff were not specialists, they were generalists; there was no task in the branch which they could not perform. They were consequently capable of keeping the branch open – for a time. Indeed, in Japan foreign staff were flown in from Hong Kong, secreted in hotels, and brought work by circuitous routes from the branch. This could not be sustained; local opinion had to be considered and staff demands at least partially accepted. In Singapore and Sri Lanka, for example, it was irrelevant that the demands on banks were part of a broader leftist movement; if the banks wished to undertake business, they had to make reasonable concessions. There were even directives from Head Office, another break in the autonomy of the branch manager. The major political battle had to be fought elsewhere. The staff, loyal during the war and returning voluntarily to help reopen, could no longer be taken for granted.

Diaspora

Portugal, in that nation's withdrawal from Asia, had left behind communities which were Portuguese and Catholic in their culture.[9] Similarly the Dutch survived in Sri Lanka as 'Burghers'. The former could be found in

Macau, Malacca and Singapore. From Macau they were early in settling in Hong Kong. From there they migrated to all the main Treaty Ports, where they retained their distinctive communal role. When the Hongkong Bank was established in Hong Kong, in 1865, the first employees came from the foreign-settled port cities, the Treaty Ports of China and they included Portuguese. However, without a trace of documentation explaining policy, the banks passed over their Portuguese employees, despite earlier management assurances that all would be treated equally. With the coming of juniors trained in the London office, *de facto* a separate 'class' was established. There were a few locally employed 'Europeans' such as building engineers but the eventual personnel policy became clear: only staff hired through London and trained there for the East would be officers of the corporation.

The post-war rise of local nationalism was not aimed at the 'European' alone, but, in varying degrees, at all non-indigenous residents. Thus the chettiars were driven from Burma, and the pressure on the Portuguese, except in Macau and Hong Kong, was such that many, including Burghers, emigrated to Australia and North America. This exodus encouraged a similar movement from Hong Kong. In consequence, by the middle of the 1950s, although Portuguese remained in Hong Kong itself, the population dwindled and made recruitment of career bookkeepers, employees without prospects, increasingly difficult. This, in turn, put pressure on the three-tier system and called, *inter alia*, for a review of the Chinese role in the corporation.

The Compradore and the 'System'

The key figure was the 'compradore' who, some would argue, ran a bank within a bank.[10] The compradore and his shroffs (note the mixture of Portuguese and Anglo-Indian heritage) were responsible for the cash, its receipt, disbursement and safety. But their role extended in two directions: (i) they were responsible for the Chinese staff, who were either vetted by them or were actually their employees, and (ii) they were responsible for contacts with the local business world, including the introduction and guaranteeing of local customers. The compradore was, then, an important figure in the business community, either in his own right or because he was related to and sponsored by someone who was.

One consequence was that the compradore was seen by nationalists as a 'running dog of imperialism', to use one phrase, and after the war the compradoric system became untenable, especially after the establishment of the People's Republic of China and of other sovereign regimes. For political reasons, therefore, bank chief executives were under pressure to find an alternative. This political pressure ran parallel to business pressure which could no longer be neglected. The very strength of the compradore, his entree to the local business world, was significant only in those cases in which there was but one dominant community in the local scene. In Hong Kong, however, the important Shanghai Chinese community, members of which had personally dealt with bank officers, became important economically in the territory. And the Hong Kong compradore had little intimate knowledge of their business.

The departure of the Portuguese blurred the distinction between the roles of the two communities in foreign business and banking houses, and the Chinese employees needed to be directly responsible individually, able to accept assignments by the foreign management. At the same time the compradore's role was seen as a political hindrance and cultural anachronism. At a practical level it followed that, since the compradore was in many instances paid by commission on business introduced, he could not be retained to perform just some arbitrary part of his role. He himself had to be transformed into a Chinese Manager, directly employed as an employee by and of the company. And this occurred at just the time that other political pressures were forcing a reconsideration of the 'London trained only' officer policy, thus making the change one part of a package which was to form the basis of a new attitude and of new personnel policies in foreign-owned businesses.

By the late 1950s, 'Juniors' new to the East must have wondered how the compradoric system could ever have operated. In additional to economic and political considerations no longer existing, the system reflected the total social separation of the Chinese and foreign communities. Despite historically interesting exceptions, the two communities did not have contacts with one another (the guest book of the Shanghai manager in the early twentieth century did not contain any Chinese names). After 1945, the social situation had changed. Wartime experiences, including intermarriage, had made possible intercommunication. The Chinese were seen more often attending foreign-style social occasions, they spoke English or French, they were capable of dealing directly with the foreign manager. It was, in brief, another world.[11]

Dissatisfaction, Head Office, and Policy: Foreign Staff

Executive staff dissatisfaction immediately following the Second World War was provoked, for example, by regulations against bringing one's wife out East (due to lack of facilities but after years of separation), unsatisfactory working conditions and assignments without regard to wartime experiences (assignment, for example, of a one-time prisoner of war to Japan or to the Dutch East Indies), inadequate provisions to improve housing, and assignment to routine work after important wartime responsibilities. Given the complexity of actual bank/finance-related problems, it is hardly surprising that personnel problems could not be immediately remedied. Lack of resources and shortage of qualified officers with the requisite health and ability forced arbitrary assignments, barely tolerated for a time.

There was still a sense of 'service' and 'life-time career' which gave management breathing space, but the concept of service in the Empire or the romance of service east of Suez had lost much of its self-apparent allure. Management had to tread more carefully. There was, however, an apparently unrelated development which had a significant impact – the improvement and the practicality of air travel. Previously, chief executives could visit outports only if the ship bearing them on home leave called at the relevant port, or managers en route to northern offices, Shanghai, Kobe, and so on could call in at Hong Kong. With air travel the chief manager could visit – and so could his wife.

The chief executives, visits were intended for banking discussions as usually defined, but, with the first lady along, the inspection might move to areas of peripheral concern. Wives with problems now had a willing ear. Thus, management in Hong Kong was directly aware of the 'limits' which managers enjoyed but also their household accounts and circumstances, a situation unheard of before the war. The beginning of specific controls would make possible – the cynic might say 'inevitable' – the formalization of controls over the whole range of branch activities.

Local Officers, Control, and Corporate Development

The breakdown of the branch manager's absolute control had a further impact. Foreign staff were still recruited in London and acculturated during months or at times years of socialization in the London office and in the sports club in Beckenham. When in the 1950s local officers were appointed, they went to London for training and for acculturation. Those that had the experience remembered it more for the camaraderie than for the technical banking training, for London itself was changing. But this was important, at least for the first career local officers. A liberal attitude in 1953 could be stated thus: while there was no reason why one could not have a junior local officer, when the big customer arrived from overseas, he expected to find an American behind the desk in the manager's office.[12] Subsequently the overseas visitor might not find a 'European' behind the manager's desk, but he soon learned that, in dealing with the London-trained local officer, he could act and talk as if there were.

Even this reform, convoluted as it was, could not continue. It had gone only part way. 'Knowing each other', 'playing sports together' were no longer an assurance of banking control once back in Asia. This was compounded by the Hongkong Bank's acquisition of the Mercantile Bank, whose officers were equally loyal but to a different chief and with different assumptions. Now the tentative measures of control found their rationale and were consolidated, providing a sounder base for the corporation's expansion.

The Mercantile Bank had recruited three Indian officers before the war and imbued them with the concept of 'British banking'. But this was an experiment. The Hongkong Bank's post-war efforts in India revealed a surprising problem. The new officer-recruits were too anxious to direct; they were unwilling to undertake the years of apprenticeship which the foreign staff had experienced. The foreign firms had to start again.

Management's reluctance to introduce local officers was the consequence of a conflicting self-image. On the one hand, they proudly claimed to be part of the local community while on the other, they saw their role as being 'British' or 'French' or 'American'. On this basis, local recruitment, which would be without prospects, would consequently be difficult. Besides, Chinese banks gave New Year bonuses; foreign banks did not. Another factor was the danger of a local officer being involved with dishonest local interests, something always mentioned quietly but never tested. It was part of the 'gentlemen's club' concept of control.

The practical and political pressures continued, however, until governments placed quotas on the number of foreign staff able to obtain a work permit. They made it unpleasant by, in some instances, preventing wives from having ancillary employment, even at the volunteer level. This is ironic; pre-war wives would not have considered employment. The practical pressure was partly the cost of the foreign employee and partly the growth of business.

The Success of Localization

The barriers to employing local officers broke down but over a period of some twenty years. If the process had not been a slow one, the political pressures of governments would have been destructive, but banks were reaching the same conclusions as governments.

The first stage was permitting a local employee to sign for the bank in those matters for which he had previously only initialled. Illustrative was the 1954 experience of a young Hong Kong University graduate, the first to be employed as a junior executive by the Dutch company Royal Interocean Lines. His assignment, usually the task of a young Dutchman, was to carry the ship's instructions out to a ship anchored in mid-stream and deliver them personally to the captain. Received courteously, he noted that the captain kept looking over his shoulder, waiting for the expected 'European'. Quietly the Hong Kong Chinese told him, 'I am all there will be, Captain!'

The second stage was the assignment of tasks previously only undertaken by 'foreign staff'. Third came independent assignments, and the first female branch manager made local headlines. By this time the overseas customer had become prepared, as his culture too had changed. Then perhaps twenty years ago, the fight was over. Even though the *Financial Times* complained that the Hongkong Bank still served curry tiffin on Thursdays, the banks were no longer 'colonial'. They had really become in attitude as well as by definition, multinational.

The Specialist

This summary has so far omitted consideration of the change in the expertise of the officer staff. Prior to the Second World War, officers employed in foreign exchange banks were generalists. Not all may have been generally qualified, but they were supposed to be. Assignments too often in the same category, for example, current accounts, might create a 'specialist', but it was the consequence of a defect in posting which would adversely affect the officer's career. Officers of mediocre ability could eventually be given responsibility in a small agency, with major decisions made in the home branch. After 1945, with work-visa quotas, there could be no foreigner in a minor post; recruitment and expectations had to change. Exceptionally, there had been two or three officers before the war who trained themselves to handle the major China loans, but they had no successors. They had been replaced by 'political advisers' seconded from the consular service.

Once again post-war political and social pressures, supplementing changes in the technology and scope of banking, forced the introduction of change. The complexities of international law and their impact on such key legal problems as 'plunder' and debt adjustment required a specialist. There would be others in insurance, in the first subsidiary companies, the trustee and nominee companies, and, with the coming of new sovereignties, in a separate company for each jurisdiction. Then there was a pause as a pre-war pattern attempted to meet the challenges of new banking and new technology. Once again the pioneers in each bank would be generalists volunteering to learn a speciality. Their successors would be newly recruited specialists, at first perhaps regarded with suspicion, but the tasks had become careers in themselves (even in archives, a qualified career archivist might replace a banker graduating from a crash course). For this major development to occur the pre-war attitude of 'they did not really belong' had to change. Integration was made easier by the broader scope of the 'officer' category and by the recognition that the role of the generalist was, rightly or wrongly, under question, if not attack.

Yet the evolution of the regionally oriented 'colonial' or foreign exchange bank into a financial multinational group of revolutionary complexity has been possible – at least in part – as a consequence of policy reaction to war-time and post-war crises, of the new political pressures which followed the end of colonialism, and of the rise of new nation states in South-East Asia and in regenerated nations to the north and northeast. 'Forced into success' might be an apt conclusion.

References

Ceylon, Government of (1934), *Report of the Ceylon Banking Commission* (1934 Sessional Paper XXII), Colombo.

Cleveland, H. van B. and Huertas, T. F. (1985), *Citibank, 1812–1970*, New York: Harvard University Press.

Green, E. and Kinsey, S. (1999), *The Paradise Bank, The Mercantile Bank of India, 1893–1984*, Aldershot: Ashgate.

Jao, Y. C. (1974), *Banking and Currency in Hong Kong, a Study of Postwar Financial Development*, London: Macmillan.

Jao, Y. C. and King, F. H. H. (1990), *Money in Hong Kong: Historical Perspective and Contemporary Analysis*, Hong Kong: Centre of Asian Studies, University of Hong Kong.

King, F. H. H. (1955), *Money in British East Asia, Colonial Research Publications*, 19, London: Her Majesty's Stationery Office.

King, F. H. H. (1979), 'The Hong Kong open market, 1954', in King, F. H. H. (ed.), *Asian Policy, History and Development: Collected Essays*, Hong Kong: Centre of Asian Studies, University of Hong Kong.

King, F. H. H. (ed.) (1983), *Eastern Banking: Essays in the History of The Hongkong and Shanghai Banking Corporation*, London: Athlone Press.

King, F. H. H. (1987–91), *The History of The Hongkong and Shanghai Banking Corporation*, 4 vols, Cambridge: Cambridge University Press.

King, F. H. H. (1990), 'Structural alternatives and constraints in the evolution of exchange banking', in Jones, G. (ed.), *Banks as Multinationals*, London: Routledge.

King, F. H. H. (1996), 'Does the corporation's history matter? Hongkong Bank/HSBC Holdings, a case study', in Godley, A. and Westall, O. M. (eds), *Business History and Business Culture*, Manchester: Manchester University Press, pp. 116–37.

King, F. H. H. (1998), '"Eastwards of the Cape of Good Hope": British Overseas Banking on the Pacific Rim, 1836–1870', in Miller, S. et al. (eds), *Studies in the Economic History of the Pacific Rim*, London: Routledge, pp. 121–54.

King, F. H. H. (2000), 'The transmission of corporate cultures: International Officers in the HSBC Group', in Latham, A. J. H. and Kawakatsu, H. (eds), *Asia Pacific Dynamism, 1550–2000*, London: Routledge, pp. 245–64.

Leiper, G. A. (1982), *A Yen for my Thoughts*, Hong Kong.

Mackenzie, C. (1954), *Realms of Silver*, London: Routledge & Kegan Paul.

Marshall, J. F. (1986), *Whereon the Wild Thyme Blows: Some Memoirs of Service with the Hongkong Bank*, Grayshott, Surrey: Token Publishing.

Standard Chartered Bank (1980), *Standard Chartered Bank: a Story Brought up to Date*, London: Standard Chartered Bank.

Thomas, W. H. Evans (1952), *Vanished China*, London: Thorsons.

Tomkins, H. J. (1962), *Report on the Hong Kong Banking System and Recommendations for the Replacement of the Banking Ordinance, 1948*, Hong Kong.

Tytler, B. (1979), *Here, There, and (Nearly) Everywhere*, London: Weidenfeld and Nicolson.

Notes

1   The duress issue is properly defined to include notes legally signed but unissued. The Chartered Bank transferred its notes to the Manager's residence before discovering that notes are hard to burn. Their problem was solved when Japanese artillery scored a direct hit on the storage area. (When referring to the

    territory, the spelling is 'Hong Kong', when to the bank it is 'Hongkong'. Reference to a single bank without name is, unless the context suggests otherwise, The Hongkong and Shanghai Banking Corporation.)

2   British North Borneo is now the State of Sabah, Federation of Malaysia. Sarawak is another such state.

3   An exception was the Mercantile Bank of India, which recruited at least three Indian officers with success.

4   The Tanglin Club was the exclusive 'European only' social club in Singapore. It survives today much reformed and Singaporean.

5   IMF regulations did not exclude trade in religious objects made of gold. Images of the Virgin Mary might be traded despite their solid gold content.

6   Central bank staff tended to be paid on a higher than civil service scale, and they tended to multiply.

7   Pre-war the Hongkong Bank had on occasion to reassure a foreign authority that *all* the assets of the bank, not simply those on the books of the local branch, were available in case of a local crisis. Post-war more than a letter from Head Office was required. The Philippines provides a case study.

8   Chettiar ('chetty'): a South Indian caste of 'native' banker found also in Ceylon, the Straits Settlements and Burma.

9   In Malacca's Portuguese settlement (racially Malay, culturally Catholic), the parish priest still came from Portugal, at least until the 1950s.

10   The terms under which a compradore operated varied significantly from port to port. If there are essentials however, they would probably be that the compradore had a range of independence beyond his position as compradore, could not use the company's regular 'chop', and was to some degree accountable for the local staff. In Japan the compradore was referred to as *banto*, in India as 'cashier *babu*', in Ceylon as 'guarantee shroff'.

11   The Goethe Institute was making every effort to add German to the list of languages.

12   The specific expression of this attitude was in fact that of the Singapore manager of the (American) National City Bank (now Citibank). Some thirty years later, Chase decided on the best of three worlds, appointing a Chinese-American female manager for their Hong Kong operations; she looked very young. By this time customers were ready to adjust, provided the banking was sound.

Crisis and Renewal in Twentieth Century Banking: The Slovenian Experience

CHAPTER 11

A Comparison of Banking Crises in Slovenia in the 1930s and 1990s

Franjo Štiblar

Introduction

Slovenia entered its two largest economic crises of the twentieth century, which had profound effects on the banking sector, in very different institutional environments. During the first crisis, between the wars, Slovenia constituted two regions (Ljubljanska oblast and Mariborska oblast) within the Kingdom of Serbs, Croats and Slovenes and, after 1929, the territory of Dravska banovina within the renamed Kingdom of Yugoslavia. In this territory of 15.85 thousand square kilometres, the population increased from 1.06 million in 1921 to 1.21 million in 1938. In the second crisis, at the end of the 1980s, Slovenia was a federal republic in SFR Yugoslavia; it became an independent country, for the first time in its history, on 25 June 1991. Both its territory (20.2 thousand square kilometres) and its population (1.99 million people) had increased significantly in the interval of sixty years. At the same time the country's Gross Domestic Product (GDP) increased immensely, although comparison is difficult. The GDP of the whole 'First Yugoslavia' was around US$1 billion at that period, of which Slovenia's share did not exceed 25 per cent. The GDP of independent Slovenia during the 1990s increased from US$12 to US$20 billion, half of it due to the revaluation of domestic currency.

Institutional change also took Slovenia in different directions between these two periods. At the start of the first period, Slovenia was transformed from the least developed region of the old Austrian Empire to the most developed region in the new Yugoslavia. In the second period, Slovenia was evolving from the most developed republic of the second Yugoslavia towards becoming one of the least developed economies in the enlarged European Union. How much will the trade patterns and the fortunes of the banking sector follow previous patterns of change? This may mean the return to concentration in the primary sectors and a stronger import dependence (in technologically advanced industries and some services, including trade and finance) on more developed Western European countries, particularly Slovenia's immediate neighbours.

Which similarities and differences can be identified in the banking sector during both of these periods? In both periods there was a sharp decline of economic activity. Slovenia's GDP decreased during the crises years by almost a half in 1930s and 22 per cent in 1990, deep enough declines to describe these crises as depressions and not only as recessions. But by almost all other accounts the two periods differ significantly: in the external economic environment, in the country's position in the world, in internal institutional arrangements, in the causes and consequences of crises, and in the renewals which followed.

The Economic Crisis of the 1930s

The pre-crisis period, 1918–24

The Slovenian economic situation after the First World War was similar to the situation elsewhere in Europe. The new Kingdom of Serbs, Croats and Slovenes suffered from a weak currency and high inflation, a lack of food and raw materials, worn-out machinery, and so on. The major goal of the economic authorities was to deal with the transition to a new economy. This entailed nationalization (nostrification) of businesses, currency reform, the concentration of cooperatives, and an answer to the problem of scarcity.

In the inter-war period, trade and finance were strongly influenced by large institutional and geographical changes. These changes included the question of Slovenia's territorial status. From being a region of the Habsburg Empire, Slovenia became a constituent region of the newly established Kingdom of Serbs, Croats and Slovenes, later renamed the Kingdom of Yugoslavia. A special administrative body for trade and crafts was formed in Ljubljana, the Slovenian capital, in December 1920 to deal with economic matters, including trade and finance. A transitional office was established to deal with exports and imports. Both the National Council – Slovenia's provisional government – and its economic council dealt at length with the problems associated with the privatization of foreign-owned businesses in Slovenia. Tax reform was high on the agenda. The transition period ended in 1924, when the dinar currency was stabilized, the budget was balanced, international agreements were signed, a new customs regime was introduced, and the country enjoyed a good harvest. The Kingdom's external debt – loans granted during the First World War and in the transition period – remained a problem. Agricultural reform was attempted twice, in 1919 and later in 1931. Industrialization (in mining, textiles, wood products, steel, chemicals, food, paper, glass and construc-tion) and the adoption of electricity as the main source of power moved forward in Slovenia during that period. Despite the fact that the government and the central bank in Belgrade, increasingly centralized and dominated by Serbian interests, channelled flows of credit toward the south and the east of the Kingdom, the other regions of Yugoslavia never caught up with Slovenia in terms of economic development. Thus in 1938 the per capita national income in Slovenia was 4000 dinars ($100 in current US dollars) in comparison with only 2400 dinars in Yugoslavia as a whole.

The institutional switch from the Habsburg monarchy to the Karadjord-jevic monarchy had a significant impact on the structure of the Slovene economy. As one of the least developed provinces of the Austro-Hungarian Empire, Slovenia concentrated its economy predominantly in the primary sectors of agriculture and the extractive industries. The province was a source of raw materials and food for other regions in the Empire as well as other countries, especially Italy and Germany. The existing heavy industry was predominantly controlled by the German population in the region or by interests in Austria and Germany. At this time territories where Slovenes predominated included Carniola (with the capital city of Ljubljana), Styria, Carinthia, Pomurje, Dolenjsko and Primorsko.

When the new South Slavic kingdom was established, Slovenia obtained partial autonomy. Slovenia instantly emerged as the most developed part of the new Kingdom. That had important consequences for the structure of the economy. Instead of expanding the primary sector – agriculture lost its former markets and at the same time met strong competition from Vojvodina, Dalmatia and other regions of the new country – Slovenia started to develop trade, to export manufacturing products and to emerge as technologically the leading region in the new Kingdom. These changes promoted the rapid development of trade and finance in Slovenia.

For a comparative evaluation of the role of trade and finance in Slovenia (namely its position within Yugoslavia and with regard to other countries), unfortunately many essential statistical data are not available. The most important missing data are aggregate statistics on the national product, exports and imports. These statistics are available only for Yugoslavia as a whole. For comparison of the constituent parts of the Yugoslav kingdom, the only available base point is that in 1931 Dravska banovina (closely corresponding to what became Slovenia) encompassed 6.43 per cent of Yugoslav territory and 8.21 per cent of the Yugoslav population. At the same time its share in Yugoslav total manufacturing was, according to one estimate, 26 per cent. According to the 1931 census in the territory of

Table 11.1   Banks in the territory of Slovenia, 1929–38

A. Joint stock banks in Slovenia

Year	Banks	Branches	Capital million dinars	Total assets million dinars	Profit million dinars
1929	9	26	94	1809	6.8
1933	12	20	75	1367	3.5
1936	no data		86	1249	7.1
1938	no data		84	1347	5.2

B. All banks in Slovenia

Year	Number	Subsidiaries	Total	Capital	Total assets million dinars Sum	Net	Profit million dinars Total
1918	10	9	19				
1919	10	9	19	7.5	107.3		0.78
1920	14	15	29	24.0	295.7		4.27
1921	14	20	34	37.6	593.0		7.97
1922	14	33	47	66.3	912.7		9.97
1923	15	43	58	103.2	1 092.7		1.59
1924	16	41	57	117.0	1 284.1		17.17
1925	15	40	55	118.0	1 498.3		15.80
1926	13	28	41	112.6	1 542.0		12.97
1927	12	26	38	98.3	1 512.1	11.4	11.95
1928	12	26	38	98.3	1 601.5	11.7	12.34
1929	12	26	38	101.3	1 688.3	11.8	11.33
1930	12	26	38	101.3	1 836.2	11.8	12.41
1931	13	26	39	103.3	1 520.6	9.5	10.21
1932	13	24	37	103.3	1 312.7	6.0	9.29
1933	12	21	33	98.3	1 193.8	4.4	8.48
1934	10	21	31	74.7	1 076.3	3.1	3.88
1935	10	18	28	84.7	1 072.8	6.7	7.49
1936	10	18	28	84.7	1 104.9	5.8	6.66
1937	10	18	28	84.7	1 116.7	8.9	10.30

Source: Spominski Zbornik Slovenije 1919–39 (1939)

present-day Slovenia, 6.8 per cent of the population (and 4.6 per cent in Yugoslavia as a whole) were employed in the sectors of trade, credit and transport. Classified by the profession of heads of households in 1921, 3.65 per cent of all families were in trade and credit in 1921, with an equivalent figure of 2.99 per cent in 1931. The comparable figures for Yugoslavia as a whole were 3.18 per cent in 1921 and 2.88 per cent in 1931.

After the First World War the first domestic bank, the Ljubljanska Kreditna Banka (LKB; established in 1900), increased its nominal share capital five-fold, thus obtaining a majority of domestic holdings and retaining the position of the largest Slovene financial institution. The Jadranska Banka, established in 1905 in Trieste, was decentralized into three units during the First World War (the Adriatische Bank in Vienna, the Banco Adriatico in Trieste and the Jadranska Banka with its central office in Belgrade). The first two branches got into difficulties due to external pressure and mismanagement and were liquidated in 1925, while the third branch was later merged with another bank. Thus the largest Slovene bank before the First World War disappeared from the scene in the 1920s.

In 1920, the Ljubljana branch of Vienna's Creditanstalt was transformed by nationalization into a Slovene institution–the Kreditni Zavod za Trgovino in Industrijo (the Credit Institution for Trade and Industry). The Creditanstalt retained a substantial 30 per cent share in the stock capital. As explained in detail in Tosti (1989), this financial institution of the universal bank type played an important role in the Slovene economy in the 1920s. It was hit hard by the crisis of the 1930s, as were other Slovene financial institutions, but it survived even through the Second World War. A similar process of reorganization due to 'nostrification' occurred in the case of the formation of the Hipotekarna Banka Jugoslovanskih Hranilnic in Ljubljana (1921–30), the Mariborska Eskomptna Banka (1918–22) and some smaller corporate banks in Prekmurje.

In addition to reorganization, some new banks were incorporated in Slovenia after the First World War. The most important of these was the Zadruzna Gospodarska Banka (Cooperative Economic Bank). It was established in 1920 on the initiative of cooperatives, as were the Zadruzna Banka (Cooperative Bank) in Ljubljana (1920) and the Celjska Posojilnica (Celje Credit Institution) in Celje (1922). At the same time, a growing number of entrepreneurs established several smaller corporate banks suited to their specific needs. Such were the Obrtna Banka (Craftsmens' Bank, 1920), the Slovenska Banka (1920), the Prometna Banka (Transport Bank, 1921), the Trgovska Banka (Trade Bank 1922), all in Ljubljana; the

Merkantilna Banka (1922) in Kocevje and the Kreditna Banka in Murska Sobota.

By 1923, the number of Slovene corporate banks and their branches reached a peak. This 'foundation euphoria' was brought to an end by the deflationary monetary policy of the Yugoslav government, which successfully stabilized the domestic currency dinar by 1925, and by the difficulties of the Slavenska Banka in Zagreb. This bank had a Slovene manager and close business connections with several Slovene banks. When the Slavenska Banka failed after its post-war speculations, several Slovene banks were liquidated and some others reduced their total assets by writing off dubious claims. Among the banks which disappeared – not all, however, in connection with the fall of Slavenska Banka – were the Mariborska Eskomptna Banka (leaving the industrial centre of Maribor without its own financial support), the Slovenska Banka, the Hipotekarna Banka, the Ilirska Banka, the Trgovska Banka, the Merkantilna Banka in Kocevje and some smaller banks.

Surprising as it may seem, the liquidation of some banks and the bad and doubtful debts of other banks contributed to a consolidation of the Slovene banking sector, creating solid foundations which would withstand the impact of the world economic crisis in 1930. The worldwide crisis had several major consequences for the Yugoslav and Slovene financial sector. Besides decreases in the volume of financial business and the number of existing financial intermediaries, there were quite significant changes in the structure of financial performance. As seen from Table 11.2, in the first half of the 1930s, the share of demand deposits decreased substantially (a typical sign of crisis in the credibility of finance). Savings deposits in Yugoslavia as well as the level of deposits and loans in Slovenia decreased and never really recovered.

Yugoslavia pursued a surprisingly prudent or restrictive monetary and fiscal policy after normalisation of the economy in the period from 1924 to 1934. Only in the period immediately before the Second World War did monetary and fiscal policy become expansionist to a certain extent, although the policy could not be described as inflationary. The general overview shows that prices doubled in Yugoslavia between 1914 and 1924, than halved in the next ten years between 1924 and 1934 and increased again by 25 per cent in the next five years. Exchange rates followed the dynamics of prices. Thus the dinar was depreciating against the dollar and sterling until 1924, after that it was appreciating until 1934 and, following official devaluation in 1935 by 28.5 per cent, it started to lose ground again, especially against sterling.

Table 11.2   Deposits and credits in Slovenia's financial institutions, 1919–39 (in million dinars)

	Deposits				Credits (Loans)			
Date	Banks	Savings banks	Cooperatives	Total	Banks	Savings banks	Cooperatives	Total
1919	96			96	94			94
1920	255		37	292	246		20	266
1921	531		114	645	507		29	536
1922	811	228	332	1 371	810		201	1 011
1923	951	260	324	1 535	958		189	1 147
1924	1 121	350	442	1 913	1 123	198	244	1 565
1925	1 333	483	589	2 405	1 331	269	385	1 985
1926	1 428	624	984	3 036	1 374	378	705	2 457
1927	1 358	728	939	3 025	983	473	650	2 106
1928	1 420	861	1 060	3 341	1 124	604	781	2 509
1929	1 524	1 025	1 307	3 856	1 254	741	1 148	3 143
1930	1 649	1 182	1 688	4 519	1 415	902	1 299	3 616
1931	1 169	1 269	1 723	4 161	1 247	1 005	1 367	3 619
1932	1 049	1 193	1 651	3 893	1 080	no data	1 316	
1933	912	1 139	1 564	3 615	880	936	1 261	3 077
1934	787	1 101	1 505	3 393	773	901	1 213	2 887
1935	788	1 072	1 454	3 314	789	863	1 138	2 790
1936	819	1 053	1 396	3 268	820	758	1 064	2 642
1937	837	1 045	1 374	3 256	817	723	890	2 430

Source: Spominski Zbornik Slovenije 1919–39 (1939)

Interest rates moved accordingly. First, in 1920 during the time of expansive economic policy, the savings rate was 4 per cent while the lending rate reached 7–8 per cent. The restrictive monetary policy caused an increase in the savings rate to 12 per cent and the lending rate to 18–20 per cent by 1924. By 1927, interest rates decreased to more normal levels, the savings rate to 4.5–8 per cent and the lending rate to 9–12 per cent. As part of reform measures in 1935, the National Bank of Yugoslavia decreased the discount rate from 6.5 to 5 per cent and limited the savings rate to a maximum of 5 per cent and the lending rate to 10 per cent.

After the First World War, the goal of Slovenia was to substitute Yugoslav overseas trade with Slovene trade and to establish the leading position in the exports of the newly established Yugoslavia. Foreign trade in Slovenia under the Habsburg monarchy had been directed strongly towards Trieste, Rijeka and to some degree Vienna. Changes in international borders changed these trade patterns. Foreign trade became more independent and links towards the east and south became more important. Wholesale export trades were situated close to production sites. Thus, the timber trade was sited near railways in the west and north-west of Slovenia and the wine trade was concentrated in Maribor.

Crisis (1925–34)

In 1930, Slovene banking capital was concentrated in Ljubljana. Within Ljubljana the three largest financial institutions (the Ljubljanska Kreditna Banka, the Kreditni Zavod za Trgovino in Industrijo and the Zadruzna Gospodarska Banka Ljubljana) accounted for over 88 per cent of the total banking assets of the Slovene banks, which reached a peak in 1930. In the following year, the Yugoslav government adopted the gold standard but this regime lasted only few months. The collapse of the Creditanstalt in Vienna (with strong financial ties with Slovenia), the outflow of capital from Austria and Germany, President Hoover's moratorium on reparations (from which Yugoslavia should have received payments) all contributed to the contraction of Slovene banking in the period from 1931 to 1934. Although this financial contraction halted after 1935, the late 1930s brought little more than the stagnation of banking assets (Jonker and Zanden, 1992).

In collecting deposits and disbursing credits, the banks were leaders and other financial institutions were followers in Slovenia, with a time lag of a year or two. In 1930 and 1931, banks felt the world economic and financial crisis first, before the savings banks and cooperatives; on the other hand, the banks were the first to feel the revival of financial activity in 1935/36.

Renewal (1935–41)

The renewal period of 1935–41 was actually a period of consolidation combined with stagnation rather than a new upswing in the activity. Just before the war, a small revival occurred in response to preparations for war. According to Hočevar's calculations (1984, p. 271), the total assets of Slovene banks decreased by 10–20 per cent each year in the period from 1931 to 1934, thus halving them in nominal terms by 1935. At the same time, the amount of outstanding bank credits decreased at a somewhat slower rate while the amount of savings deposits decreased more rapidly. In the period from 1935 to 1940, the total banking assets of the Slovene banks increased by approximately 10 per cent; cash holdings in banks more than doubled; outstanding bank credits increased by 10 per cent; basic capital stock increased by 20 per cent, and profits steadily increased from year to year. The profit rate increased from 8 per cent in 1935 to close to 10 per cent in 1940. In nominal terms, however, the total banking assets of Slovene banks in 1940 remained much smaller than in 1930, even if one takes into account deflation during the 1930s.

Regular incorporated private banks had competitors from the two different groups of financial institutions in the Slovene financial market: from larger and more protected privileged state banks, and from smaller and less organized regulatory savings institutions with savings and credit cooperatives. The latter were organized into three groups in Slovenia: members of the Cooperative Association in Ljubljana, members of the Union of Slovene Cooperatives and members of the Cooperative Association in Celje.

The Crisis of the 1990s

The pre-crisis period (1985–91)

A two-tier banking system had emerged in Slovenia by the late 1950s, in the framework of post-war socialist Yugoslavia (the 'second Yugoslavia'). Former branches of the central bank had become independent bank units and some new banks were established in different sectors of the economy (Štiblar, 1994). The economic reforms of 1962 and 1965 enabled banks to become increasingly independent and by the late 1960s banks were licensed to undertake profit-based international operations.

In the early 1970s, the political leadership's alarm at the increasing independence of the 'technocratic' economic sector, combined with rising nationalist sentiments, led to the defeat of the economic reforms. Several managers and republican political leaders were replaced. The fledgling market system was replaced with a new system of 'associated labour' in which forces of supply and demand were replaced by a number of association agreements. In this system, banks lost their previous independence. Instead, they were treated as 'a service of associated labour'. Business enterprises became founders and 'owners' of banks. In practice, the political leadership had a direct influence on the banks' lending policies; large businesses with their representatives on the banks' managing and supervisory boards were becoming at the same time net debtors of those banks. Obvious conflicts of interest, and opportunities for insider dealing, were thus institutionalized.

Each federal unit or republic in the second Yugoslavia established one strong bank – in Serbia there were two – and all other banks in the federal units became quasi-affiliates. These banks in the republics were quite large, some of them among the 300 largest banks in the world at that time. Only two banks (Ljubljanska Banka from Slovenia and Jugobanka from Serbia) had offices in all parts of former Yugoslavia. At the end of 1980s, before the collapse of Yugoslavia, there were 169 banks in the country; of the 16 banks in Slovenia, 13 were affiliates of Ljubljanska Banka.

The need for the rehabilitation of banks in independent Slovenia derived from the adverse consequences of the country's separation from ex-Yugoslavia and the transformation to a fully-fledged market system. Financial consequences (the 'price of independence and transformation') were concentrated in the banking sector, which was from 1960s in the ownership of socially-owned enterprises and not the state. Slovene banks lost their assets in other units of ex-Yugoslavia, while foreign exchange deposits were frozen in the central bank in Belgrade. At the same time, Slovene enterprises suffered by losing 40 per cent of the market, including their own branches in the rest of ex-Yugoslavia. A transitional depression in the domestic market and privatization under the new economic system added to this burden. Slovene companies were therefore less able to repay their banking loans.

Banking problems followed from the illiquidity and insolvency in the enterprise sector, leading to rapid deterioration of banks' loan portfolios. Other factors adding to banking crisis in Slovenia were financial liberalization, including freeing of interest rates and liberalized entry of new banks (domestic rather than foreign). In 1992, 13 out of 26 banks counting for more than 70 per cent of total deposits reported losses and a bank rehabilitation programme duly started at the beginning of 1993.

The large majority of non-performing loans originated in the period before 1992. After that, small additions to the problem came from the worsening situation in some business enterprises which already had outstanding bank loans. For that reason banks were directly involved in business reconstruction. Only occasionally was there pressure from the government on banks placed under state ownership to help finance larger corporations which were also in state ownership. In Slovenia, a 'restructuring first, privatization later' approach was adopted for loss-making enterprises.

Crisis and rehabilitation (1991–94)

Slovenia suffered a significant crisis under transition and separation crisis between the end of 1980s and the beginning of the 1990s. GDP first decreased by 100 per cent in 1987 and by 78 per cent in 1992, but then recovered by 115 per cent in 2000 and 119 per cent in 2001. From its peak value in 1986–87, industrial production (in real terms) decreased by 37 per cent to a low point in 1993; construction activity was halved, retail trade decreased by a third, transport by 30 per cent, and the number of tourists more than halved. Employment totals fell from 964 000 in 1987 to 752 000 in 1994 while the number of unemployed increased from 15 000 in 1987 to 137 000 at the end of 1993. Inflation reached its peak in 1989 with a yearly rate of 1413 per cent but then declined in independent Slovenia to below 10 per cent in the second half of the 1990s. Slovenia's balance of payments was in surplus at the end of the 1980s and became negative in the second half of 1990s. Internal retail trade did not decline substantially during the pre-crisis period from 1986 to 1991; while the number of employees decreased from 70 000 to 53 000, the number of registered legal units actually increased from 1342 to 1980. In external trade, values increased. In 1986, exports were $2.5 billion and imports were $2.7 billion (a deficit of $200 million) while in 1991 exports amounted to $3.9 billion and imports $4.1 billion (a deficit of $200 million).

After the separation and proclamation of the independence of Slovenia, the Banking Law and the Law on the Bank of Slovenia were among the first 'independence laws' enacted on the day of independence on 25 June 1991. Banks in Slovenia now answered to a new monetary authority. Linkages with the old system had, however, left an important question unresolved. Under the former Yugoslav banking system, 85 per cent of banks' foreign currency deposits had to be deposited physically in the central bank in Belgrade. They were never returned to the banks which deposited them. The amount of these deposits in the case of the Ljubljanska Banka, the largest Slovene bank, was around $1 billion and their repayment to its depositors became a major problem for the bank. For depositors in Slovenia, a gradual repayment was applied but not for depositors of the Ljubljanska Banka's branches outside Slovenia (the amount in question was over $500 million, mostly in Croatia and some in Bosnia). The repayment of these foreign currency deposits remains a political problem. The Ljubljanska Banka itself cannot solve the problem. Slovenia's position is that claims should be directed towards Narodna Banka Jugoslavije and eventually solved in the negotiations among former Yugoslav federal units.

At the time of Slovenia's proclamation of independence in June 1991, the banking system in Slovenia faced serious problems of non-performing loans due to the disintegration of the former Yugoslavia, the retention of foreign exchange assets in the central bank in Belgrade and political influences on lending policies. At the proclamation of independence in 1991, the share of bad debts in total banking assets was over 10 per cent and the share of non-performing bank loans was over 30 per cent. In each of the three large banks that were put into formal rehabilitation, the share was above 40 per cent. In addition, there was little competition in the banking sector. Certainly banking regulation and supervision did not develop according to the international standards.

These circumstances in the banking sector demanded radical action. New legislation and other measures were adopted in 1991 and subsequently in order to rehabilitate old banks and establish new banks, and to improve and strengthen of banking regulation and supervision. Slovenia has introduced the Bank for International Settlements' 8 per cent capital-to-risk assets ratio, as well as other international standards with regard to liquidity and the diversification of risks.

Renewal (1994–2000)

The Slovene economy recovered quickly, with the second fastest pace among transition countries (Poland was the first, until 2000). The country's GDP per capita remained at least 25 per cent higher than in any other transition country and at 73 per cent of the European Union average.

Commercial banks needed restructuring because of non-performing loans but also to assure the competitive position of domestic banks once capital controls are removed and integration with the European Union begins. At the beginning of 1993, the two largest banks were put into rehabilitation and the third followed at the beginning of 1994. The first two banks, which counted for more than 50 per cent of the total banking sector, were also hit by 'joint and several liability' clauses regarding ex-Yugoslav debts to foreign private creditors.

The rehabilitation of the banking sector in Slovenia was narrowly defined as the process of solving the problem of non-performing loans. It concentrated on rehabilitating the largest 'old' banks with problems created

Table 11.3 Main macro-economic indicators for Slovenia, 1992–2000 (Area: 20 000 square km; population: 2 million; GDP US$20 billion)

	1992	1993	1994	1995	1996	1997	1998	1999	2000
GDP growth	− 5.4	2.8	5.3	4.1	3.5	4.6	3.9	5.0	4.6
Inflation (average)	93.9	22.9	12.3	8.6	8.8	9.4	7.9	6.1	8.9
Balance of payments (million US$)	926.0	192.0	573.0	− 99.0	31.0	11.0	− 148.0	− 783.0	− 594.0
Unemployment rate per cent	11.6	14.6	14.5	14.0	13.9	14.4	14.4	13.0	12.0
Ditto, ILO standard, per cent	7.3	7.4	7.9	7.6	7.0				
Budget balance/GDP per cent	0.0	0.3	− 0.2	0.0	0.3	− 1.2	− 0.8	− 0.6	− 1.3

Sources: National Statistical Office, Bank of Slovenia, Institute of Macroeconomic Analysis and Development

before the separation and transition of Slovenia. Rehabilitation meant returning these banks to solvency, profitability and liquidity.

This Slovene experiment in bank rehabilitation was unique in the sense that no previous experience from other countries existed for the rehabilitation of more than 50 per cent of the banking sector at once. A mixture of centralization and decentralization was chosen for the rehabilitation of these three banks. The state swapped bonds for the banks' bad debts (providing solvency and thus taking over the ownership of banks) but not to the full amount of existing bad assets, thereby reducing moral hazard and forcing banks to play their part in the internal rehabilitation process. In addition, the central bank helped banks in their rehabilitation by providing additional liquidity. After four years, the rehabilitation was successfully concluded in June 1997. The two banks became solvent, profitable and liquid.

Slovenia's approach was a mix of centralization and decentralization and it was gradual in effect. It took into account the specific conditions of Slovenia. The state's main policy responses to the bank crisis included:

- stricter supervision by the Bank of Slovenia
- prudential regulation, embodied in the new 1991 banking law and consequent by-laws
- the introduction of minimum capital levels (in absolute terms) and minimum capital adequacy rules
- strict laws on credit provision
- the creation of a special Bank Rehabilitation Agency
- improved coordination between state authorities (the Ministry of Finance, Bank of Slovenia and the Bank Rehabilitation Agency) and the banks.

Specific techniques used were:

- the takeover of banks in rehabilitation by the state through the Bank Rehabilitation Agency
- the partial exchange of foreign exchange deposits in the former National Bank of Yugoslavia and bad debts with Bank Rehabilitation Agency (later State) bonds
- the temporary relaxation of supervision ratios for banks in rehabilitation, ending in 1994.

The burden of losses was paid by:

- former owners (shareholders) who had their shares replaced with subordinated claims on the Bank Rehabilitation Agency

- the repayment of foreign exchange deposits of customers in Slovenia
- the issue of government bonds in the range of 1.8 billion DM for all three banks in rehabilitation (Parliament allowed for upper limit of 2.2 billion) to be repaid by the sale of rehabilitated banks and the retrieval of some of the bad debts transferred to the Bank Rehabilitation Agency.

Based on the decrees of the Bank of Slovenia, three banks were put into rehabilitation: the Nova Ljubljanska Banka in January 1993, Nova Kreditna Banka Maribor in April 1993 and Komercialna Banka Nova Gorica in January 1994 (the Komercialna Banka was subsequently acquired by the Nova Kreditna Banka Maribor in 1995). Four key state measures were adopted for establishing financial health in state-owned banks:

1. a swap of bad debts for rehabilitation bonds in January 1993
2. the re-establishment of Nova Ljubljanska Banka and Nova Kreditna Banka Maribor in July 1994
3. exchange of rehabilitation bonds in October 1995 (valid from January 1995)
4. resolution of the issue of unconfirmed foreign debt swaps under the 'New Financial Agreement' in February 1996.

About one third of bad debts (15 per cent of their total loans) remained in the balance sheets of banks in rehabilitation. Through intensive-care units, banks in rehabilitation were forced to participate directly in the process of business restructuring (Štiblar, 1995b). In 1996, the share of non-performing loans in these banks was below 5 per cent, a strong indication that they were rehabilitated.

The collaboration of these banks in business reconstruction included the following actions (Deželak, 1995):

- rescheduling old businesses' obligations to banks, with longer maturity
- allowing moratoria on principal debts and more favourable interest rates
- enabling firms to settle obligations to banks by discount
- discharging some businesses from their obligations by specific
- swapping bad debts for stakes in enterprise equity.

The results were striking. At the start of rehabilitation, swaps of bad debts for the state (Bank Rehabilitation Agency) bonds were made in three banks under rehabilitation in the following amounts:

- issued bonds for balance claims: 1 482 500 million DM
- bonds for out of balance liabilities: 391 837 million DM
- Total: 1 874 337 million DM

The outcome was that the banks which had begun the rehabilitation procedure in 1993 with a negative capital balance of 1.5 billion DM achieved a positive capital balance of 850 million DM by 1996. The improvement of 2350 million DM was 420 million DM more than the value of bonds swapped plus an additional injection in 1994 of about 50 million DM. The additional value was created by the banks' own profitable activities during that period.

In the rehabilitation period from 1993 to 1997, the size of the banking sector in Slovenia increased moderately, as measured by number of banks, capital and assets (see Table 11.4).

The share of bad debts in the total assets of the banking sector decreased from over 10 per cent in 1992 to only 3.9 per cent at the end of 1995. Bad debts did not fall dramatically as a share of the total loan portfolio, not because there are new loans going bad, but because in Slovenia loans have been indexed. Indexation implies that bad debts will not be decreased by inflation (as they were for example in Poland) and the total corporate loan portfolio has not expanded significantly.

The financial performance of the banking sector has improved significantly since 1991 and the sector has experienced increased aggregate profits in the second half of the 1990s. In 1997, the aggregate profit of the banking sector was 0.7 per cent of GDP. When the profit of the central bank is added, that contribution amounts to 1.2 per cent of GDP. At the end of

Table 11.4   Development of the banking sector in Slovenia, 1991–2000

Years	Number of banks	Capital	Total assets Billion SIT	Billion $	As percent of GDP
1991	26	63	327.3	5.8	—
1992	30	103	628.0	6.4	62.0
1993	32	142	937.4	7.1	65.3
1994	33	220	1174.0	9.3	64.6
1995	31	263	1493.0	11.9	67.9
1996	30	285	1799.1	12.4	72.0
1997	29	320	2094.1	12.5	73.4
1998	27	354	2412.7	14.5	74.1
1999	25	392	2763.2	15.2	75.9
2000	26	445	3267.5	14.7	80.2

Source: Bank of Slovenia, Monthly Bulletins and Yearly Reports.

1997, the total assets of the banking sector counted for 73 per cent of GDP, its Return on Equity was 7.18 per cent and Return on Assets 1.0 per cent; its operating costs were 60 per cent covered by net non-interest income. In 2000, the banking sector's assets accounted for 80 per cent of GDP, its Return on Equity was 11.4 per cent and its Return on Assets was 1.4 per cent. These results have continued to improve.

A very conservative provisioning policy has shielded the capital base of banks in rehabilitation almost completely from any down-side risk in this respect: bad debts are provided for almost 100 per cent. The restructuring of the recapitalization instruments has resulted in major improvements in terms of foreign currency exposure. Banks approached zero net foreign exchange exposure, maturity mismatches have been reduced, and the recapitalization bonds became tradable. The banks had become profitable in spite of continuing conservative provisioning practices. The outlook for strong profit growth was promising, given the relatively low share of profits stemming from the foreign exchange part of the balance sheet and the likely reduction in provisioning charges.

Accounting standards and information systems have improved significantly, while a strict loan classification system in line with Western practice led to confidence in the assessment of capital value for calculating capital adequacy ratios. This ratio exceeded 12 per cent in both banks – following the Basel Convention – which was clearly a dramatic improvement. Return on Equity and Return on Assets coefficients attained for both the banks in rehabilitation have been above the average in the Slovene banking sector and above world standards. Liquidity has improved, operational costs were under control and provisioning was, in relation to conservative risk assessment, above standard.

Corporate governance has also been reformed and modern organisational structures have been put in place. Slovenia's banks have been introducing the newest and more sophisticated financial products and services and their information technology meets international standards. They have succeeded in achieving an adequate capital base, introduced sufficient provisioning, developed sound financial and lending policies and procedures, and they have developed well-qualified and motivated management teams.

The three major consequences of rehabilitation were:

- an increasing public debt for the whole country of 1.8 billion DM (less than 10 per cent of GDP), partly reduced by bad debt recoveries
- for the entire banking sector, a decreasing share of bad debts from 10 per cent to less than 4 per cent, an increasing share of A-classified loans from

less than 80 per cent to 89 per cent, aggregate profits of over \$110 million in 1995, and a more normal structure of balance sheet
- for banks in rehabilitation, a decreased share in banking sector assets from over 50 per cent to 40 per cent, a positive capital balance of 850 million DM instead of a negative capital balance of 1 500 million DM; Return on Equity and Return on Assets financial results above the average of the banking sector, and significant institutional reforms and much improved management of human resources.

The rehabilitation status of the two major banks was formally terminated in June 1997, when management boards were appointed and supervisory boards were nominated. Conditions to terminate the rehabilitation of banks, prescribed by the Bank of Slovenia in a special decree of June 1995, had been by and large fulfilled. Both banks then took legal action to clear themselves from rehabilitation status. The Bank Rehabilitation Agency was merged with the Slovenian Development Association (which is losing its independent status). Despite several efforts, only small steps in privatization had been made before 2001, when it was expected that privatization programmes would begin in earnest.

The evaluation of the results of Slovenia's bank rehabilitation leads to the following conclusions:

- The programme, while slow in getting started, was well thought out and pragmatic, with 'learning-by-doing' as one of its important features.
- The partial removal of bad debts has had more positive effects (namely a smaller public debt and stronger discipline for the banks) than negative effects (such as leaving banks with a larger proportion of sub-standard assets).
- After initial uncertainty, a cooperative approach was adopted by key actors, including the Ministry of Finance, the Bank of Slovenia, the Bank Rehabilitation Agency, and the top management of the banks. Cooperation with institutions responsible for business restructuring and privatization, including the Ministry of Economy, the Privatization Agency and the Development Fund) has been less fruitful.
- The programme imposed tight controls on the rehabilitation banks and their management, leading to considerable improvement in corporate governance, organization, lending procedures, loan monitoring and recovery.
- Given a significant share of over 50 per cent of the banking sector in Slovenia under rehabilitation and a rather restrictive (and successful) monetary policy, the Bank of Slovenia's liquidity support to the

programme was not totally adequate, leading to adverse effects on interest rates.

- The programme has significantly benefited from external advice and technical assistance from bilateral and multilateral sources, although this advice has been used selectively taking into account local conditions and constraints dictated by political realities and bearing that in mind the bank rehabilitation in Slovenia was a 'home-grown' program.

Comparison

The historical dimension

Institutional financial intermediation appeared in Slovenia early in the nineteenth century, initially in unincorporated form and, after 1900, in company form on a universal banking model. Although lagging behind the Austrian financial centres, the Slovenes developed their own banking sector. It played an important role in the country's somewhat late industrial development and modernization, similar to the experience elsewhere. Again, at the start of second crisis in 1990, all banks were in Slovene ownership. During rehabilitation, foreign ownership of banks increased gradually but, unlike other transition countries, the majority of banks remained in domestic ownership.

The period between 1919 and 1925 was a 'Grunderzeit' of Slovene banking, 50 years after the equivalent period in Austria. Through nostrification, the power of branches of foreign banks decreased after the First World War but at the same time Slovene banks obtained an enlarged Yugoslav economic hinterland, enabling fast development. That expansion ended with the restrictive monetary policy in 1924. In contrast, in the second period of crisis in the 1990s, the number of banks more than doubled but their internal market contracted from the whole of Yugoslavia to only Slovenia.

Slovenia did not escape the economic and financial crisis in the 1930s, partly due to strong financial ties with German-owned banks and with Slovene banks operating in the financial centres in Austria and Germany, which were both strongly hit by the banking crisis. The financial weight of the banking sector was more than halved during the first half of the 1930s and then merely stagnated in the second half of 1930s. Similarly, Slovenia could not avoid the effects of the transition crisis at the end of 1980s, when there was the additional dimension of the secession crisis. The financial power of existing banks again decreased substantially but the recovery was rapid. From 1994, a stronger banking sector emerged, with the largest bank,

Nova Ljubljanska Banka (NLB Group) holding a 40 per cent share in the domestic market, a strong presence in international banking and the highest international rating among domestically owned banks in countries in transition in 2001.

The political dimension

In the bilingual territory of Slovenia before the First World War, language differences resulted in the parallel emergence of Slovene and foreign banking at the beginning of the twentieth century. The economic spheres of the two traditions differed significantly. The first was smaller in its scale, but closely connected with local interests. Within Slovene banking, further divisions appeared along political lines. The foreign banking presence, however, was only in the form of branches of banks centred in Vienna and in Berlin. Thus, they induced an outflow of capital (saving deposits were channelled into central offices) and at the same time an inflow of capital (by financing investments in the German-dominated industries). This approach was especially evident before the emergence of domestic corporate banking in 1900 and during the occupation in the Second World War. In the independent Slovenia of the 1990s, foreign banks are again parallel to Slovenian banks in the internal market. The foreign presence in banking is increasing, both institutionally and by business. Of 25 banks in 2001, half had some foreign ownership and four of them were in majority foreign ownership.

The role of the government in banking was important even before the crisis of 1930s, when the restrictive monetary policy of the central government in Belgrade caused financial contraction but at the same time helped to consolidate the banking sector. During the crisis, additional state intervention did not have as severe impact on the performance of banking sector as it did in world financial centres (except during the unsuccessful short-term introduction of the gold standard in 1931). In the 1990s, in comparison, the state-led rehabilitation of over 50 per cent of the Slovene banking sector in 1990s shared features with programmes applied in developed economies. It was successful, since only Slovenia among all countries in transition did not suffer from a major banking crisis after rehabilitation during 1990s (*The Economist*, August 1999). Privatisation of the two largest banks will more than repay the costs of bank rehabilitation.

There remains the question of the correlation between universal banking and national interests in a less developed region, seeking independence, such as Slovenia. In the 1930s, to counter the economic dominance of foreigners and to establish an economic foundation for political autonomy, an independent Slovene model of universal banking was established. This was not nationalism but it was an instrument to preserve national identity and to prevent economic, political subordination to powers outside the region. Today, after renewal, a similar question arises: how much foreign banking ownership should Slovenia have in its home market? In 2001, Slovenia was the only country in transition among EU candidates which had a majority of its banks in domestic ownership. In contrast, all member countries of the EU (including the smallest and poorest among them) still have at least 80 per cent of their largest banks in domestic ownership.

References

Anderson, R. W. et al. (1996), *Banking Sector Development in Central and Eastern Europe*, London: CEPR.

Bole, V. (1995), *Sterilization in the Slovene Monetary Sector*, Ljubljana: EIPF Working Paper.

Bollenbacher, G. M. (1992), *Bank Strategies for the 90s*, Dublin: Bankers Publishing Company.

Bomhoff, E. J. (1992), 'Monetary reform in Eastern Europe', *European Economic Review*, 36, pp. 454–8.

Borak, N. (ed.) (1995), *Banke na razpotju*, Portorož: ZES.

Deželak, J. (1995), 'Effectiveness of the Slovenian banking system rehabilitation program', in Simoneti, M. and Kavelec, S. (eds), *Bank Rehabilitation and Enterprise Restructuring*, Budapest: CEEPN.

Gospodarstvo med vojnama, v: Zgodovina Slovencev (1988), Ljubljana, pp. 687–99.

Granda, S. (1987), 'Poskus organiziranja slovenske Ljubljanske obče banke', 1872, in *Zgodovina denarstva in bančništra na Slovenskem, Zgodovinski časopis*, Ljubljana, pp. 47–52.

Guštin, D. (1987), 'Finanečni viri in denarništvo NOB na Slovenskem, 1941–1945' (Financial sources and monetary matters in national independence struggle in Slovenia, 1941–1945), in *Zgodovina denarstva in bančništra na Slovenskem, Zgodovinski časopis*, Ljubljana, pp. 81–103.

Hočevar, T. (1984), 'Slovensko poslovno bančništvo,1913–1941' [Slovene Business Banking, 1913–1941], *Bančni Vestnik*, Ljubljana, 33, pp. 7–8, 230–4; 9, 267–72.

Hočevar, T. (1986), *Financial Intermediation in a Multilingual State: The Case of Slovene Corporate Banking in Austria, 1900–1912*, New Orleans: Slovene Studies, University of New Orleans, 8, 1, pp. 45–56

Hočevar, T. (1987), 'Slovensko poslovno bančništvo kot inovacijski dejavnik' (Slovene Business Banking as an Innovation Factor), in *Zgodovina denarstva in bančništva na Slovenskem, Zgodovinski časopis*, Ljubljana, pp. 61–74.

Jonker, J. and van Zanden, J. L. (1992), *Method in the madness? Banking crises between the wars. An international comparison*, Report from the International Conference on 20th Century Universal Banking, International Comparisons, Budapest, Volume I, pp. 1–16

Jugoslavija 1918–1988, Zvezni zavod za statistiko (1989), Belgrade: Republic of Yugoslavia.

Michel, B. (1976), *Banque et banquiers en Autriche au debut du 20e siècle*, Paris: Presses de la Fondation nationale des sciences politiques.

Mishkin, F. S. (1996) 'Understanding financial crises: A developing country perspective', *Annual Conference on Development Economics*, Washington DC: The World Bank, pp. 1–71.

Potocnik, D. (1939), *Slovensko denarnistvo 1918–1938, v Spominski Zbornik Slovenije 1919–1939, Jubilej*, Ljubljana, pp. 444–57.

Radzynger, O. and Havlik, P. (eds) (1996), *Monetary Policy in Central and Eastern Europe: Challenges of EU Integration*, Vienna: Institute for Comparative Economic Studies.

Repanšek, B.(1994), 'Regionalna analiza poslovanja bank v Republiki Sloveniji', *Prikazi in analize*, II/4, BoS, Ljubljana.

Ribnikar, I.(1993), 'Rehabilitation of banks in Slovenia, *Studii e ricerche*, 5, Trieste.

Shleifer, A. (1995), 'Corporate governance: a survey', *Harvard University Working Paper*.

Simoneti, M. and Kavalec, S. (eds) (1995), *Bank Rehabilitation and Enterprise Restructuring*, Budapest: CEEPN.

Štiblar, F. (1992), 'Universal banking on Slovene territory, 1900–1945', paper at the Conference on Universal Banking in Europe, Budapest, pp. 1–13.

Štiblar, F. (1994a), 'Banking in Slovenia', *Vienna Institute Monthly Report*, 1, pp. 32–9.

Štiblar, F. (1994b), 'Tuje neposredne nalobe v slovenski bančni sektor', *GG, EIPF*, 6/1994; Ljubljana, pp. 24–40.

Štiblar, F. (1995a), 'Development of the Slovene banking sector', *Banking Newsletter – some features of the Slovenian financial system development*, December.

Štiblar, F. (1995b), 'Nova Ljubljanska banka d.d. – A case study in bank rehabilitation and enterprise restructuring', in Simoneti, M. and Kavalec,

S. (eds), *Bank Rehabilitation and Enterprise Restructuring*, Budapest: CEEPN, pp. 125–35.

Štiblar, F. (1996), 'Financial restructuring goes forward: The Slovenian case', Woodrow Wilson Centre – East European Studies, Washington DC, May.

Tosti, A. (1989), 'Denarni zavodi v Sloveniji po prvi svetovni vojni' (Monetary Institutions in Slovenia After the First World War), *Bančni Vestnik*, Ljubljana, pp. 1–158.

Voljè, M. (1995), 'Bank rehabilitation and private sector development', in Simoneti, M. and Kavalec, S. (eds), *Bank Rehabilitation and Enterprise Restructuring*, Budapest: CEEPN,

Wijnbergen, S. (1996), 'Privatizing Nova Ljubljanska banka: strategy and implementation', Mimeograph, Ljubljana.

Other Sources

'Banking in Central Europe', a special sponsored section in *Institutional Investor*, 1955.

Bank of Slovenia, *Monthly Bulletins*.

Bank of Slovenia, *Prikazi in analize*.

European Bank for Reconstruction and Development (1995), *Transition Report*.

Nova Ljubljanska Banka (1996), Final report on rehabilitation of NLB, internal material, pp. 1–40.

CHAPTER 12

Slovenian Banking in Transition

Ivan Ribnikar

Under the socialist system in Slovenia, as in all countries that have emerged from former Yugoslavia, banks were owned by socially-owned non-financial business enterprises. They were owners on the principle of unlimited liability. Unlimited liability was in accordance with the role which banks had in the functioning of an economic system that involved socially-owned, non-financial business enterprises; limited liability ownership would have been contrary to the logic of the system and its ideological basis. The question of how banks performed financial intermediation, given the peculiar role they had, is discussed in the first part of this chapter. Because of the large outright and hidden losses among their assets, almost all of them were insolvent at the beginning of transition in the early 1990s. Hence the second step in their transition, after their quick transformation into stock companies, was their rehabilitation. Previous owners that had unlimited liability were not, as they should have been, called on to pay in money or capital. That is the topic of the second section of the chapter.

The next step in the transition of banking was the rehabilitation and immediate post-rehabilitation period, when banks were relatively well protected from foreign competition, not so much for the sake of protection itself but in order to make the central bank's sterilized foreign exchange transactions effective. They were, of course, controlled and supervised prudently by the central bank as well. But even during that period the banks were exposed to some competition. Their competitors were not domestic financial markets – they would never be a serious threat – but foreign banks. There was also competition amongst the banks. What the banks have actually achieved and whether they are fit enough to survive in a much more or completely competitive environment is the topic of the third part of this chapter.

The survival of banks depends not only on their efforts and achievements. There are serious obstacles beyond their control which may render useless all their efforts to become efficient and competitive banks. In particular, the Slovenian banks have only been able to collect predominantly short-term funds because of the very high propensity of their depositors and other suppliers of funds to hold liquid assets. The banks are also relatively limited as to how big they can become in a small country. With Slovenia's population of two million and a Gross Domestic Product of some US$20 billion, large banking institutions cannot emerge without the expansion of business beyond the country's borders. But big foreign banks are already waiting for that business or they have already taken it over. How important these obstacles or limitations might be is the topic of the fourth section of the paper.

Will the ultimate solution in Slovenia be the same as in other transitional economies, whereby banks become branches or subsidiaries of foreign banks? The chapter closes with some speculation as to whether there are other ways in which banks can succeed as financial intermediaries while also managing the transformation of assets.

Yugoslav Banks and Socially-owned, Non-financial Business Enterprises

Besides debts, socially-owned business enterprises also had non-debt or non-borrowed funds amongst their liabilities and these funds did not belong to anybody. Here, it was possible to declare that such funds belonged to society as a whole and to establish an economic system that was neither capitalism (where non-debt funds belong to private individuals) nor the Soviet type of socialism with state ownership (where non-debt funds belong to the state). In the absence of owners of the non-debt funds – that is, in the absence of business enterprises – it was possible to have workers' self-management. This had nothing to do with workers' management but with workers exercising some rights that otherwise would have belonged to the owners of business enterprises. Workers' self-management was a misnomer for two basic reasons. At the beginning of the 1950s, the distinction between management, in the hands of hired professionals, and control, to be exercised by owners, was not yet known or perceived in Yugoslavia.

The declaration of social ownership, limited to non-financial businesses, or the abolition of state ownership did not turn people into altruists. Altruism would certainly have been required if the non-debt funds of business enterprises were to increase externally in a normal way. Only altruists would be prepared to put their money into socially-owned business enterprises when knowing that, as soon as they did this, the funds so created would belong to society as a whole.

The need for altruism was a clear manifestation of the utopian characteristics of the third economic system, as part of the grand design to have something that was neither capitalism nor a centrally planned economy. That necessity had not been recognized at all either by politicians or economists because banks were heavily involved in the financing of business enterprises and business enterprises apparently had sufficient funding (Ribnikar, 1989). They had enough not only of debt capital or 'capital' but also of non-debt funds. Non-debt funds were created on the basis of bank loans that were given to business enterprises at a negative real interest rate. A high enough inflation level with low nominal interest rates did the job.

Behind the scenes, bank loans were mostly in fact grants, not only allowing the functioning of a utopian economic system but also permitting better functioning than would have been possible in a centrally-planned or Soviet-type economic system. The model later came to be highly regarded, with substantial support from Western economists. In particular, it enabled Yugoslavia to rid itself of the Soviet-type economic system and to run a softer kind of dictatorship.

An economic system that relied on banks as providers of debt and non-repayable funds to non-financial businesses was very efficient in enabling business enterprises to keep increasing their non-debt funds, until rising inflation in the mid-1980s forced the introduction of indexation of bank loans. While it was impossible for non-debt funds of non-financial businesses to appear and/or to increase externally, and although business enterprises had no cash flow available to increase their non-debt funds internally, business enterprises had on average more non-debt funds than business enterprises in market economies. The process of the ongoing accumulation of non-debt capital – the 'primitive accumulation of capital' in Adam Smith's terminology – and the accumulation of capital via bank loans that were predominantly grants had been running very efficiently. In this role the banks were crucial for the functioning of a utopian economic system that was, at the same time, the best then available. But if banks were required to give non-financial businesses loans that were predominantly grants, then necessarily the banks faced problems with their assets or solvency. Similarly, the financial system of such a country risked instability because of the huge gap between desired or required investments and available savings.

So long as banks were giving loans on the basis of domestic currency deposits, their assets and liabilities were depreciating in real terms at the same rate. Banks' net assets did not decrease because they incurred no losses on the basis of their loans that were predominantly grants. Banks were merely vehicles for transferring wealth from depositors to borrowers and they were not directly affected. They were affected indirectly because domestic currency deposits did not grow or began to decrease. How much wealth had been transferred from depositors to bank borrowers could not be seen in the banks' balance sheets.

It was quite a different story when banks were allowed or required to accept foreign currency deposits. This happened in the mid-1960s when Yugoslavia opened its borders for economic emigration. At the same time a solution was thought to have been found in that foreign currency bank deposits would be sufficiently attractive as financial assets for individuals and others. But because nothing changed in the functioning of the economic system, the banks were still required to give loans to business enterprises that were predominantly grants. They were forced to expose themselves to foreign currency risk and, because of high domestic inflation and nominal deprecation of the domestic currency due to their short net position in foreign currencies, losses started to appear and increase. Those losses, kept on the books as 'other claims' or claims on the National Bank of Yugoslavia – for which there was some justification – were visible evidence of the amount of wealth transferred to bank borrowers, especially loans to non-financial businesses on the basis of foreign currency deposits. This was the first difficulty which existed in the make-up of bank assets before transition started.

The second difficulty with bank assets when transition started was the potential losses due to bad debts. These barely featured during the period when loans were predominantly grants. But when indexation started, new loans were no longer grants and it was impossible to alleviate the debt burdens of highly indebted business enterprises by simply postponing the repayment of their debts, as had been done before. Bad debts or non-performing assets started to accumulate among the banks' assets. They were at first, of course, hidden.

The banks therefore had negative net assets before transition started and before they converted into joint-stock companies. Among their assets there were accumulated losses due to foreign currency deposits and potential losses due to bad debts. Both balance sheet items were largely hidden so that banks could change overnight from unlimited liability into limited liability stock companies.

Rehabilitation of Banks Converting from Unlimited Liability to Joint-stock Companies

The conversion of banks into joint-stock companies was necessary but it was undertaken too hastily. Previously, the liability of their owners was unlimited and the valuation of banks did not take place at all. Banks simply changed into joint-stock companies. Those behind the quick change were probably so enthusiastic about the newly rediscovered joint-stock company that they simply could not wait for the relatively long and tedious procedures which might have unpleasant consequences for bank owners.

Only a small part of the wealth that had been transferred via bank loans to non-financial businesses left any trace among bank assets in the form of losses due to foreign currency deposits or potential losses due to bad debts. The equivalents of both items among bank assets were non-debt funds among the liabilities of non-financial businesses. Their non-repayable funds or quasi-equity were created almost exclusively on the basis of bank loans which were predominantly grants. It would have been appropriate not only from the legal point of view but also from the economic point of view – and simply out of fairness – that the non-financial businesses which owned the banks should have been called upon to rehabilitate their banks before they changed into joint-stock companies. Business enterprises then had on average many more non-debt funds (later changed into equity when social ownership was abandoned) than business enterprises in the West. Bank owners were not called upon and therefore the banks that had already changed into joint-stock companies had black holes, empty spaces or losses among their assets on one hand, while on the other hand, non-financial businesses had huge inflated amounts of non-debt funds which were changed into equity.

Figure 12.1 shows the large losses incurred by Slovenian banks and the proportion of funds or bonds which the government provided to rehabilitate them. There were two phases of rehabilitation in which almost all banks were affected. In the general rehabilitation, banks received government bonds in the amount of their losses due to foreign currency bank deposits (1318.7 million DM) and for part of potential losses due to bad debts (248.7 million DM). With the exception of three banks (two of which later merged), other banks were rehabilitated in this way by the general rehabilitation. There was, of course, no need to privatize them because they were never in state ownership. The remaining banks underwent individual rehabilitation. Their main problems were potential losses due to bad debts. These bad debts were exchanged for government bonds (1647.9 million DM) and taken over by the Agency for Rehabilitation. These banks came into state ownership, which is always the case if a government rehabilitates banks.

No bank received any cash, only long-term government bonds; therefore their liquidity situation did not improve much through their rehabilitation.

Assets   Liabilities

Government bonds for General rehabilitation 12.8 per cent SIT 118.6 billion	Capital and reserves 16.5 per cent SIT 152.2 billion
Government bonds for individual rehabilitation 13.5 per cent SIT 124.7 billion	
	Other liabilities 83.5 per cent SIT 771.7 billion
Other assets 73.7 per cent SIT 674.6 billion	

SIT 923.9 billion   SIT 923.9 billion

Source: Bank of Slovenia Bulletins.

Figure 12.1 Slovenian bank balance sheets at the end of 1993, showing losses replaced by government bonds

In Yugoslavia, the banks had approximately the same amount of non-performing assets, but they were kept liquid via a large amount of funds flowing into them from the central bank. The central bank in Belgrade was therefore obliged to pursue a very expansionist monetary policy. But with monetary independence, the Bank of Slovenia immediately needed to change monetary policy from being expansionist to restrictive in stance. Special channels of the supply of liquidity to banks or special instruments of monetary policy had to be introduced so that the banks, then in a most precarious liquidity situation as a result of the rehabilitation procedures, were kept liquid.

Rehabilitation of Slovenia's banks ended in 1997, when the two banks that underwent individual rehabilitation were declared fit for the same treatment on the part of the Bank of Slovenia as other banks. From that time on, it was not only possible to allow more competition in banking but it was desirable to promote it. This was not only a question of new entrants. Even before October 1991, there were some new entrants in the banking sector. Some were domestic and some foreign-owned. But even foreign-owned banks did not have any perceivable impact on the banking sector. They were just happy to earn more; they could achieve that without great effort because they did not have the non-performing assets that burdened the old domestic banks.

Bank rehabilitation, while it could have been done without public funds, was an important second step in the transition of the banking sector and the economy as a whole. Once rehabilitation was over, competition within the Slovenian banking sector became more important. Somewhat later, perhaps even more important was the competition from foreign banks which did not have branches in Slovenia with their branches but which did their business in Slovenia across the border by giving loans to large and successful enterprises that sold most of their products abroad.

Bank Restructuring, Consolidation and Performance in the Post-rehabilitation Period

The number of banks did not increase significantly above the total of 26 in 1991 (Figure 12.2), even though banking was for some time after 1991 a rather attractive business activity. The Bank of Slovenia increased and kept at that high level the minimum capital requirements in order to prevent too big an increase in the number of banks before and during the rehabilitation process. Later it was accepted as normal for the minimum amount of capital for banks in a small transitional economy to be higher than in other economies.

Concentration in Slovenian banking has not been excessive absolutely or compared to other countries (Figure 12.3) But there is one peculiarity that should be kept in mind. One relatively large bank (Nova Ljubljanska Banka) has grown even larger as other banks were acquired as subsidiaries, partly owned to begin with and later wholly owned, and were later changed into branches. This has been the principal way in which consolidation in banking has taken place in Slovenia, albeit in friendly rather than contested fashion.

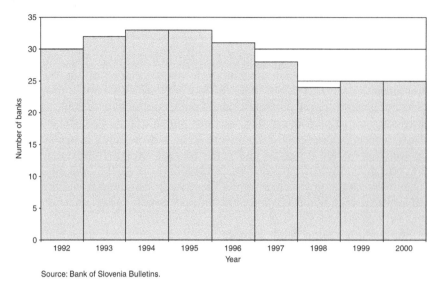

Source: Bank of Slovenia Bulletins.

Figure 12.2   The number of banks in Slovenia, 1991–2000

Other banks that sought to increase their market share through mergers or acquisitions have had much more difficulty in avoiding conflict. While it may be desirable that other banks do not become even smaller compared to the largest bank, this has certainly occurred. However, until Slovenia enters the European Union or the European Monetary Union, the competitiveness of its banking sector – represented not so much by how many banks there are but by the strength of its largest bank – remains high. Consolidation in banking via mergers and acquisitions remains attractive for the small banks whose consolidation increases their cost efficiency. Economies of scale and scope reduces their costs (Košak, 2000, 2001).

Return on assets has been more or less the same since 1995 at around 1 per cent. The relative size of bank capital (tier 1 and tier 2) in comparison to their risk-weighted assets has been decreasing, from 21.5 per cent in 1995 to 13.6 per cent in 2000. Return on equity has been volatile, moving from 7.8 per cent in 1999 to 12.2 per cent in 2000. The net interest margin has not fallen and in 2000 it was still 4.6 per cent (Table 12.1).

We have seen that banks in Slovenia have so far not achieved very much in increasing their cost efficiency. Their net interest margin remains at a high level. One reason for this is relatively high inflation in combination with the indexation of financial assets and liabilities, excluding short-term bank

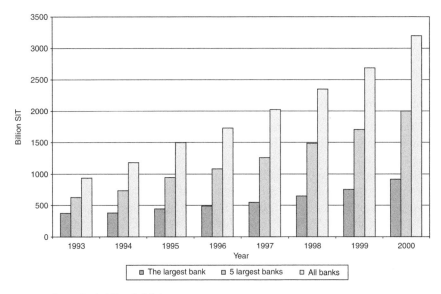

Source: Bank of Slovenia Bulletins.

Figure 12.3 Concentration in Slovenian banking, 1993–2000

liabilities (with maturity up to 30 days). The banks have been postponing their genuine restructuring and consolidation until the last minute, when cross-border competition from foreign banks may force them to cut their loan interest rates to the level that bank borrowers pay abroad.

After the beginning of 1999, the banks had already begun to lose their best borrowers when restrictions on borrowing abroad were removed,

Table 12.1 Percentage return on assets, return on equity, relative size of bank capital and the net interest margin in Slovenian banking, 1994–2000

	1994	1995	1996	1997	1998	1999	June 2000
Return on assets	0.4	1.0	1.1	1.1	1.2	0.8	1.2
Return on equity	4.0	9.2	10.3	10.3	11.3	7.8	12.2
Net interest margin	3.7	4.9	5.6	4.9	4.5	4.0	4.6
Relative size of bank capital	20.5	21.5	19.7	19.0	16.0	14.0	13.6

Source: Bank of Slovenia Bulletins

making the banks aware that they must cut their loan interest rates. The pressure to restructure and consolidate was increasing – as perhaps the only way to survive as independent banks and not change into branches of foreign banks.

Outside Limits on Banks as Asset Transformers

Whatever the banks can achieve in their cost or revenue efficiency, they will not be able to obtain longer-term funds either through deposits or through the sale of long-term bonds, at least in the foreseeable future. Similarly, they will be unable to substantially transform the maturity of those predominantly short-term funds because they are and will remain small. Total bank assets in Slovenia amounted to SIT 3178 billion or approximately 28 billion DM at the end of 2000. If we exclude the assets of those banks that are already or will in the near future be subsidiaries of foreign banks, this amount falls to about SIT 2600 billion (or 24 billion DM). Even if there is only one bank that is not a subsidiary of a foreign bank, it will still be a small bank by European standards.

If domestic banks cannot become big banks in the domestic market, there is little chance that they can compensate by expanding beyond the national

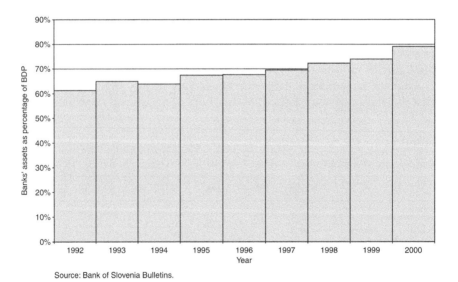

Source: Bank of Slovenia Bulletins.

Figure 12.4   Slovenian bank assets as percentage of GDP, 1991–2000

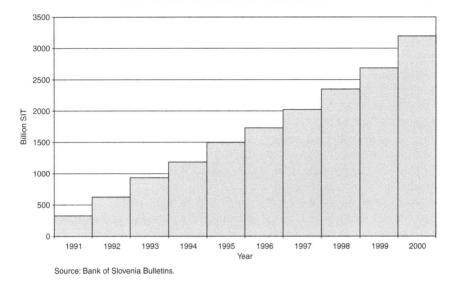

Source: Bank of Slovenia Bulletins.

Figure 12.5   Bank assets in Slovenia, 1991–2000

border. In countries to which they could expand, in most cases the banks there are already branches or subsidiaries of Western European banks. There is simply not much space left for other foreign banks.

Nevertheless there is a place for small banks, as in any other country, if their advantages and disadvantages are properly taken into account. Domestic banks have a disadvantage *vis-à-vis* both foreign-owned banks at home which are the subsidiaries of foreign banks and banks abroad in the supply of longer-term funds to domestic borrowers; domestic banks are small in size and suffer from the high preference of households and others for liquid assets or liquid financial investments. The banks cannot perform financial intermediation properly. Because of their size and the much shorter average maturity of their liabilities, they cannot and will not supply enough longer-term funds. Such banks, if they cannot find means of supplying longer-term funds, will be crowded out of business (Ribnikar, 2000).

Banks or financial intermediaries in general and the financial markets of a small country where there is demand for financial assets of short maturity may provide the longer-term funds required by business enterprises, households and others – but only if they do not isolate themselves from banks and financial markets abroad, particularly in the European Union or the European Monetary Union. What they need, namely the transformation of the maturity of funds, is available in the European banking sector and its financial markets almost like a public good.

The majority of banks in other European transitional economies were bought by foreign banks at the very beginning of transition or were sold later. Hence these banks immediately and somewhat radically addressed the negative effects of their small size and the short maturity of their liabilities in their financial intermediation. They simply became branches or subsidiaries of foreign banks. The problems discussed here simply did not arise because of the 'pre-emptive' measures taken by the governments, as owners of the banks, in their need for cash.

The foreign assets of a small country like Slovenia – the majority of which are central bank international monetary reserves and commercial banks' foreign exchange reserves – are short term or liquid. Its foreign liabilities, which were at least until recently of almost the same size, are of a much longer maturity. Looking at foreign assets and liabilities, banks and financial markets abroad have not been as important as providers of funds for business enterprises and others in Slovenia. Also, as financial intermediaries, they have not been able to channel a net import of funds or capital (a preoccupation of international financial 'experts') to complete the job that domestic financial intermediaries and financial markets have not been able to do.

Because the government of Slovenia has so far not been in such a need for cash, 'pre-emptive' measures have not been taken and (at the time of writing in 2001) the two banks that are in state ownership had not yet been sold.[1] Other banks were never state-owned. If there are possibilities for domestic banks to overcome the two outside obstacles to appropriate financial intermediation, Slovenia should at least try to turn to their benefit the 'public good' nature of varieties of asset transformations which are undertaken by banks or financial intermediaries in general and financial markets abroad, as for example, in the European Monetary Union countries.

The banks should have liquid foreign assets and be indebted abroad in the longer term. Domestically the situation should be just the opposite: they should be short-term or shorter-term indebted at home and be a lender in the long term or longer term. In this way, the banks could provide long-term funds despite their small size and the preference of lenders, depositors and domestic bondholders for liquid financial assets.

To reach this outcome, there should be complete freedom of international financial transactions. What the banks or the economy in which those banks operate need is not so much the import of capital or net imports of capital but freedom of financial transactions in both directions. International financial transactions in both directions would enable banks to perform financial intermediation with the help of the financial intermediation of banks and financial markets abroad. It is a different, more difficult and precarious way of integrating the banks of a small transitional economy in the world banking and financial markets but it should at least be tried. Whether the funds provided in such a roundabout way would be cheap enough is probably the most important question.

Banks as Branches or Subsidiaries of Foreign Banks?

Banks in small and transitional economies can quickly become conventional financial intermediaries if they become branches or subsidiaries of foreign banks. This has occurred already with the majority of banks in all other transitional economies. Because the economies of small countries are and will remain banking economies, this means that control of domestic business enterprises will be predominantly in the hands of foreign banks (Gregorič et al., 2001). This is a result that large and non-transitional economies try hard to avoid in their own markets, for instance by mergers between the biggest domestic banks. Their economies are already market economies to a great degree. At the same time, they advise the small and/or transitional economies to accept that result, for their own benefit.

The point is that the small transitional economies did not and do not have a choice, even when the outcome may not be in their best interests. The case of Slovenia has so far been rather different. Technically, from the very beginning of transition, the banks were not as weak as they were in other transitional economies. Bank rehabilitation took place relatively early and was thorough, so that the banking sector became sound comparatively quickly. In contrast to other transitional economies, the banking sector in Slovenia did not offer foreign investors big profits in the short term. Initially, foreign investors rushed where profits were expected to be highest. Besides, Slovenia was geographically so close to them that in their vision of Eastern Europe they did not even discern the country. Its territorial size, the small population size and its present and expected economic size probably played some role in why it has been 'invisible' to foreign investors. As another important point, banks were never in state ownership with the exception of the two which were nationalized during rehabilitation. Private owners, mostly business enterprises, were not in any hurry to sell bank shares and the government has not been eager, partly for political reasons, to press ahead. There has so far been no need on the part of the government for any 'pre-emptive' sale as was the case in other transitional economies.

The banking sector in Slovenia has had almost ten years to prepare itself for what we might call the second wave of foreign capital entering the banking sectors of transitional economies. This new wave differs from the first. The big opportunities have already gone, probably with the exception of Yugoslavia or Serbia, and therefore investors will search in much greater depth. If the detailed examination is important in this way, then Slovenia will not be overlooked as a target for purchases by foreign banks.

Will banks in Slovenia become branches or subsidiaries of foreign banks only five to ten years later than banks in other transitional economies, with only the price paid by foreign banks being higher? The answer is no if two conditions are fulfilled. Banks in a small transitional economy have problems as financial intermediaries in the maturity transformation of assets or funds. But if banks are able to provide long-term funds to their borrowers cheaply enough through the additional or secondary financial intermediation of banks and financial markets abroad, for instance in the European Monetary Union countries, then the first condition will be met.

If only this first condition is met, that simply means that small banks can exist if they are banks (with predominantly short-term liabilities) which can still give enough long-term loans to their customers. But, as a second condition, a small bank will only become a branch or subsidiary of a foreign bank if its owners sell their shares. This, of course, is not just a question of whether it will become a public instead of a private bank but who its owners or shareholders will be. If we know who a bank's shareholders are and they are predominantly non-financial businesses, then that bank's shares will be for sale. On the other hand, there might be some banks whose shareholders would be firm holders of shares and these banks would not be for sale, at least not quickly or cheaply.

However, it is important that the first condition which we have discussed is met. Who will be the bank owners? Will they be merely branches or subsidiaries of foreign banks or will they be independent banks? This will depend more or less on the same causes, influences, factors, or events that occur in other small economies. In this, the outcome will no longer be determined by the fact that the country and its financial sector are in transition; it will also mean that banking is no longer in transition. That result is probably the most that the banking sector in a small transitional economy can expect or achieve.

References

Gregorič, A., Prašnikar, J. and Ribnikar, I. (2001), 'Corporate governance in transitional economies: the case of Slovenia', *Economic and Business Review*, Ljubljana, 2, 3.

Košak, M. (2000), 'Učinkovitost in tržna struktura v bančništvu – primer Slovenije', PhD thesis, Faculty of Economics, University of Ljubljana, p. 185.

Košak, M. (2001), 'Učinkovitost slovenskih bank', *Bančni vestnik*, 50, 5.

Ribnikar, I. (1984), 'Financiranje gospodarstva in inflacija', *Bančni vestnik*, 33, 9.

Ribnikar, I. (1989), 'Kako ohraniti, kako je to mogoce, kapital v inflaciji – na primer zrevalorizacijo ali indeksacijo', *Bančni vestnik*, 38, 11.

Ribnikar, I. (2000), 'Financial intermediation in a small (transitional) economy', *Economic and Business Review*, Ljubljana, 2, 2.

Note

1   KBC Bank NV, Belgium, acquired a 34 per cent share in Nova Ljubljanska Banka in September 2002 (editors' note).

PART VI

Rupture and Reconnections

South-eastern European Banks and Western Banking: Twentieth Century Connections and Crises

John R. Lampe

Identifying the entire region running southeast from Slovenia to Greece and Turkey as South-eastern Europe, rather than subdividing it between Central Europe and the Balkans, makes sense across the economic history of the entire twentieth century if we concentrate on modern banking. Both industry and agriculture fall too far short of European aggregates in production and vary too much in practice across the region to merit early membership in a modern, integrating European economy. But domestic central and commercial banking, interconnected with Western banks and bank practice, has belonged to that economy since the 1920s.

This brief inquiry cannot attempt a full account of those connections. Existing scholarship has addressed that account in appropriate detail (Notel, 1986, pp. 170–295; Lampe and Jackson, 1982, pp. 202–309, 329–482, 549–56). The purpose here is to concentrate on the political and economic crises that periodically confronted those connections and the responses which they prompted from both sides. This account will provide no comfort to the two simplified approaches that have characterized too much of the attention previously paid to the region's economic history. One is the originally Marxist assumption of control and exploitation flowing from Western financial contact with the region. As articulated by Immanuel Wallerstein in the 1970s, this still influential critique rejects any reciprocal, comparative advantage to trade. It defines international capitalism as nothing more than the Western 'core's' penetration to capture the higher surplus value available from low-wage labour in the non-Western 'periphery' or 'semi-periphery' (Wallerstein, 1979, pp. 1–118). But we may also be wary of an Anglo-American approach that assumed, after the collapse of Communist regimes in 1989, that an inter-war framework for a market economy had existed and could easily be revived. Stock markets, stable exchange rates and newly privatized banks would mobilize the private capital needed to effect a smooth transition. During the Cold War, Western analysis had concentrated on Soviet-bloc economies where banks were dependent and basically incidental institutions. In the process, the former Yugoslavia's more complex financial structure and its socially-owned commercial banks received too little early attention, and non-Communist Greece's, none at all. As we shall see, Greece's experience in particular supports neither the Wallerstein nor the market assumptions just noted (Turkey's experience is omitted here solely for lack of space).

This paper examines five periods of crisis in relations between South-eastern European banks and Western banking, beginning with the 1920s and ending with the 1990s. The decade following the First World War was a period of crisis despite the apparent spread of Western bank presence and enterprise investment. Western banks counted for less, it is argued here, than the combined failure of Western governments to resume the pre-war level of state lending and of newly established or reconstituted regional governments to avoid overvalued exchange rates all the same. The crisis of the 1930s derived from the retreat of Western commercial and investment banking but was also significant for the reforms, sometimes with French or British technical assistance, by the region's central banks. The wartime that followed was longest for Greece, from 1941 to 1952, and involved its central bank in first German and then similar British measures which, ironically, helped to constrain any significant Western presence in Greek banking until the 1990s. For the 1970s and 1980s, I focus on Yugoslavia's debt crisis and the role of Western and Yugoslav banks in first creating and then responding jointly to it. Both the Bulgarian and Romanian economies would face similar repayment problems during the 1980s, but their governments would respond only with administrative restrictions on imports, disastrously deep ones in Ceausescu's Romania. Then in the first post-Communist decade, central banks – even in the new successor states to the former Yugoslavia – established convertible currencies more easily than expected. The region's commercial banks still struggled to find the legal framework that would mobilize badly needed domestic capital and also attract the sort of Western investment that has advanced the Hungarian economy to the front of the line for admission to the European Union.

The 1920s

We are not accustomed to think of the 1920s as a decade of crisis for South-eastern European banks and their Western connections. Indeed more Western commercial banks showed more interest in the region than they had before the First World War, and more of them used new affiliates or branches to hold stock in or extend credit to local industrial or mining enterprises. The picture provided by Liuben Berov for Bulgaria is too easily taken as representative of a larger European financial connection in a time of overall expansion (Berov, 1999, pp. 19–25). Italian, Czech, French, Belgian and German banks established affiliates in Sofia during the early 1920s. By 1927, the five biggest banks held paid-up capital that was almost twice that of the four largest domestic banks, making the foreign share of Bulgaria's bank capital 31 per cent. All seven foreign affiliates owned or sold stock in and extended current account credit to networks of ten to twenty industrial firms or mines. So far, so good, but where is the case for crisis?

First, as Berov himself admits, even in Bulgaria all but two of the seven foreign banks began to retreat from their Bulgarian engagement in general and from their industrial interests in particular between 1923 and 1927. It was during those years that the interest rates of 20 per cent or more that had doubtless played a leading role in attracting foreign banks in the first place began to decline to levels closer to the European norm.

Second, when we look inside the financial structure and foreign investment of the two largest European economies, Germany and France, we find their external activity much reduced from levels of the pre-war period. Richard Tilly recognizes the efforts of the *Grossbanken* to promote German trade with their South-eastern European branches and affiliates, even speculating on their possible role as an intermediary for American capital. But he reminds us that, overall, Weimar Germany had probably become the world's largest debtor. It was certainly Europe's largest debtor, with net capital imports of $4.2 billion for 1924–30, from a total of $7.8 billion of which our four economies accounted for less than $1.0 billion. Germany's foreign investment mediated by banks would remain limited and its presence in our region weak (Tilly, n.d.; Feinstein et al., 1997, p. 91). The Austrian presence in the region also rested on a doubtful foundation (Weber, 2001).

French bank presence included Bulgaria, and its tobacco exports in particular, and also extended to Greece and Romania. But, as Olivier Feiertag points out, the period 1918 to 1926 was largely one of retreat for French banks and their foreign interests. The export of capital from a France which was still working to rebuild its own northeastern region after the ravages of the First World War would remain under administrative control until 1928 (Plessis and Feiertag, 1999, pp. 221–3). France's net export of capital for 1924–30 totalled $1.3 billion, barely more than our region's net capital imports. For Greece, the two French banks respectively involved in the Bank of Salonica and the Bank of Athens had both pulled back from their initial commitments by 1927. In Yugoslavia, the pre-war commitment to the Banque Franco-Serbe was not renewed even at the start of the decade, and we find no French interest in the major Zagreb banks. Despite a strong French diplomatic interest in Romania throughout the interwar period, and despite some ambitious plans for industrial investment from the Paris-Bas and the Banque de l'Union Parisienne, Feiertag calls their activities 'hesitant' and dismisses them as 'backtracking' and 'poor man's imperialism' (Plessis and Feiertag, 1999, p. 224).

The crisis that confronted commercial banking across South-eastern Europe during the 1920s did not come solely from the weakened position of the major German and French investment banks but also from a restrictive framework for central banking. The central banks of Bulgaria, Yugoslavia, Romania, and to a lesser extent Greece, had dutifully stabilized their currencies by the mid-1920s at exchange rates that would supposedly attract foreign loans and investment. While their economies waited in vain for that inflow, the overvalued rates made their exports more expensive and their imports less costly, prompting protective tariffs that further restricted the well-known failure of inter-war trade to return to pre-1914 levels.[1]

I have previously detailed the restriction not only of trade but also of central banks' currency issue. The constant value of per capita note issue for 1926–30 was roughly half that of 1920 for all four economies and less than that for 1911 for three (where Yugoslavia is excepted because we must take the earlier figure for Serbia as representative). Only such restriction could accommodate the combined Western pressures to adopt a fixed, convertible exchange rate enforced by newly empowered central banks and at the same time allow governments to repay war debts (Lampe and Jackson, 1982, pp. 383–94). While the debt burden applied to Bulgaria in the form of reparations, loans from Britain and the United States to support the war efforts of the other three left virtually the same obligation to be repaid. Until terms for that repayment could be negotiated, the US government in particular barred significant access to its capital market, by then the largest in the world. Even Standard Oil found that its pleas to the State Department to pressure the ruling National Liberals to grant their company an exception to the new Mining Law of 1924 were rejected on grounds that Romania had still not settled on repayment of its wartime debts. Eventual negotiations with the Romanian government and the others demanded adherence to the deflationary gold exchange standard but did not generate the tide of new long-term state loans (beyond the modest League of Nations loans of the mid-1920s) that would have been needed to compensate the supply of domestic credit. The absence of new long-term lending would leave the region just as dangerously dependent as Germany by 1929 to cover what Charles Kindleberger has aptly called a 'mare's nest of reparations, war debts and commercial debts' (Kindleberger, 1984, p. 360).

The 1930s

We have long been familiar with the crisis prompted first by the end of short-term Western lending and then by the withdrawal of Western European commercial banks from their South-eastern European connections, reducing their activity in branches, affiliates and attendant networks of enterprise investment. But the crisis was not common to all four sets of commercial banks and had the neglected consequence of promoting reforms for the central banks. At the centre of the retreat by Central European banks was the collapse of Vienna's Creditanstalt in 1931 (Weber, 2001). Its failure hit Romania hard, helping to take down the large domestic Banca Marmarosch Blank, and also the large Zagreb banks, as Ivo Bicanic explains in his chapter in this volume. The French and Belgian retreat came later, most significantly in Bulgaria, but the breach was not filled by Nazi German banks, contrary to one of the long-held assumptions of post-war Marxist economic history in Bulgaria in particular. The small German Kreditna Banka did increase its assets and activities in the late 1930s but not enough to keep the foreign share of Bulgaria's bank assets, both state and commercial, from falling from 21 to 7 per cent between 1931 and 1939 (Lampe, 1986, p. 93; Grenzbach, 1988). For Yugoslavia, the German share of foreign investment, banks and enterprises combined amounted to only 6 per cent in 1939, even after Austria and the Czech lands had been absorbed into the Reich. In Greece, continuing British support explains an inflow of capital per capita for 1931–37 which was three times that of Romania, the nearest regional rival (Mazower, 1991, pp. 179–202; Lampe and Jackson, 1982, pp. 476–82, 504–19).

It was nevertheless a French connection with central rather than commercial banking that provided a positive response to the Depression's financial crisis, at least for Romania and Yugoslavia. Once the franc had been officially stabilized in 1928, the Bank of France began a programme of stabilization loans and technical assistance to smaller European countries that reached Bulgaria before the Depression descended but not Romania and Yugoslavia. There the large stabilization loans came too late to have much effect on the two economies' structural vulnerability to the Depression or to keep their attendant adherence to a gold-exchange standard that

Britain and other countries abandoned in 1931 from becoming a deflationary handicap. But the French connection did serve two other purposes. One was to continue the policy of Emile Moreau as governor of the central Banque de France until 1930, that is, the policy of using the bank's leverage to counter British or German influence, diplomatic as well as economic. The second was to provide technical advisers to the central banks of both Romania and Yugoslavia who worked with their increasingly able staffs to codify and further reform the entire framework for commercial banking. For Romania, these efforts extended into the Ministry of Finance and the badly needed revision of the tax code. For Yugoslavia, the French presence prompted a rival team of British advisers to appear in Belgrade by 1934 (Plessis and Feiertag, 1999, pp. 226–7; Lampe and Jackson, 1982, p. 479).

For Bulgaria and Greece, we find a similar process of financial reform under way, proceeding from the central bank and consolidating the number of commercial banks. Bulgaria's brief Zveno regime of 1934 none the less left a lasting economic imprint with the merger of 19 domestic commercial banks into a new state bank, the Banka Bulgarski Kredit. The central Bulgarska Narodna Banka acquired new powers for trade premiums while giving up its role as a commercial lender. But here was reform that, as I have argued elsewhere, set the stage for the post-war Communist regime rather than private enterprise and a market economy (Lampe, 1986, pp. 92–3). Greece's reaction to the Depression crisis also set the stage for its post-war financial framework of private concentration. Mergers of smaller commercial banks played a lesser part, although such combinations had reduced their total number from 48 to 31 between 1930 and 1938. More important was the predominance, further encouraged by their intense rivalry, of the new central Bank of Greece and the longstanding National Bank of Greece. Their combined assets approached 80 per cent of the Greek total by 1934. With their aforementioned access to British credit as well, they were able to provide the support for industrial enterprise that other regional banking systems had to leave to the state during the 1930s. Partly for this reason, Greek industrial production already exceeded its 1929 level by 41 per cent in 1935 (Mazower, 1991, pp. 100–12, 250–6; Pagoulatos, 1999, p. 116).

The 1940s and 1950s

Everywhere in South-eastern Europe with the exception of Greece, post-war Communist regimes quickly took power following Axis occupation or collaboration during the Second World War. These Soviet-style regimes,

Tito's Yugoslavia included, put an end to private commercial banks and the practice of independent central banking. Only Greece's experience with preserving both, in the face of German occupation and then the civil war of 1946–52, is relevant to the present inquiry.

That experience with first German and then British support for the drachma not only reinforced the predominance of the central bank and one large commercial bank, the Bank of Greece and the National Bank of Greece. It also encouraged the virtual isolation of Greek banking from Western connections that ensued through the 1950s. The isolation derived in part from the desire of the central bank and the venerable National Bank, the bank of note emissions until it lost that power to the former in 1928, to maintain their predominance. Yet it also drew wider support in Greece from the curiously similar experiences that Nazi and then British gold sales had afforded in supporting the drachma but also in prolonging the hyper-inflations of the period 1941–46.

What came to be seen in Greece as a single experience, now described in full financial detail by Michael Palairet, began in 1943 on the initiative of Hermann Neubacher (Palairet, 2000). Appointed to head the Axis economic mission to Greece in October 1942, the former mayor of Vienna and executive of I. G. Farben faced the immediate problem of funding Wehrmacht expenses in Greece from local resources as much as possible. How could these expenses be paid with a currency increasingly discounted by a hyperinflation that had begun in 1941? He rejected another halving of existing notes, issuing new ones for full value of one half and keeping the other for official purposes, as the Greek government had successfully done in 1922 and 1926. Instead, Neubacher diverted gold sovereigns brought in to pay army bills directly to the Athens Stock Exchange, where they were auctioned off for drachmas. Forcing the Bank of Greece to augment these notes with additional credits, this 'gold auction' allowed German authorities to preserve the Greek currency as a means of payment expanded by the gains from seigniorage (that is, printing new notes beyond the purchased amount). In the process, drachmas covered 65 per cent of Wehrmacht occupation costs from November 1943 to October 1944.

However, Greek hyperinflation persisted for another two years beyond the end of the occupation. A Greek government already challenged by the Communist insurgency of December 1944 tried and failed to establish an egalitarian regime of property tax collection from private business while fixing food prices but allowing wage increases to continue. After the collapse of the initial Varvaressos reform, a successor government returned to relying on the exchange of gold for drachmas. These gold sales supported an exchange rate that allowed it to print new notes that the public would accept and thereby award the resulting addition to the state budget. The Anglo-Greek Agreement of January 1946 created a Currency Committee including British and American members with veto rights to supervise the activities of the Bank of Greece. Within this framework, first Britain and then the United States accepted gold from Bank of Greece reserves in return for sovereigns that went directly into the Greek currency market. Their ready exchange for drachmas, to a sum that was double the previous German total by the end of 1946, slowed inflation and allowed the government budget to live off new note issue (whose depreciation was kept under control by gold sales).

Our concern here is not the immediate effect of this seigniorage arrangement but rather the system of credit rationing through the Bank of Greece to commercial banks that the post-war crisis served to leave in place until the late 1950s. On the positive side, this system channelled United States aid and subsequently 10–15 per cent of total lending to industrial enterprises. At the same time, it also demanded that commercial banks should keep 10–20 per cent of their deposits on reserve at the Bank of Greece and place another 10 per cent or more in government bonds. Under these restrictions, some 90 per cent of commercial bank assets remained in two bank networks and foreign banks were greatly discouraged. The dozen foreign banks active in Greece were limited to no more than 40 per cent of share capital, and no foreign branches were even allowed until the 1960s. By then, the increase in private savings was sufficient to force open commercial banking and leave the Currency Committee to wither, although it lived on formally until 1982 (Ferris, 1986, pp. 142–50; Halikias, 1978, pp. 14–15). It should be noted that the subsequent deregulation of Greece's commercial banking, even after further encouragement from accession in 1981 to what is now the European Union, has not increased the share of Western banks in Greece's commercial bank assets to more than 13 per cent (Pagoulatos, 1999, pp. 104–16).

The 1970s and 1980s

No Western bank could hold assets, let alone shares in any bank in Yugoslavia. Yet Western commercial banks soon developed connections to a variety of entities following the economic reform of 1965. That reform replaced the mushrooming network of 380 communal banks with a set of no more than 40 regional institutions each intended to operate as commercial banks with principal enterprise depositors becoming shareholders. The three large state banks in Belgrade designated for investment, foreign trade and agriculture were also restructured on commercial lines.

By the late 1970s, a number of these banks plus new ones had been established in the republics' capitals to replicate the Investment Bank in Belgrade. They led the way in a surge of short- and medium-term borrowing from leading US and Western European banks. The use of these loans was not sufficiently productive during the 1970s to slow a rising rate of inflation or to prevent the debt-servicing crisis of the early 1980s. Inflation climbed in the 1970s by an annual average of 18 per cent and foreign debt rose more, by 20 per cent, versus a mere 5 per cent average increment for Gross Domestic Product. Worse was yet to come. Harold Lydall, the prescient Western pessimist about Yugoslavia's economic prospects throughout the 1980s, aptly dubbed the period 1979–85 'the great reversal', citing annual average changes for real production and investment and real per capita consumption and income that now were uniformly negative (Lydall, 1989, pp. 40–71).

We confine our concern here to the role of Western and Yugoslav banks in this crisis. The former are hardly free of responsibility. Awash in petro-dollars from the first Oil Shock of 1973, German, British and especially American banks could not resist the higher interest rates of return that were available from loans to borrowers outside the circle of Western development – from Brazil to Poland to Indonesia as well as Yugoslavia. Most, including Yugoslavia, offered the prospect of repayment inflated by overvalued currencies. Most were secured by the presumption of official guarantee rather than the project's immediate prospects. For Yugoslavia, moreover, the period 1970–79 witnessed the transition of its foreign debt from 56 per cent official with 74 per cent guaranteed to 71 per cent private with 68 per cent unguaranteed. Manufacturers Hanover Trust and Chase Manhattan Bank in New York were the largest American contributors to this new private majority. While they may have been reassured by Yugoslavia's spotless record in repaying its low-interest loans from the World Bank, none of their commercial loans of the 1970s were accorded to that single federal government. The multitude of borrowers was sufficient to leave the federal authorities in Belgrade unable to determine total indebtedness – some $19 billion – without the assistance of an American accounting firm. The debt crisis came to a head (as detailed by Russell Prickett, the US Embassy's Economic Counselor at the time) when Manufacturers Hanover could not find other backers for a $500 million loan to allow the central National Bank of Yugoslavia to service the sizeable repayment due in 1982 (Lampe et al., 1990, pp. 148–89). How appropriate that the same now significantly exposed US lender would take the lead among the Western banks that joined the officially coordinated US effort to obtain support from the International Monetary Fund (IMF), the World Bank and the Bank for International Settlements. These 'Friends of Yugoslavia' provided rescheduling, consolidation and new credits that totalled $4.5 billion for 1983. The immediate result of this effort was to allow Yugoslavia to reverse its current account deficit of recent years and record a small surplus for 1983, thereby receiving another $3 billion package from the same Western consortium in 1984.

The subsequent failure of this assistance and the considerable conditions attached to it are well known. IMF conditions stipulating the repayment of principal as well as interest served no constructive purpose in the short run. It would have helped to assure continued Western support by 1989, when a mandate for sweeping internal change in Yugoslavia's economic framework brought Ante Markovic and his plans for full-scale market reforms to head the federal government. By that time, however, the political possibility for carrying it through with enough consensus among the republics no longer existed (Lampe, 2000, pp. 325–31).

However the internal problem could not have been addressed by any other IMF or Western response. That problem was the continuing inability of the central bank in Belgrade to limit the money supply by controlling credit to the complex of commercial banks in Yugoslavia. The IMF Standby Agreement of 1983–85 had at least ended the negative interest rates for domestic borrowers. But the IMF condition of interest rates set at 1 per cent above the rate of inflation did not prevent new National Bank emissions to the rest of the banking system nor did it keep inflation from resuming in 1986 once other IMF guidelines had been set aside. The briefly successful diktat of the Markovic government to the central bank in 1990, however, would show what a central bank independent of republic political influence might have done sooner and with some chance of a lasting effect.

The 1990s and Beyond

The challenges of the post-Communist period since 1989 invite an appraisal of the experience of South-eastern European banks and European banking earlier in the twentieth century. Which experiences are still relevant, whether exemplary for continuing connections or cautionary tales for economic crises?

This chapter offers the following tentative conclusions. The debt burdens of the post-1989 period have proved less severe and prompted a more flexible Western response than after the First World War. Still, the Croatian central bank's restrictive emissions of the 1990s in order to maintain an overvalued exchange rate had no more success in attracting a large inflow of Western capital than did the region's central banks during the 1920s, both acting under direct political control rather than independently. The fixing of Bulgaria's exchange rate permanently to the German mark since 1997 (under the independent Currency Board set up at Western urging) runs the danger of similar overvaluing while making central bank policy irrelevant.

At the same time, the road to political independence pioneered by South-eastern European central banks and encouraged by Western technical assistance from the late 1920s into the Depression decade is a direction essential for membership in the European Union of today. The establishment of new currencies in Slovenia, Macedonia and Croatia and the stemming of hyperinflation in Bulgaria – and even Milosevic's Serbia – proved to be less difficult than predicted, in part because of the domestic expertise in central banking which had already accumulated.

But as in Greece after the Second World War, simply ending hyperinflation could not create a competitive set of commercial banks. Indeed, that process did not begin in Greece until the privatization required by the European Union finally took place in the late 1980s (Niarchos, 1999, pp. 85–102). Here the entire region cannot draw on an inter-war legacy of healthy domestic competition and constructive Western assistance. The privatization of commercial banks in the post-Communist states has thus proved doubly difficult; it still eludes Romania and Bosnia-Herzegovina.[2] Although official assistance is now available and often accepted for privatization, the regional temptation remains to resist Western bank branches and affiliates. Yet their belated arrival in Greece has not, as we have seen, swamped domestic rivals. The competitive framework within which domestic commercial banks operate most efficiently is only strengthened, as in Hungary, by the arrival of Western banks; these banks are far removed from the dominating networks of industrial investment of the 1920s and also prudently wary of repeating their reckless lending of the 1970s. Their recent presence in Croatia, hopefully forcing down high rates of interest that have limited domestic access to credit, and their interest in Serbia should prove instructive. So should the initiative of the Nova Ljubljanska Banka to acquire one existing bank in Macedonia and another in Bosnia, plus a share in a third in Serbia.

References

Berov, L. (1999), 'Foreign capital in the Bulgarian banking system, 1878–1944–1997', in Kostis, K. P. (ed.), *Modern Banking in the Balkans and West-European Capital in the Nineteenth and Twentieth Centuries*, Aldershot: Ashgate, pp. 15–33.

Eichengreen, B. (1992), *Golden Fetters: The Gold Standard and the Great Depression, 1919–1939*, London: Oxford University Press.

Feinstein, C., Temin. P. and Toniolo, G. (1997), *The European Economy Between the Wars*, London: Oxford University Press.

Ferris, A. F. (1986), *The Greek Economy in the Twentieth Century*, London: Croom Helm.

Grenzbach, Jr, W. (1988), *Germany's Informal Empire in East-Central Europe, 1933–1939*, Stuttgart: Franz Steiner Verlag.

Halikias, D. J. (1978), *Money and Credit in a Developing Economy, The Greek Case*, New York: NYU Press.

Kindleberger, C. P. (1984), *A Financial History of Western Europe*, London: Allen & Unwin.

Kostis, K. (ed.), (1999), *Modern Banking in the Balkans and West-European Capital in the Nineteenth and Twentieth Centuries*, Aldershot: Ashgate.

Lampe, J. (1986), *The Bulgarian Economy in the Twentieth Century*, London: Croom Helm.

Lampe, J. (2000), *Yugoslavia as History, Twice There Was a Country*, 2nd edn, Cambridge: Cambridge University Press.

Lampe, J. and Jackson, M. (1982), *Balkan Economic History, 1550–1950*, Bloomington, IN: Indiana University Press.

Lampe, J., Adamovic, L. and Prickett, R. (1990), *Yugoslav-American Economic Relations since World War II*, Durham, NC: Duke University Press.

Lydall, H. (1989), *Yugoslavia in Crisis*, Oxford: Clarendon Press.

Mazower, M. (1991), *Greece and the Interwar Economic Crisis*, Oxford: Clarendon Press.

Niarchos, N. A. (1999), 'Privatization in the banking sector and its effect on the Greek stock market', in Sevic, Z. (ed.), *Banking Reform in Southeast European Transitional Economies*, Greenwich, UK: University of Greenwich Business School, pp. 85–102.

Notel, R. (1986), 'International finance and monetary reforms', in Kaser, M. C. and Radice, E. A. (eds), *The Economic History of Eastern Europe, 1919–1975*, 2 vols, London: Oxford University Press.

Pagoulatos, G. (1999), 'The Greek banking system and its deregulation', in Kostis, K. (ed.), *Modern Banking in the Balkans* ..., Aldershot: Ashgate.

Palairet, M. (2000), *The Four Ends of the Greek Hyperinflation of 1941–46*, Copenhagen: Museum Tusculanum Press, University of Copenhagen.

Plessis, A. and Feiertag, O. (1999), 'The position and role of French finance in the Balkans from the later nineteenth century until the Second World War', in Kostis, K. P. (ed.), *Modern Banking in the Balkans and West-European Capital in the Nineteenth and Twentieth Centuries*, Aldershot: Ashgate, pp. 215–34.

Tesche, J. (2000), 'Bosnia and Herzegovina: The Post-Dayton economy and financial system', *MOCT-MOST*, 3–4, pp. 311–24.

Tilly, R. (n.d.), 'German banks and foreign investment in Eastern and Central Europe before 1939', unpublished paper.

Wallerstein, I. (1979), *The Capitalist World-Economy*, Cambridge: Cambridge University Press.

Weber, F. (2001), 'The failure of the Austrian Creditanstalt and its consequences', unpublished paper, European Association for Banking History.

Notes

1 The wider case against the generally deflationary and export-inhibiting consequences for most European economies of the mid-1920s adjustment to, if not yet adoption of the gold exchange standard, may be found in convincing detail in Eichengreen, 1992.

2 On the prolonged Bosnian struggle to turn too many small existing banks into a viable set of private commercial banks capable of lending at affordable rates, see Tesche, 2000, pp. 311–24.

CHAPTER 14

Reconstructing National Identities: The Banknotes of Central and Eastern Europe in the 1990s

Virginia Hewitt and Tim Unwin[1]

The central aim of this chapter is to examine the ways in which the dramatic transformations that have taken place over the last decade in Central and Eastern Europe have been reflected in the restructuring of financial instruments. It focuses particularly on the creation of new currencies, and the ways in which banknotes have been used to express a renewed interpretation of national identity in the region during the 1990s. The crisis it addresses is thus the dramatic upheaval in banking systems following the disintegration of the Soviet Union and the collapse of the command economy; the renewal is reflected in a renewed search for national identities in the wake of the introduction of so-called liberal democracies.

The chapter begins with an overview of the context of political and economic 'transition' within which the introduction of new financial instruments has played such an important role. This is followed by a brief discussion of the significance of the new currencies and series of banknotes that have been introduced in the region, and a broad analysis of the imagery depicted on the notes that have been issued therein since 1989. The second half of this chapter focuses on particular case studies which illustrate the variety of ways in which banknote designs have reflected the diversity of crisis and renewal experienced in Central and Eastern Europe over this period, and the consequent re-emerging national identities.

The Context of Transition[2]

There is a rapidly growing literature that seeks to understand or explain the changes that have occurred in the so-called transition economies of Central and Eastern Europe (see, for example, Pickles and Smith, 1998; Roberts, 1999; Bradshaw and Stenning, 2001; Hall and Danta, 2000). In essence, the transition economies are most usually defined simply as those previously centrally planned economies – together with the decentralized economies of the former Yugoslavia – that are currently undergoing a process of reform to create market economies (Bradshaw and Stenning, 2001). Much of the early literature on transition adopted a specifically programmatic stance (Callinicos, 1991; Miliband, 1991; Burawoy, 1992). Thus, the statements of many of those liberal academics supporting transition in the early 1990s were concerned more to advocate the free market than they were to provide a rigorous appraisal of the various alternative models of social, political and economic change that governments in Central and Eastern Europe might have pursued (Åslund, 1992, 1995; Blanchard et al., 1992). This is typified in the work, for example, of Sachs (1990, 1995), whose shock-therapy model, with its advocacy of a free market hand-in-hand with liberal democracy, was to be so influential in shaping the political and economic paths followed by many new governments in Central and Eastern Europe. As Gowan (1995, p. 9) has argued, this model sought to create a very specific kind of political economy, with 'a state as open as it is possible for it to be to the forces of international economic operators: a state with a globalized institutional structure, through which the resources of what he calls "the global mainstream economy" can be'. It was also a transition that had to happen as quickly as possible. As Lynn (1999) has emphasized, 'The new post-Soviet governments were encouraged by neo-liberal strategists to cash in on their immediate post-independence legitimacy and remove as much of the previous system as they could while they had the chance: transition had to be comprehensive and it had to happen all at once in a seamless web.' It was as part of this speedy rejection of the recent past that new financial systems and banknotes were issued across the region, both in the former Soviet Union and also in those parts of Central and Eastern Europe outside the rouble zone.

One of the most trenchant advocates of the neo-conservative case was Fukuyama (1992), whose book *The End of History and the Last Man* sought to explore the apparent historical victory of capitalist 'democracy' over communism. Such arguments were premised on the need to show that the collapse of communism was a direct result of the economic superiority of capitalism, and they had the specific political objective of encouraging governments to adopt capitalism's twin pillars of liberal democracy and the free market. Moreover, the IMF and World Bank (see, for example, World Bank, 1996) played a significant role in helping countries to follow this path through the economic reviews that they conducted in the region, and their subsequent support for structural adjustment packages designed to incorporate these fledgling market economies into the global capitalist economy. Central to such policies was the need to adopt new macro-economic instruments, prime among which was the importance placed on financial stability.

Many of the problems associated with this simplistic model of a clear-cut and uniform path of transition that would rapidly lead states from their former centralized and/or planned economic system to a liberalized free market economy have been highlighted by more recent research (see, for example, Pickles and Smith, 1998; Smith and Pickles, 1998; Bradshaw and Stenning, 2001). In particular, Stark (1995; see also Grabher and Stark, 1997) has argued forcefully that it is not as easy as many commentators have assumed to create capitalism by design through the creation of a few key institutional and structural transformations (see also Smith and Swain, 1998). A second set of criticisms has focused more explicitly on the spatial and temporal diversity of transition. Karl and Schmitter (1991) have thus stressed the importance of identifying different kinds of transition, not only in Southern and Eastern Europe, but also drawing on experience from Latin America. This is a theme echoed by Lynn (1999, p. 824), who emphasizes the importance of adopting what he terms 'a critical geographical perspective' on these changes, noting the need for a more contextual, place- and time-specific, interpretation of transition. As this present chapter illustrates, transition has most certainly not been a monolithic construct, but has instead reflected a myriad of different colours and nuances; contrasting variations around a single theme (Unwin, 1999).

At the heart of theoretical debates over transition, there is a fundamental tension between the ideas of capitalist economic modernization and political freedom. This is of crucial significance to the present paper, because the economic instruments we consider are the new banknotes introduced in the transition economies of the region in the 1990s, and yet these also express a dimension of political freedom through their representations of national identity. Habermas raises the key question of whether the countries of Central and Eastern Europe possess the necessary cultural conditions to ensure that there is positive, rather than negative, feedback between the political and economic structures emerging through their re-incorporation into the capitalist world economy. As he argued in the mid-1990s, 'the evidence continues to mount that there is no automatic relationship between capitalist modernization and political freedom' (1994, p. 84). One of the central purposes of this paper is thus to explore the interactions between the economic and the political that are expressed in banknotes.

The idea that individual freedom, in the guise of liberal democracy, and capitalism, in the form of the market economy, are each essential for the success of the other, is long-established. Nevertheless, as Held (1991, 1995) has emphasized, the linkages between forms of political representation, national sovereignty and economic system have not always been as clearly differentiated as they might have been. In particular, Held (1995) stresses that there are many alternative kinds of democracy, each of which is related to the global political and economic system in significantly different ways (for Latvian and Estonian examples, see for example, Smith, 1996). What is important here is that the rhetoric of 'democracy' has been used by those in power across Central and Eastern Europe as a means of legitimizing their political and economic control. Habermas (1994) thus stresses that we need to understand and distinguish carefully between various economic and political interests and processes. It is with just such interests and processes that we engage in this paper.

Financial Restructuring in Central and Eastern Europe in the 1990s[3]

Central to the reforms associated with transition were aspirations to create new and stable currencies. As Klagge (1998, p. 194) has argued, 'The development of financial markets in eastern Europe is an important part of the transformation from planned to market Economies. Banks play a central role in this process, as banking functions such as payment, clearance and the provision of finance are at the heart of a capitalist market economy' (see also Bonin and Székely, 1994; Caprio and Levine, 1994; Dittus, 1994; Hall and Danta, 2000). Surprisingly, though, major surveys of the 'new' Europe (see, for example, Graham, 1998; Pinder, 1998; Hall and Danta, 2000) have paid remarkably little attention to the establishment of new currencies and financial systems in the region.

At the heart of the macro-economic policy recommended for the newly emergent states of Central and Eastern Europe by the IMF were three key instruments: stable currencies, balanced budgets and liberal foreign trade (Unwin, 1998a, 1998b). While different states have had varying fortunes in implementing these policies, all of them have created new banking systems and issued new currencies as they have sought to create economies compatible with the free market liberal-democratic hegemony that has come to dominate the global economic system. As Surga and Pekárek (1998, p. 163) have commented in discussing the introduction of new currency in the Czech Republic, 'Currency is one of the fundamental expressions of the sovereignty of any state.' Estonia provides a classic example of the processes of currency reform and the transformation of monetary policy that were such an essential element of 'transition' during the early 1990s (Kallas and

Sõrg, 1995; Kelder, 1997; Sõrg and Vensel, 1999). In describing this transformation Kallas and Sõrg (1995, p. 52) have thus recorded that

> The need to introduce its own currency resulted from the re-establishment of political independence in Estonia that had to be supported by economic sovereignty. But a groundwork of economic independence is an independent monetary system. On the other hand, a successful transition to a market economy requires a solid currency as a medium of exchange, unit of account and a store of value.

This quotation neatly stresses the fundamental interconnectedness of the political and economic processes that have shaped the creation of new states from the fragmentation of the Soviet Union, and the key role played in this by the new currencies. What is of most significance about this for the present paper is that, whilst new currencies were of fundamental economic importance to the restructuring of states throughout Central and Eastern Europe, these currencies also had very great tangible and symbolic significance. As Brozoviç (1994) has noted, 'Money is the foundation of the national economy, but also the mark of national sovereignty and it mirrors the State which issues it. The symbolic role of money is one of its essential characteristics, and the name of the currency its salient feature.'

The introduction of these new currencies and the designs on the banknotes themselves were generally accepted quite positively by people in most of the countries of Central and Eastern Europe so far examined. However, in the case of Croatia, the name of the new monetary unit to be adopted was highly contested. Article 34 of the Law on the National Bank of Croatia (National Gazette 74, 4 November 1992) specified that the new monetary unit should be called the Croatian crown (kruna) divided into one hundred banica. This led to considerable public protest, primarily on the grounds that the 'crown' was a foreign, international name, and that an indigenous Croatian name should be used instead. It was then suggested that the new currency should be called the kuna (literally meaning 'marten'), divided into lipa (Croatian for 'lime tree'). Marten skins had been used as a means of payment in early medieval times, and a figure of the marten had been used on Croatian coinage in the thirteenth and fourteenth centuries. However, there was also criticism of the choice of the name kuna by many of those opposed to the far right, because it had been used as the name of the currency adopted by the Independent State of Croatia allied to the Axis countries during Second World War. As Brozoviç (1994, p .7) comments, 'The critics claimed that the name was not founded on older Croatian tradition, but only linked with the 1941–1945 Independent State of Croatia and that this was detrimental to Croatian interests because it jeopardized Croatia's image in the modern world, built on foundations created in the 1939–1945 antifascist war against Axis powers.' This criticism was eventually overruled by the government, primarily because it was argued that the term kuna had indeed been used historically, and that the leaders of the Independent State of Croatia in the early 1940s had merely utilized this older tradition. In Brozoviç's terms, the kuna 'links different periods and it is historically neutral, and characteristic and representative of Croatia' (Brozoviç, 1994, p. 40). Nevertheless, the ethnic diversity of Croatia provided a source of continued friction during the mid-1990s, as some minorities felt frustrated by this imposition of a particular kind of Croatian identity; this frustration was voiced primarily in the name of anti-fascism. From a Croatian viewpoint, though, the use of the kuna-lipa pairing provided a clear break with the more recent past of Serbian domination.

Banknotes are therefore not only of interest for purely economic reasons, but because they also reflect a wide range of political, social and ideological interests (see, for example, Hewitt, 1995a). Gilbert and Helleiner (1999a, p. 1) have stressed that 'Most existing literature addressing contemporary monetary transformations has been written by economists who are inclined to view money primarily as an economic phenomenon' (see also Gilbert, 1998). This paper seeks to adopt a more culturally sensitive approach to the understanding of banknotes and the creation of national identities. Moreover, it also focuses on a particularly significant period, because for those countries in Central and Eastern Europe aspiring to join the European Union, their currencies may soon be subsumed within the Euro.[4] This efflorescence of artistic representations of national identity in the 1990s therefore reflects a brief and poignant moment in these states' development. They are all reasserting very specific kinds of national identities following their separation from Soviet domination, but these will in turn have to be discarded upon their accession to the Euro zone.

The Banknotes of Central and Eastern Europe Issued Since 1989

The banknote database

In order to examine the linkages between banknotes and national identity in Central and Eastern Europe, we first created a database portraying information about all of the banknotes issued in the region since 1989. As of April 2001, complete information has been obtained on 280 banknotes from 17 countries.[5] In the absence of previous attempts to develop rigorously structured databases for the analysis of banknote imagery on this scale, the choice of information to include within the database required some considerable deliberation (for wider discussion of the analysis of visual imagery, see Ball and Smith, 1992; and for geographical interpretations of the visual, Rose, 1996). The key themes of interest for our examination of the notes as expressions of national identity were thus taken to be not only the images on both sides of the notes themselves, but also textual descriptions about the images represented as well as the colours, languages, and epochs depicted. Information on the designers, printers, sizes of the notes, and sources of information about them was also included. The use of a FileMaker Pro 4.1 relational database (currently 129.2 MB) enables the entire set of data to be searched for any words or phrases in which a user is interested, and for the database to be sorted accordingly. In its standard form, the entries are sorted by country, and then within each country by denomination and date of issue. Once the database had been largely completed, all of the information was then checked for consistency, and a two-tier categorization of the descriptive data entries introduced. This was particularly pertinent to the entries for the dominant images, which were rewritten to indicate, for example, woman (opera singer), man (poet), or building (church). This then enabled the category to be searched system-atically, both at a generic level (woman, man, building), and also at the more detailed level of opera singer, poet or church. At the most detailed level, it is possible to search the text descriptions of the banknotes, each of which is usually between 50 and 100 words in length, for any words included within them, thus enabling the whole database to be searched at a fine level of resolution.

Themes in banknote imagery

Prior to a more detailed exposition of the ways in which crisis and renewal have been explored in the banknote imagery of particular states, this section of the chapter provides a short overview of the images depicted on the banknotes of Central and Eastern Europe, focusing on five main themes: the types of series used, the features depicted on the notes, their colours, gender, and epoch. Most countries have issued more than one version of many of their banknotes over the last decade, and therefore only the most recent version of each note is included in this analysis.

Series

The dominant theme for most of the banknote series examined here has been depictions of artists and scientists who have played a significant role in the emergence of a state's national identity. Thus, three of the eight Estonian banknotes depict people who played a central role in the republic's period of national awakening in the nineteenth century, namely Jakob Hurt, Lydia Koidula and Carl Robert Jakobson. Likewise, Bulgaria's banknotes include depictions of Stefan Stambolov, Peter Beron and Pagisios of Chiliandar, all of whom played important practical roles in the emergence of a Bulgarian national identity.[6] Other banknotes depict people who became national heroes, such as the Lithuanian pilots Steponas Darius and Stasys Girènas who attempted to fly from New York to Kaunas in 1933, but crashed in uncertain circumstances in Poland. In contrast, three countries (Hungary, Poland and Ukraine) have banknote series that depict past rulers on them, and in the case of Moldova all of the banknotes have the image of a single person, Stefan the Great, on their fronts. This imagery evokes memories of past periods of greatness, when their territories and political strength were either emergent or expanding.

The exceptions to these broad generalisations are interesting. While Slovakia and the Czech Republic combine images of rulers with those of other famous personages from their pasts, Latvia, Macedonia and Armenia have adopted a different approach to their banknote series. The Armenian series issued in 1993 depicts material objects such as buildings, coins and sculpture, although its most recent series, first issued in 1998, has adopted the more usual practice of using famous artists and scientists. Latvia and Macedonia nevertheless continue to provide alternative strategies, and their notes include some of the most visually beautiful examples of those being considered here. Macedonia's brightly coloured notes thus illustrate a range of archaeological features, sculptures and buildings, and half of Latvia's notes depict aspects of rural landscapes as represented by an oak tree, a river landscape, and a farmstead on their fronts.

Dominant images

Within the broad parameters determined by the choice of material to be depicted in the banknote series, there remains a wide diversity of particular images that have been adopted by their designers. The most obvious and significant feature to note about these images is the dominance of human faces (for a wider discussion of portraiture on banknotes, see Pointon, 1998). Some 81 per cent of all of the banknote fronts thus had human faces as their dominant image, with the vast majority (92 per cent) of these images being of men. Of the people depicted on the fronts of the notes, 18 per cent were kings or princes, 12 per cent were writers, 11 per cent poets, 8 per cent statesmen or politicians, 7 per cent priests or monks, and 5 per cent painters or artists. The lack of representation of politicians and statesmen from the recent past on banknotes from all of the countries examined reflects a widespread feeling that the people chosen to be depicted on the notes should reflect wider interests than those of any one political party. As one person interviewed concluded, present-day politicians change too quickly to be included, and only represent a transient impression of national identity.

While the imagery on the fronts of the banknotes is dominated virtually to the exclusion of all else by people's faces, it is much less easy to draw generalized conclusions concerning the imagery on the backs of the notes. In most instances, such imagery reflects a conscious attempt to depict a scene or object related to the person shown on the front of the banknote, although frequently more than one such image is used. Among these diverse images, it is very evident that buildings, and urban imagery in general, vastly overwhelm the depiction of rural landscape imagery. Some 40 per cent of all the dominant back images are thus of urban buildings, and approximately one third of these are in some way related to Christianity.

Colour
Surprisingly little research has been undertaken on the ways in which colour is related to national identity. At its most obvious, though, this is of clear importance to such expressions of national identity as expressed in flags and the clothing worn by sports teams. In the past, many banknotes were clearly identifiable with a single colour. However, advances in printing technology, and a desire to keep one step ahead of the forgers has meant that notes now include a much wider diversity of colours. Indeed, it is often difficult to tell precisely which colours dominate any particular banknote. Many different factors have contributed to the spectra of colours used in the banknote series under examination here, including the choices made by the designers themselves, the decisions of various central bank committees, and the contributions of staff in the companies which actually printed the notes. In some instances, the colour of banknotes reflects the choice of subject matter depicted. Thus blue is an obvious colour to choose for the sea scenes depicted on the 100 kroon Estonian note and the 200 litas Lithuanian note. Likewise, green is highly appropriate for the Latvian 5 lats note depicting an oak tree, as well as for the Estonian 25 kroon of a farmstead set in a rural landscape. In other cases, such as the notes of the Czech Republic, the new series has followed an established convention of using certain colours for each denomination.

There is no evidence that banknotes systematically replicate the colours depicted on national flags, or indeed on other heraldic representations of national identity. However, in a few instances particular notes do indeed convey something of a nation's heraldic representation. Thus, the 1000 kuna note for Croatia has on its left side the red and white chequered pattern of the state's flag, and a chequered background, although in different colours is also encountered in this position on all of the other notes in the series. Furthermore, some designers have deliberately sought to incorporate certain colours that they associate with their national identities into the design of their notes. Thus the lowest two denominations of Lithuania's banknotes were deliberately printed in brown and green to represent the state's brown earth and green forests.

Gender

One of the most marked features of the new series of banknotes issued in Eastern and Central Europe has been the predominance of male figures. Not only are most of the people represented on the notes men, but all but one of the designers were also men; likewise, the vast majority of people responsible for making decisions concerning the imagery depicted on the notes were men. Focusing just on the images depicted on the fronts of the notes, there are some 121 portraits of men but only 11 portraits of women.

This male dominance in the imagery cannot be attributed simply to the male composition of the decision-making processes that led to the creation of the notes. Rather, it is in large part an artefact of the strategies adopted in determining the overall content of the series. Once it was decided that the dominant images on the notes should be people, and that these should be either former rulers, artists or scientists, then this almost by default generated a set of men to be depicted on the notes. Interestingly, at least in the Hungarian case, some members of the committee responsible for determining the images to be depicted had specifically sought to identify a woman of equivalent status to the group of men being considered, but commented that they were unable to find one. However, where significant figures from the arts, especially literature, have been chosen, the number of portraits of women increases (for a wider discussion of the depiction of women on banknotes, see Hewitt, 1994, 1995b).

Epoch

One of the most interesting features of the banknotes being considered here is that with the exception of only a single note they all seek to represent national identity through a representation of the past. In general, images of people from the nineteenth century dominate the fronts of the banknotes, with 60 per cent of all such images being from this century alone. This reinforces the wealth of research that emphasizes the significance of the nineteenth century in the formation of national identity across Europe (see, for example, Hooson, 1994 and Gilbert and Helleiner, 1999b). However, it is also important to recognize that there is considerable divergence from this generalization, and that there is an interesting spatial variation in its applicability. Furthermore, when the imagery on the backs of the notes is considered, a much wider spread of epochs is represented.

Case Studies: The Processes of Choice in the New Order

As noted at the start of this chapter, new issues of paper currency have occurred as part of much wider processes of political and constitutional change: as the president of the Bank of Estonia during the negotiations for independence emphasized, planning a new currency was a prerequisite for the economic foundation without which there could be no separate Estonian nation. But mass-produced banknotes for people to use in daily life may also be tangible manifestations of change, agents for disseminating images of a redefined or reinstated national identity, and it is clear that in the countries we are studying, there were conscious decisions to have note designs conveying a sense of identity.

The processes of choosing designs and implementing production varied according to the circumstances of different countries, including whether or not they had already been issuing their own notes. In Hungary, for example, the National Bank had an established tradition of note issue, and could draw on the expertise of its own banknote printing house (Garami, 1999). None the less, the new series introduced in 1997 was the result of much deliberation and consultation from 1992, involving committees with representatives of the bank, the printing house, the paper mill, the Academy of Scientists, historians and art-historians, among others. The Hungarian Premier was also consulted. Ultimately the bank chose great Hungarians of the past as the theme, and the designer was chosen by a limited competition, won by the bank's artist, Károly Vagyóczky, because he best understood how to marry aesthetic appeal and security features. In this respect, renewal has been compatible with continuity of tradition: the designer told us that, for him, earlier Hungarian banknotes were like 'sacred papers'.

Czechoslovakia also had existing notes, but began planning a new note series in 1989 partly because of their unpopularity; the public wished to move away from outdated socialist symbolism, and disliked the inclusion of a portrait of the Communist Party secretary Klement Gottwald on the then recently issued 100 kroon note. The designer was chosen by the traditional method of a public competition, in which the subject for the imagery was left open, though there was a recommendation to use important figures, on the grounds that portraits would offer good security against forgery. The original jury comprised representatives from Czech and Slovak institutions, and a short-list of both Czech and Slovak artists was drawn up. The final choice of the graphic designer Oldrich Kulhánek was strongly influenced by the preference of the Union of Artists. This choice in itself marked a new political order, for under the old regime Kulhánek was arrested for his political satire, and had had a proposed note design rejected. The people to be portrayed on the notes – originally equally representing Czechs and Slovaks – had to be reconsidered once it became apparent that the country would divide; this provided an opportunity for the Czechs to introduce three women to the series of portraits. In this case, then, plans for the new notes were adapted as further political change occurred and new states were created.

In contrast, the Baltic states could not draw on recent practice, since as Soviet republics they had used roubles as currency. Estonia set up an open competition, with great Estonians as the design theme, to be assessed by a jury representing institutions ranging from the Supreme Soviet Parliament to the Union of Estonian Artists. Advertised in newspapers, the chance to design the national currency for an independent Estonia attracted a large number of entries, from schoolchildren and pensioners as well as professionals. The chosen designer, Vladimir Taiger, had no previous experience of working on banknotes, and found it a challenge: the Estonian notes issued during the brief period of independence from 1919 to 1920, with their now old-fashioned and unacceptably socialist imagery, offered no guidance (Leimus, 1993). In Latvia, seeds for the note designs were sown even before independence, when the Cultural Foundation structured informal discussions among artists and others into a competition to look for ideas for symbols of an independent Latvia. After independence and the establishment of the current Bank of Latvia, the results of that competition were used in choosing the new Latvian notes. As in Estonia, the notes had to break new ground; as in Czechoslovakia, artists played a significant role in the creative process.

Reconstructing Identities

In most countries today, national currency is designed to reflect national identity. Indeed, this is so common that in many places it is taken for granted. But the imagery is of particular interest in countries undergoing change, where there is a conscious process of creating or re-establishing a distinct identity, for there the designs on the currency may be a part of legitimizing that identity. The broad themes chosen to proclaim nationhood and the ways in which these are depicted vary across the region we are studying, but several dominant trends emerge, which may be illustrated with examples from the countries we have visited.

History

A recurring thread is the association of identity with history, especially the glorious past. This is evident on banknotes across the world, and for good reason. It is easier to choose historical subjects that are uncontroversial than contemporary ones, and it is natural for us all, as nations or as individuals, to look to our roots to understand who we are, but this ancestry has particular resonance in regions that have known scattered or limited periods of independence or have recently experienced dramatic change. Countries that can do so may choose to emphasize their early origins or golden ages of power. Thus in Hungary, the highest denomination when the new series was issued carried a portrait of St Stephen, the king who established the medieval kingdom of Hungary around AD 1000. The dates of the rulers and statesmen depicted on Hungary's notes span ten centuries, so taken as a group they convey the longevity and survival of a Hungarian nation, however often it has been challenged. The designer believed the National Bank felt this long tradition of powerful statesmen gave a positive message in the current climate of change; significantly, one reason the bank preferred rulers as a group was that they would furnish portraits of men with strong faces.

A similar approach may be found on some of the notes of the Czech Republic. For example, the 100 korun note shows Charles IV (1316–78), the monarch of Bohemia under whom Czech lands received equal rights with other regions of the Holy Roman Empire. Like Stephen, his reign is associated with a flowering of religious and cultural development, and he is known as 'the country's father'. The metaphor of father-figures and the importance of building the infrastructure of the state is also evident in more recent figures. Czech banknotes portray Frantisek Palacky (1798–1876), a politician known as 'the father of the nation' (indeed, the designer felt that it was with the nineteenth-century national movement that 'we found our identity') and Tomáš Masaryk (1850–1937), the first president of the Czechoslovak Republic. Hungary has Count Széchenyi (1791–1860), 'the greatest Hungarian' who founded the Academy of Sciences and developed a modern economy and transport system, including the famous Chain Bridge linking Buda and Pest.

As the nineteenth century witnessed a rising sense of national consciousness across our region, it is not surprising that it should be a key epoch in
the banknote designs, often illustrated with portraits of cultural figures
renowned in the fields of literature, art and music. Both the period and the
theme are particularly important on notes of countries that do not have an
earlier history of independence. As a Baltic state, Estonia has experienced a
long history of rule by various foreign powers, the brief period of
independence in the 1920s and 1930s being followed by German occupation,
then Soviet authority. For their new notes, the country has chosen cultural
heroes, most of whom were part of the celebrated National Awakening in
the nineteenth century. Language and literature predominate, with figures
such as Jacob Hurt (1839–1907), a theologist, folklorist and linguist who
recorded the stories, songs and dialect which expressed ordinary people's
sense of identity; Anton Hansen Tammsaare (1878–1940), a major novelist
whose works include a family saga as a metaphor for the lives of Estonians
from the National Awakening to independence during the 1930s; and the
poet and playwright Lydia Koidula, known as the Nightingale and so much
loved that the 100 kroon note bearing her portrait is colloquially called a
'koidula'.

Culture

The association of language and literature with the preservation and
dissemination of a distinct identity is an important theme in our region.
Indeed, some have seen parallels in the functions of language and money:
the writer Aphra Behn said 'money speaks a language all nations
understand', but within a country money can have its own meaning. As
Gilbert and Helleiner (1999a) have observed with regard to the 1930s,
'National currencies also came to be seen as significant for bolstering
national identities ... Money was thought to be like language, a tool that
would facilitate "communication" among members of the nation.'
Significantly, several of those depicted on notes in this region are honoured
for promoting literacy. For example, Lydia Koidula worked as an editor on
the first Estonian language newspaper, founded by her father. An earlier
figure in Slovenia is Primoz Trubar (1508–86) who produced the first
Slovene book in 1550; a detail of the first page of his *Abecedarium* appears
next to his portrait. Perhaps the most poignant image is that on a
Lithuanian note showing a famous statue of a mother and child by a
spinning wheel; the woman is secretly teaching her child to read at a time
when the Czarist regime prohibited Lithuanian books printed in the Latin
alphabet. Writers such as Preseren (1800–49) in Slovenia or Bozena

Nemcova (1820–62) in the Czech Republic wove their country's folklore into their work and helped to create a romantic national ideal, sometimes in contrast to difficulties or political activities of their personal lives.

The invocation of cultural heritage as another way of defining national identity through past achievements is a common practice on banknotes in the West, but designs of the new currencies of Central and Eastern Europe are more likely to be politically charged. Those chosen to be portrayed are often respected both for their artistic work and for their association with national causes and values. In the Czech Republic, the opera singer Ema Destinnová (1878–1930) was persecuted during the First World War for her anti-Austrian stance; in Slovenia, the writers Preseren and Cankar campaigned for political freedom, and in Estonia, the works of the composer Rudolf Tobias (1873–1918) and the novelist Tammsaare were suppressed during the Soviet era. Thus these currencies not only define identity in terms of cultural heritage but also reassert that heritage, and therefore identity, as quite distinct from those of former foreign oppressors. Furthermore, they present current identity as evolving from earlier expressions of patriotism. The incidence of Christian imagery may also be acknowledgement of renewed freedom, in this case to worship openly. Designs may feature portraits, such as St Agnes of Bohemia in the Czech Republic or Bishop Valancius in Lithuania, or buildings, ranging from an eighteenth-century wooden church, again in Lithuania, to the splendour of St Vitus Cathedral in Prague, views of which appear on two of the Czech notes.

Rural identity and tradition

While the fronts of notes are dominated by portraits, the backs of notes often show places, buildings or monuments associated with the person depicted. Many of these are urban views, perhaps linking nationhood with the power and cultural activity centred in and disseminated from towns and cities. But the lives of ordinary people have often been lived in the countryside; indeed, the novelists and poets portrayed on notes are often famed for writing about such traditional ways of life. In Latvia, rural traditions, still valued in all the Baltic states, are illustrated on their notes to represent the nation. The 5 lat note carries the 'sacred oak', such an important symbol that a small, stylized oak leaf appears on each denomination as a security feature. On the 20 lat note, a neat farmstead represents the ideal of a settled rural family life, while the 10 lat depicts the River Daugava, not for its undoubted economic importance, but because it is known as the River of Destiny and is seen as a mother, nurturing and uniting the people of Latvia. This rural identity and the reverence in which it is held suggest the wish to restore confidence after political crisis by reminding people of simpler ways of life, and enduring values that may be retained in the current period of renewal, preserving distinction in the face of westernising and globalising influences. Judicious placing of traditional emblems can help to legitimize modern currency: for example, the name 'kuna' for the Croatian denomination; a knight on horseback from the Lithuanian coat of arms, which appeared on the currency from 1918 to 1940; or the head of a Latvian folkmaid in traditional headdress. This last image was on the highest denomination Latvian coin, the 5 lat, which was cherished in the first republic and during the Soviet period as a symbol of protest. Many older people kept these coins, as they had a significance far beyond their monetary value; when the new banknotes were issued, it was therefore decided again to place the folkmaid on the highest denomination, the 500 lat note.

Dilemmas of Reconstruction

Of course the choice of such emblems, or indeed any aspect of the past, involves careful selection and interpretation, not least because the nations in question have experienced such turbulent histories. The problem of shifting boundaries is demonstrated in Hungary by the 2000 forint note portraying Gábor Bethlen (1580–1629), prince of Transylvania, a region which was once part of the kingdom of Hungary but is now in Romania. Unlike the other Hungarian notes, the back of the 2000 forint note does not show a place associated with the portrait but reproduces an image of Bethlen with his scientists taken from a painting. There is also the sensitive question of different ethnicities within a country: for example, in rejecting the Soviet era completely, Estonian notes now contain no Russian elements, even though almost 30 per cent of the population is Russian. Both territory and ethnicity have posed difficulties in the modern republic of Macedonia, formed in 1992 after the break-up of former Yugoslavia. Though now more or less accepted, the very name has been controversial, prompting fears in Greece that it indicated a potential claim on areas of northern Greece which contain most of ancient Macedonia – a worry firmly denied by many Macedonians. For this reason, one of the most popular suggestions for a note design, an image of Alexander the Great, could not be entertained. Intense debate among Slav Macedonians shows how hard it would be to agree on candidates for portraits. In an attempt to avoid dissension yet create a distinct imagery, the commission appointed to choose the designs opted for artistic representation of the cultural and historic past as a theme. The commission selected a series based on archaeological artefacts and buildings from the geographical area now known as Macedonia. In bold and colourful designs they depict Christian symbols such as a serene Madonna and Child based on a fourteenth-century icon, or a peacock from the mosaic floor of a basilica, while even older beliefs are recalled by a beautiful torso of the Egyptian goddess Isis, from a third-century BC marble figure in the Archaeological Museum in Ohrid, or a sixth-century BC dancing Maenad from a grave in Tetovo.[7] These archaeological subjects neatly embrace both distant history and current boundaries, but they are not immune from controversy. The 100 denar note has on one side an elaborate ceiling rose carved from wood, and on the other, a view of Skopje, based on an engraving, seen through a window. In the publicity material from the bank, both the ceiling rose and the house are described as Albanian, but an alternative, forceful view is that they were not Albanian, but merely typically 'Balkan'. The bank's leaflets at least show a wish to be seen to acknowledge the Albanians, who make up some 25 per cent of the population, but it is salient to note that this note was the least popular in the series amongst Macedonians. We were told repeatedly that the designs did not represent a national identity, but cultural heritage. Here, the apparently joyful images of the banknotes reflect continuing tensions in a country which is not so much renewing statehood as creating it, and where the threat of crisis is not over.

Conclusions

The thought, sometimes even passion, which has gone into designing the new paper currencies in Central and Eastern Europe is all the more significant because most of the countries hope to join the European Union and therefore the single currency: some of these national currencies may last only a few years. But designs proclaiming past glory or rural tradition need not be a romantic retreat from modern realities. Rather, they are invoked to lay a firm foundation for membership of a wider economic community as acknowledged independent nations. The Estonian president, opening a conference to mark five years of the Estonian kroon, said that 'the history of Estonian money is closely related to the history of Estonian independence'; 'our kroon is not a historical symbol void of contemporary value – no, much more than that, it is our real effective financial instrument, which supports us on our way to Europe' (Eesti Pank, 1997, pp. 5–6). It is precisely at times of change that we are forced to question and seek to reaffirm our identities;

so after profound political change, in the 1990s these countries proclaimed their reconstructed identities in the imagery of their paper currencies, asserting historic origins and laying claim to their future independence. In many of the designs there is implicit recognition that this may not always be easy, for amongst the pride in past glory there are also heroes who died young or in exile; troubled lives; scars of war and oppression. In February 2001, Hungary issued a 20 000 forint note, bearing a portrait of Ferenc Deák, Minister of Justice in the first independent Hungarian government during the revolution and war of 1848–49. The press release for the new note quotes Deák's words after the failure of the revolution and the imposition of Hapsburg rule: 'the nation shall endure all miseries to preserve our constitutional freedom for posterity', evidence perhaps that current freedoms are not taken for granted. The currency on which Deák is now portrayed is a vindication of his faith, his words a reminder of the powerful need to preserve and renew identity in the aftermath of crisis.

References

Åslund, A. (1992), *Post-Communist Economic Revolutions: How Big a Bang?*, Washington DC: CSIS.

Åslund, A. (1995), *How Russia Became a Market Economy*, Washington DC: Brookings Institute.

Ball, M. S. and Smith, G. W. H. (1992), *Analyzing Visual Data*, London: Sage.

Blanchard, O., Dornbusch, R., Krugman, P., Layard, P. and Summers, L. (1992), *Reform in Eastern Europe*, London: MIT Press.

Bonin, J. P. and Székely, I. P. (eds) (1994), *The Development and Reform of Financial Systems in Central and Eastern Europe*, Aldershot: Elgar.

Bradshaw, M. and Stenning, A. (2001), 'Introduction: transformation and development', in Bradshaw, M. and Stenning, A. (eds), *The Transition Economies of East Central Europe and the Former Soviet Union*, London: Addison, Wesley, Longman.

Brozoviç, D. (1994), *The Kuna and the Lipa: the Currency of the Republic of Croatia*, Zagreb: National Bank of Croatia.

Burawoy, M. (1992), 'The end of Sovietology and the renaissance of modernization theory', *Contemporary Sociology*, 21, 6, pp. 774–85.

Callinicos, A. (1991), *The Revenge of History: Marxism and the East European Revolutions*, Cambridge: Polity Press.

Caprio, Jr, G. and Levine, R. (1994), 'Reforming finance in transitional socialist economies', *World Bank Research Observer*, 9, pp. 1–24.

Dittus, P. (1994), *Corporate Governance in Central Europe: the Role of the Banks*, Basle: Bank for International Settlements (BIS Economic Papers, 42).

Eesti Pank (1997), *Five Years of the Estonian Kroon. Papers of the Academic Conference held in Tallinn on 18 June 1997*, Tallinn: Bank of Estonia, Tallinn.

Fukuyama, F. (1992), *The End of History and the Last Man*, New York: Free Press.

Garami, E. (1999), *The 75th Anniversary of the National Bank of Hungary. Issue between 1924–1999*, Budapest: National Bank of Hungary.

Gilbert, E. (1998), '"Ornamenting the façade of hell": iconographies of nineteenth century Canadian paper money', *Environment and Planning D: Society and Space*, 16, pp. 57–80.

Gilbert, E. and Helleiner, E. (1999a), 'Introduction – nation-states and money: historical contexts, interdisciplinary perspectives', in Gilbert, E. and Helleiner, E. (eds), *National-States and Money: The Past, Present and Future of National Currencies*, London and New York: Routledge.

Gilbert, E. and Helleiner, E. (eds) (1999b), *National-States and Money: The Past, Present and Future of National Currencies*, London and New York: Routledge.

Gowan, P. (1995), 'New-liberal theory and practice for eastern Europe', *New Left Review*, 213, pp. 3–60.

Grabher, G. and Stark, D. (eds) (1997), *Restructuring Networks in Postsocialism: Legacies, Linkages and Localities*, Oxford: Oxford University Press.

Graham, B. (ed.) (1998), *Modern Europe: Place, Culture, Identity*, London: Arnold.

Habermas, J. (1994), 'Europe's second chance', in Pensky, M. (ed.), *The Past as Future: Jürgen Habermas Interviewed by Michael Haller*, Cambridge: Polity Press, pp. 73–98.

Hall, D., and Danta, D. (eds) (2000), *Europe goes East: EU Enlargement, Diversity and Uncertainty*, London: The Stationery Office.

Held, D. (1991), 'Democracy, the nation-state and the global system', *Economy and Society*, 20, pp. 138–72.

Held, D. (1995), *Democracy and Global Order*, Cambridge: Polity Press.

Hewitt, V. (1994), *Beauty and the Banknote: Images of Women on Paper Money*, London: British Museum Press.

Hewitt, V. (ed.) (1995a), *The Banker's Art: Studies in Paper Money*, London: British Museum Press.

Hewitt, V. (1995b), 'Soft images, hard currency: the portrayal of women on paper money', in Hewitt, V. (ed.), *The Banker's Art: Studies in Paper Money*, London: British Museum Press, pp. 156–65.

Hewitt, V. and Unwin, T. (2000) 'Past perfect: reconstructing national identities on the paper currencies of Hungary, Estonia and Lithuania', in *Approaching a New Millennium: Lessons from the Past – Prospects for the Future*, Bergen: University of Bergen HIT Centre [CD-ROM publication].

Hooson, D. (ed.) (1994), *Geography and National Identity*, Oxford: Blackwell.

Kallas, S. and Sõrg, M. (1995), 'Currency reform', in Lugus, O. and Hachey, Jr, G. A. (eds), *Transforming the Estonian Economy*, Tallinn: International Center for Economic Growth, pp. 52–69.

Karl, T. L. and Schmitter, P. C. (1991), 'Modes of transition in Latin America, Southern and Eastern Europe', *International Social Science Journal*, 43, pp. 269–84.

Kelder, J. (1997), *Eesti Rahareform 1992*, Tartu: Postimees.

Klagge, B. (1998), 'The development of regional banks in Hungary and the Czech Republic', in Unwin, T. (ed.), *A European Geography*, Harlow: Longman, pp. 194–7.

Leimus, I. (1993), *Eesti Vabariigi 1918–1992*, Tallinn: Olion

Lynn, N. (1999), 'Geography and transition: reconceptualizing systemic change in the former Soviet Union', *Slavic Review*, 58, 4, pp. 824–40.

Miliband, R. (1991), 'What comes after communist regimes?', *Socialist Register 1991*, pp. 375–89.

Pickles, J. and Smith, A. (eds) (1998), *Theorising Transition: the Political Economy of Post-communist Transformations*, London and New York: Routledge.

Pinder, D. (ed.) (1998), *The New Europe: Economy, Society and Environment*, Chichester: Wiley.

Pointon, M. (1998), 'Money and nationalism', in Cubitt, G. (ed.), *Imagining Nations*, Manchester: Manchester University Press, pp. 229–54.

Roberts, G. (1999), *The Soviet Union in World Politics: Coexistence, Revolution and Cold War, 1945–1991*, London: Routledge.

Rose, G. (1996), 'Teaching visualized geographies: towards a methodology for the interpretation of visual materials', *Journal of Geography in Higher Education*, 20, pp. 281–94.

Sachs, J. (1990), 'What is to be done?', *The Economist*, 13 January 1990.

Sachs, J. (1995), 'Consolidating capitalism', *Foreign Policy*, 98, pp. 50–64.

Smith, A. and Pickles, J. (1998), 'Introduction: theorising transition and the political economy of transformation', in Pickles, J. and Smith, A. (eds), *Theorising Transition: the Political Economy of Post-communist Transformations*, London and New York: Routledge, pp. 1–24.

Smith, A. and Swain, A. (1998), 'Regulating and institutionalising capitalisms: the micro-foundations of transformation in eastern and central Europe', in Pickles, J. and Smith, A. (eds), *Theorising Transition: the Political Economy of Post-communist Transformations*, London and New York: Routledge, pp. 25–53.

Smith, G. (1996), 'When nations challenge and nations rule: Estonia and Latvia as ethnic democracies', *Coexistence*, 33, pp. 25–41.

Sõrg, M. and Vensel, V. (1999), 'Currency Board arrangement in Estonia', in Ennuste, Ü. and Wilder, L. (eds), *Harmonisation with the Western Economics*, Tallinn: Estonian Institute of Economics, pp. 11–40.

Stark, D. (1995), 'Not by design: the myth of designer capitalism in Eastern Europe', in Hausner, J., Jessop, B. and Nielsen, K. (eds), *Strategic Choice and Path-Dependency in Post-Socialism*, Aldershot: Edward Elgar.

Unwin, T. (1998a), 'Rurality and the construction of nation in Estonia', in Pickles, J. and Smith, A. (eds), *Theorising Transition: the Political Economy of Post-communist Transformations*, London and New York: Routledge, pp. 284–308.

Unwin, T. (ed.) (1998b), *A European Geography*, Harlow: Longman.

Unwin, T. (1999), 'Contested reconstruction of national identities in eastern Europe: landscape implications', *Norsk Geografisk Tidsskrift*, 53, 2–3, pp. 113–20.

World Bank (1996), *From Plan to Market: World Development Report 1996*, Oxford and New York: Oxford University Press for the World Bank.

Notes

1 We are particularly grateful to The British Academy for grants which have enabled us to conduct this research, and to all our colleagues in Central and Eastern Europe who have supported our visits to the region. A considerable debt of gratitude is also owed to all those artists, bankers, politicians and academics who have responded so willingly and generously to our many questions.

2 This section of the chapter draws heavily on Tim Unwin's chapter 'The context of transition' in his forthcoming book edited with Bettina van Hoven entitled *Lives in Transition* (Pearson, forthcoming).

3 This section of the paper incorporates much material from Unwin, T. and Hewitt, V. (forthcoming) 'Banknotes and national identity in central and eastern Europe', *Political Geography*. See also Hewitt and Unwin, 2000.

4　At the time of writing, in April 2001, the collapse in the value of the euro, which has lost approximately 20 per cent of its value (against the dollar and the pound) since its introduction, makes this assertion somewhat tentative. However, it does seem likely in the long term that countries now aspiring to join the European Union will indeed lose their own currencies and banknotes. Certainly central bank officials throughout the countries visited have expressed the view that it is merely a matter of time before their currencies are indeed subsumed within the euro.

5　Detailed information for Albania, Belarus and Serbia has so far proved difficult to obtain. For further details of the project, please look at <http://www.gg.rhul.ac.uk/tim-banknotes>.

6　Note that other people depicted on Bulgaria's and Estonia's banknotes also had significant influences in shaping their nations' identities. Anton Hansen-Tammsaare, for example, wrote Estonia's classic literary work *Tõde ja õigus* (Truth and Justice), but did so in the twentieth century. In contrast, Paul Keres, an Estonian international grand master in chess, was depicted because of his fame as an Estonian who had achieved success in the international arena.

7　As Tetovo is an Albanian city, with the Albanian University, this design indirectly has an association with the Albanian population of Macedonia.

Index

*For Product Safety Concerns and Information please contact
our EU representative GPSR@taylorandfrancis.com Taylor & Francis
Verlag GmbH, Kaufingerstraße 24, 80331 München, Germany*

T - #0019 - 160425 - C0 - 234/156/16 [18] - CB - 9780754633587 - Gloss Lamination